Financial Instruments

DAVID M. WEISS

FINANCIAL

• Equities, Debt, Derivatives, and Alternative Investments •

INSTRUMENTS

Portfolio

PORTFOLIO
Published by the Penguin Group
Penguin Group (USA) Inc., 375 Hudson Street, New York, New York 10014, U.S.A.
Penguin Group (Canada), 90 Eglinton Avenue East, Suite 700, Toronto, Ontario,
Canada M4P 2Y3 (a division of Pearson Penguin Canada Inc.)
Penguin Books Ltd, 80 Strand, London WC2R 0RL, England
Penguin Ireland, 25 St. Stephen's Green, Dublin 2, Ireland
(a division of Penguin Books Ltd)
Penguin Books Australia Ltd, 250 Camberwell Road, Camberwell,
Victoria 3124, Australia (a division of Pearson Australia Group Pty Ltd)
Penguin Books India Pvt Ltd, 11 Community Centre, Panchsheel Park,
New Delhi – 110 017, India
Penguin Group (NZ), 67 Apollo Drive, Rosedale, North Shore 0632, New Zealand
(a division of Pearson New Zealand Ltd)
Penguin Books (South Africa) (Pty) Ltd, 24 Sturdee Avenue, Rosebank,
Johannesburg 2196, South Africa

Penguin Books Ltd, Registered Offices: 80 Strand, London WC2R 0RL, England

First published in 2009 by Portfolio,
a member of Penguin Group (USA) Inc.
1 3 5 7 9 10 8 6 4 2

Publisher's Note
This publication is designed to provide accurate and authoritative information in regard to the
subject matter covered. It is sold with the understanding that the publisher is not engaged in
rendering legal, accounting or other professional services. If you require legal advice or other
expert assistance, you should seek the services of a competent professional.

LIBRARY OF CONGRESS CATALOGING IN PUBLICATION DATA
Weiss, David M., 1938–
Financial instruments : equities, debt, derivatives, and alternative investments /
David M. Weiss.
p. cm.
Includes index.
ISBN 978-1-59184-227-9
1. Investments.   2. Financial instruments.   I. Title.
HG4521.W378 2009
332.63'2—dc22
2009001725

Printed in the United States of America
Set in Fairfield Light
Designed by Kate Nichols

TO MY FAMILY

To: Marcia, Randi, Craig, Nicole, Jenna, and Carly.
Thank you for your support, patience, and understanding.

TO MY COLLEAGUES

To my colleagues both past and present: Some of us have
traveled a long road together; others are fairly new
acquaintances, yet it has been my honor to know and, in
many cases, to have worked with you. Some have educated
me and some of you I have educated. I thank you for your
friendship and adding to an interesting career.

It is my hope that you find this book informative
and worthy of your time.

Contents

DEBT PRODUCTS

Financial Instruments

Introduction

Products, products, products! Each day there seem to be new financial products being offered into the market or older ones gaining new features. Some are direct obligations of the issuer, others are derivatives, and still others are derivatives on derivatives. We trade instruments that range from bonds that have a direct claim against the issuer to options whose underlying products are futures, whose underlying products are indexes, which are three derivatives, the base of which does not have any direct value. We trade collateralized debt obligations that are composed of various types of loans and mortgages, which have been pooled and securitized and shares issued against the basket of debt without the ability to determine which loans are against which shares. With this onslaught of products comes new terminology and strategies, followed by books, periodicals, and other media sources dedicated to the particular product, and the proliferation continues.

This book was written to provide a base from which the reader can gain a foundation for the major products traded. Each product—what it is and how it functions in the marketplace—is explained in a straightforward manner. Due to the book's wide panoramas of products it is general in nature, keeping the more in-depth mathematics, analytics, and complex strategies to the more productcentric documentation.

With the constant march forward of technology, we are able to execute large block trades in less time than it took to enter an order a few years ago. We can make an indexes portfolio into deliverable product and trade against the actual basket of stock, and we can still buy one share of stock. We have come a long way from marking quotes on chalkboards or looking up prices on the "pink sheets," and fifty years from now someone will communicate a financial dissertation into an education tablet that can be taken with a beverage, and it will reference today as the "old days."

This book takes the reader from equities and debt instruments to derivatives and structured products. It concludes in the working of the markets and the different forms of margin; all parts are aimed at "what it is" and "how it works."

I hope it is of value to you.

EQUITIES

I

Common Stock

· INTRODUCTION ·

Known as ordinary shares in other parts of the world, common stock is probably the best known of all the financial products. To most people it is the ticket to wealth. They come to make a "killing" in the market, yet in the long term, many of them are no longer with us and the market is still here. So who killed whom? Bernard Baruch has been credited with the following two statements;

"Nobody ever lost money taking a profit."

"The main purpose of the stock market is to make fools of as many men as possible."

The common-stock market spans the length and breadth of the financial spectrum, from a new start-up company to a mature conglomerate, from a "mom and pop" shop to an international giant, from a domestic corporation to a foreign company. All want to do the same thing—get the public to invest in them. This is a way for a company to raise capital. It is literally selling shares of itself to the public.

· CORPORATE FORMATION ·

The issuance of its shares and its capitalization structure, as well as what a corporation may or may not do in the carrying out of its business model, is covered by the corporation's charter and bylaws. The charter and bylaws also spell out the rights of its shareholders. Who is empowered to act on behalf of the corporation and in what capacity is detailed in the corporate resolution. These three documents are the basis under which the corporation will exist.

Most common-stock issues come to market through a formal underwriting. The company and its investment managers negotiate the terms of the underwriting. The reason for the underwriting is for the company to raise capital (cash). A key question is why it needs cash; is it to expand the company or to pay off debt or just to keep the company afloat? Each answer would take the investor down a different path. Another question, especially in the case of a new issue, is how much of the capital infusion is going to pay the company "insiders" for the private stock they received in lieu of cash compensation. There is nothing wrong with this practice, but the amount could be abusive.

When a young company starts up, one item that it is usually short of is cash; it therefore enters into agreements with lawyers, accountants, and anyone else who will accept shares of stock in lieu of cash. The understanding is that they will sell the stock (all, some, or an amount that is up to the recipient) at a later time when the company is established. The sale of the stock will bring in the cash the recipient was denied originally. This is a gamble on the part of the recipient. If the company fails before the recipient has a chance to convert those shares, he or she did all the work for nothing. On the other hand, the offering could be a huge success (known as a hot deal) and the recipients could convert their stock at a dollar amount far in excess of what they originally negotiated. The percentage of the new offering that will benefit these individuals, and much more information, can be found in the prospectus that is sent to the buyers of newly issued securities and can be requested by a potential buyer from an underwriter or the firm the individual has an account with. The prospectus is required under federal law as part of the Securities Act of 1933 (the "1933 Act"). Unfortunately, most people do not read the prospectus, so it is possible for unscrupulous individuals to get away with some fictitious or misleading story about the issuer.

When a company seeks out an underwriter, it is looking for definable qualities and services. Likewise, when an underwriter takes on a client, it too is looking for definable qualities and characteristics. The adage "birds of a feather flock together" is very true in this relationship. A start-up company does not need all the services that a global underwriter can offer, and a small underwriter with limited contacts cannot properly service a large, privately held company issuing its stock to the public. However, as with anything else we do, there is the best of the small and the worst of the big. It is up to each to seek out the appropriate other.

A new company or a small company going public can raise up to $5,000,000 without a formal underwriting. It is known as a Reg. A offering. Regulation A of the 1933 Act exempts some issues from formal registration. If an issue is for not more than $5,000,000, including no more than $1,500,00 being sold by insiders, it may qualify under this regulation. It cannot be made in addition to a prior offering or sale of the company's security. Form 1-A notice must be filed with the Securities and Exchange Commission (SEC) and qualified by the SEC. The form must state:

1. the name of the issuer of the security;
2. the title of the security, the amount being offered, and the per unit offering price to the public;
3. the general type of the issuer's business; and
4. a brief statement as to the general character and location of its property.

A preliminary or final offering circular must be furnished to a perspective buyer forty-eight hours before a transaction confirmation is sent. A dealer, including an underwriter turned dealer, must provide a final offering circular for ninety days after the initial offering.

Formal Underwriting

Corporate securities are brought to market through negotiated underwriting. The investment bankers that will assist in the underwriting meet with the corporation management and other interested parties to discuss the vehicle that will be used to raise capital. If the company is issuing its common stock to the public for the first time, of interest to the underwriters is what percentage of the "offering" will be made up by insiders looking to convert their shares into cash. As mentioned elsewhere, even before a company commences operation, it is incurring expenses. These are usually classified as start-up costs. Some of these expenses will be paid with shares of unregistered stock. The recipients of the stock are taking a gamble that the company will be successful and they will be able to sell the stock at a later date. When that sale takes place, they are said to be "cashing out." The first time holders of this stock have an opportunity to "cash out" at fair market value is during the initial offering period.

As the underwriters will be risking their capital when they "take down" the issue to sell, they want to make sure that the public will receive the issue and view it as fairly priced in the marketplace. Some of the buyers of this new stock will be their own customers, so they want to offer it at a justifiable price and one that the market will support or (even better) find attractive as an investment so that the price of the shares will rise. Once the amount of capital that the company wants to raise has been determined and the underwriters agree that it can be raised, an offering price range will be determined. That price, divided into the amount of money that the company hopes to raise, will determine the number of shares in the offering.

Next, a preliminary prospectus, known as the red herring, is drawn up and used to solicit other underwriters and investors into the offering. The prospectus tells the terms and conditions of the offering. A preliminary prospectus does not include the offering price, the concessions, or who the underwriters are. The final prospectus does.

In addition, a registration statement is filed with the SEC. The SEC has twenty days, known as the cooling-off period, to review the registration statement. It will issue a "stop order" if it believes that there is a misrepresentation or omission of material facts. The SEC has the right to perform an audit of the issuer to determine if such is the case. While the stop order is in effect, the issue may not be brought to market until an amended registration statement is filed and accepted by the SEC. During the cooling-off period, the underwriters and anyone else involved with the offering or the issuer cannot discuss the issue with the public.

The lead underwriter, sometimes known as the managing underwriter, solicits other underwriters into the "deal." Other underwriters are invited in to participate for four reasons.

1. As the underwriters "buy" the issue from the issuer and turn around and sell it to the public, the amount of money required to acquire the issue may be too large for one underwriter to take on.
2. The lead underwriter wants to share the market risk of the issue.
3. Adding underwriters opens more conduits that can absorb the new issue.
4. The lead underwriter wants to be invited into the other underwriters' future deals.

The underwriters agree to operate severally but not jointly, which means that each underwriter is responsible for its allotted shares but not for the other's share.

In addition, firms will be invited in just to help sell the issue. These firms do not commit capital to the underwriting and therefore are not underwriters. They receive the underwritten shares to sell to their clients. This is done for two reasons:

1. To open even more conduits that can absorb the new issue
2. To be invited into these selling firms' own deals

The underwriters and those firms that were invited in form the selling group. Compensation falls into three categories.

1. Selling concession: A fee for each share the firm sells
2. Underwriting fee: A fee for the cost of funds and the market risk taken by the underwriters.

3. Management fee: A fee paid to the underwriting manager or managers to cover expenses, et cetera, involved with managing the deal.

Example: Lucerne Corporation is going to issue 20,000,000 shares of common stock and receive $10 per share. The underwriters and the company have agreed to sell the stock at $11 per share. The $1 compensation will be divided as follows:

Selling concession $.75 per share
Underwriting fee $.15 per share
Management fee $.10 per share

Assume one manager will oversee the entire offering. Including the manager, there are five underwriters, each underwriting 4,000,000 shares. The five underwriters will pay Lucerne Corporation $40,000,000 each, once the deal passes SEC qualification. Including the five managers, there are five members who will just help sell the issue, making a total of ten members of the selling group, each of which is to sell 2,000,000 shares. The five underwriters will give half of what they underwrote to the five firms that are assisting in the selling group. Please note that while the underwriters have committed capital to the offering and will sell stock to their clients, the assisting firms' sole function is to sell the issue to their clients.

Note: The $10.00 per share that the selling group has belongs to the underwriters, as they have prepaid the issuer. It will be sent to the manager, who will allocate it among all five underwriters.

Customer A bought 100 shares at $11 per share from a broker-dealer that was also an underwriter. The firm deducts a $.75 selling concession, a $.15 underwriting fee, and $10.00 to replenish the $10 paid to Lucerne Corporation as part of the underwriting. The remaining $.10 is the fee that is sent to the manager for managing the deal.

Customer B bought 100 shares at $11 directly from the managing underwriter. The firm deducts a $.75 selling concession, a $.15 underwriting fee, and $10.00 to replenish the $10 paid to Lucerne Corporation, and the remaining $.10 is the fee due for managing the deal.

Customer C bought 100 shares at $11 from a broker-dealer who is only selling the security. The firm deducts a $.75 selling concession and sends the $10.25 remaining to the managing underwriter, which allocates the $10.15 amount to the underwriters that will, in turn, keep the $.15 underwriting fee and $10.00 to replenish the $10.00 paid to Lucerne Corporation. The managing underwriter keeps the $.10 as its compensation for managing the deal.

New issues are supposed to be placed in clients' accounts in accordance

Example of the Cash Flow

Underwriter's Customer	Underwriting Manager's Customer	Selling Participant's Customer
Customer A Buys 100 @ $11	Customer B Buys 100 @ $11	Customer C Buys 100 @ $11

Customer's $11.00

−$.75 Selling Concession
−$.15 Underwriting fee
−$10.00 Underwritten amount

Underwriter retains $10.90

Selling Group Only

| −$.75 | Selling Concession |
| $10.25 | Owed Underwriters and Manager |

−$.75 Selling Concession
−$.15 Underwriting fee
−$10.00 Underwritten amount
−$.10 Manager's fee

| −$.15 | Underwriting fee |
| −$10.00 | Underwritten amount |

$.10 | Management fee

All Underwriter retains $10.15

$.10 Management fee

Manager

with the clients' investment habits. Underwriters will protect the new issue from "flippers." Flippers are individuals who buy a new issue as a speculation, not as an investment. They sell the new issue soon after buying it, hoping to take a quick profit. As the new issue has not had a chance to establish its market presence, these sales could force the market price down, even below the public offering price. Once this happens, the syndicate selling firms, which must offer the stock at the "offering price," can no longer sell the issue because the market price is below the offering price. The managing underwriter will place a "syndicate penalty bid" into the market. With this bid for the stock, the manager will buy each and every share being sold below the offering price. The syndicate penalty bid is only in the market for a short period of time. The manager will track down any seller into the syndicate penalty bid, contact the broker-dealer whose client sold the issue, and cancel the selling firm's selling concession, then reoffer the stock to another broker-dealer, who will sell it at the offering price and get full compensation.

When new issues come to market, the demand may exceed the supply. If there is a large imbalance of demand over supply, it is referred to as a hot issue. As explained above, firms are allocated an amount of stock to sell. This is further allocated by the firm to its branch offices and from the branch office to its sales force. The composition of the firm determines how the allocations are made. Adjustments are made intrafirm, as one registered representative may need more stock while another representative may be having some problems disposing of his or her allocation. This generally occurs when the company going public has its home office in one city or state and is well known there or its products are well known in one geographical area and not in others. The syndicate manager of the firm will constantly rebalance the distribution to make sure the new issue is placed. Actually, to be technically correct, the industry considers any new offering where demand is equal to or slightly greater than the supply a hot issue (*hot* as in *good* and not *way oversubscribed*).

At times this reallocation transcends broker dealers. One firm may need more shares than it was allocated, whereas another firm's interest in the new issue may be lukewarm. The firm with the lukewarm attitude may be willing to give up some of its allocation on a reallowance basis. Of the $.75 selling concession mentioned above, the two firms negotiate the terms of the reallowance. Let's assume the firm giving up the stock will keep $.25 of the $.75 selling concession and the firm that needs the stock will retain the remaining

$.50. Assume the firms involved are both only assisting in the selling of the stock as part of the selling group. When the firm receiving the additional stock sells it to its clients, the firm will subtract $.50 from the proceeds of the sale and send the remaining $10.50 to the manager as part of normal course. The manager then sends $.25 per share to the originally allocated firm.

Special note: As the issue is being allocated, clients wanting the new issue may receive all, part, or none of what was requested. Therefore, the request for a new issue is referred to as an indication of interest and not an order. An order expresses definite criteria. An order for a round lot of common stock, which is 100 shares, is either executed or not. The client would never get a report that he or she bought 56 shares of the 100, or something like that. In the case of new issues, because of the allocation process it is quite possible that a client wanting 100 shares of a new issue may only receive 56 shares or 27 shares or even 5 shares and it is a valid report.

While the allocation begins to trade in the market, its price should be the neutralizer between supply and demand. Basic economics state that if demand is greater than supply the buyers will force the price up, and if supply is greater than demand the supply will force the price down. However, there are many different agendas at play in the market. It's not as simple as buyers and sellers. The best stock in the world would most likely drop in price if some direct or indirect misfortune was perceived.

· SOURCES OF INFORMATION ·

Today, with the information superhighway, there are plenty of opinions, recommendations, and theories available. One only has to watch the various business channels or listen to radio stations to get more information than one can handle. In some cases, experts discuss various companies, with one recommending a stock as a good investment and the others disagreeing with that choice. Listening to these experts gives viewers a lot of valuable information that they will be able to sort out. Besides the TV and radio, there are many periodicals and newspapers from which one can extract all types of information. Investors have to do their homework.

Another main source of information about companies is research reports, available from the client's financial institution or by subscription. Research falls into two primary categories. One is fundamental research;

the other is technical research. Fundamental research studies many aspects of the company, from its competitive products to its management to its financials to its industry to the overall economic conditions. Good research reports include the company's strong and weak points and attempt to project the future outlook of the company. Technical research focuses on the stock's market activity. A technical analyst uses many tools, such as charts and graphs, to study the movements of a stock's price and volume historically and currently. Through changes in a stock's movement or characteristics, the technical analyst attempts to project future outcomes.

· RESEARCH ·

Fundamental Research

Fundamental research uses the financial statements of a company as a base. These are the balance sheet, the profit and loss statement, and the statement of cash flows.

Under accounting rules every entry must have two sides. One side is known as debit, and the other side is known as credit. The two sides for each entry must equal each other, regardless of the number of entries on each side. The totals must equal each other. The company maintains a chart of accounts. The chart of accounts can be broken down into five categories of accounts, of which three (assets, liabilities, and net worth) are part of the balance sheet and two (revenue and expense) belong to the profit and loss statement. These accounts will have either debit balances or credit balances, and the total of all the debit balance accounts must equal the total of all the credit balance accounts. That's called the trial balance. If the debits do not equal the credits, then some error in processing has occurred and an accountant will review the entries from that period, find the mistake, and correct it. From these balanced accounts the following reports are extracted.

Balance Sheet

The balance sheet derives its name from the fact that the side with debit balances (assets) must equal the side with credit balances (liabilities plus net worth).

For those who are not accounting savvy, assets are that which is owned by or owed to the company, liabilities are that which the company owes, and net worth is the value of the company (i.e., assets minus liabilities). (Note: In corporations, net worth is referred to as stockholders' equity.)

Assets can be separated into three categories:
   Liquid assets (e.g., cash, accounts receivable, inventory)
   Fixed assets (e.g., buildings, furniture, fixtures)
   Intangibles (e.g., goodwill)
Liabilities can be separated into two categories:
   Current liabilities (obligations that must be met within a year, e.g., utilities payable, salaries payable, notes payable, taxes payable)
   Long-term liabilities (e.g., mortgages payable, company's issued bonds)
Net worth (known in corporations as stockholders' equity)
   Noncorporation
      ownership classes
   Corporation
      preferred stock
      common stock
   Both
      retained earnings

The balance sheet is always prepared with the notation "as of month/ day/year." It is a snapshot of the firm's financials as of a specific date.

Profit and Loss Statement

The profit and loss statement (P&L) is composed of all revenue (credit balances) and expense (debit balances) accounts.

Revenue: Sources of income, e.g., sales, compensation for services rendered.
Expenses: Direct and indirect usage of funds and materials in attempting to generate revenue, e.g., inventory expense, utilities expense, salary to employees, tax expense, marketing expense, advertising, and sales expense.
Net profit or loss: Revenue minus expenses.

A profit and loss statement is prepared with the heading "for the period ending month/day/year." It is like a report card on how the company performed from the last balance sheet report to the one being prepared currently. In accounting, all entries require two entries (a debit side and a credit side, which equal each other) for the accounting of entries to stay in balance. From this balanced environment, revenue and expense accounts are extracted to produce the P&L. This step breaks up the balanced environment, as the offset to many of these entries may have been with accounts belonging in the balance sheet report. The revenue and expense accounts are netted to produce the profit or loss incurred by the company. Once done, these accounts are closed out, with the results added to (in the case of profits) or subtracted from (in the case of losses) the net worth (stockholders) section of the balance sheet report. In other words, the profit or loss obtained when the equilibrium is broken in the preparation of the P&L should be the difference that will appear when the balance sheet accounts are totaled and the credit balance accounts are subtracted from the debit balance accounts. To reinstate the equilibrium, the balance in the P&L must be added to or subtracted from retained earnings in the balance sheet report.

Statement of Cash Flows

The third report, the statement of cash flows, is more of an analytical report, as it shows where funds came from, where they went, and the result. Its heading includes the phrase "for the year (period) ending month/day/year." It is divided into three parts. It begins with the net earnings figure taken from the profit and loss statement. Then it shows the effects of cash movements on three different aspects the company's activities namely:

1. Cash flows from operations
2. Cash flows from investing activities
3. Cash flows from financing activities

The entries on the report are only those that actually used cash. For example, the sum deducted for annual depreciation is added back into cash flows from operations, as depreciation is a bookkeeping entry and not a real cash movement entry. Changes in accounts receivable and accounts payable from the last period are recorded, as they affect cash and so on. Cash flows from operations should be a positive number. Cash flows from investing activities is generally a negative number, as it represents cash spent on expansion or updating or replacing equipment. The exception is where the investment is in securities or other assets that can appreciate as well as depreciate in value. Cash flows from financing could also be a negative number, as it represents the company's cost of borrowing. The net of these three areas is added to or subtracted from the cash and cash equivalent balances on the corporation's balance sheet from the previous accounting period. The result should be the balance for cash and cash equivalent appearing at the end-of-the-year balance sheet. In effect, the balance shows how well the company is doing and how well the management is utilizing its cash resources.

From the various reports the analyst extracts information similar to what the statement of cash flows reveals. The analyst is interested in such items as:

Ratios

Debt-to-Equity ratio: This ratio reflects how dependent the company is on financing or how much leverage the firm is using. *Leverage* is defined as the use of other people's money to increase or generate profits. The use of the borrowed funds must outperform the cost of borrowing (interest) for the leverage to work in the borrower's favor. Leverage is said to be a double-edged sword. While it can increase profits, it can also increase losses, as the cost of the borrowing may exceed the return.

Price-Earnings ratio: This is defined as the number of times the price of a stock exceeds its annual earnings per share. Growth companies should have a higher ratio than mature companies. When the dot-com bubble was in full swing, the public was paying high prices, prices of $50 or more for companies that did not have any earnings at all. In those cases and in cases where an established company is operating at a loss, the price-earnings ratio is useless.

Earnings per Share (EPS): EPS is defined as earnings divided by common shares outstanding. While the earnings of a corporation per year is an important figure, when it is broken down to a per-share basis it becomes very significant. For example, say two companies each earned $100,000,000. One company has 100,000,000 shares outstanding, and the other has 1,000,000 shares outstanding. All other things being equal, which company's stock would the analyst expect to be trading at a higher price? What if they were trading at the same price? Is their product mix the same? These and many other investigatory questions can be pulled out of EPS that wouldn't be seen in just a corporate earnings figure.

Earnings per Share Diluted: This figure takes into account what effect all warrants, rights, company-issued compensation stock options, and convertible issues would have if they were converted into common stock. What is the impact of these potential additional shares on the earnings per share?

Earnings Before Interest and Taxes (EBIT): Interest and taxes are two expenses that are not directly related to the operations of the business. As interest is subtracted from earnings before taxes, a company with debt obligations could present a misleading profile if compared to one that had little or no debt.

Earnings Before Interest, Taxes, Depreciation, and Amortization (EBITDA): This figure is used for companies that have heavy investments in fixed assets.

Dividend Payout Ratio: This is defined as how many times the earnings available for dividend exceed the dividend payment. Even though the board of directors must approve a dividend payout, the larger the amount by which earnings exceed the amount needed to make the payment, the better the ratio and the more secure the payment is likely to be in the future. It also shows the impact that the dividend payment has on the overall financial condition of the corporation (i.e., what percentage of earnings is being paid the stockholders).

Times Fixed Charges Earned: This number tests the firm's ability to pay its annual interest and related charges. How secure are those payments? Whereas dividends on stock can be passed over, interest must be paid on debt. Of importance to the bondholder or other lender is how secure the interest payment is. The safety of the interest payment (as well as that of the principal of the loan, for that matter) is directly related to the company's earnings. A potential investor would be more willing to lend a company money if the current earnings covered the current annual interest payments by a ratio of five to one than he or she would be if the earnings just barely met the payment needs.

Margin-of-Profit Ratio: This ratio reveals the amount per dollar of revenue that flows to the company's bottom line. Has it improved over the last years? What are the results of the company's competitors? This ratio tells how efficiently the company is operating. The ratio can then be compared to other companies with the same business mix and any glaring differences investigated.

There are many more ratios and tests that the fundamental analyst uses to determine inter- and intracompany comparisons and relationships. Some ratios are used to compare the current year to prior years. Others are used to compare one company against others in the same field. These in turn may be used to compare one industry to a similar or competing industry.

Analysts examine the management and weigh the management's assessment of the company's future. They then compare this assessment to other industries, the economy, and the market in general and project the results into the future. Analysis of the results of these tests and ratios and the management's vision of the future gives the analyst a picture of how the company and its management are doing against prior years, against competitors, and against competitive industries on a national or global basis and what the future looks like. Based on all of this, the analyst makes a recommendation.

Through these research reports, the investor can see "into" the company and through them, and other sources, make an informed decision about an investment.

Technical Research

Technical research involves the use of charts and graphs. Technical analysts use these tools to try to understand the markets, an industry, and or a security. Many people use charts to track securities. Some do a thorough job charting various aspects of a situation, whereas others simply plot activity. These individuals are chartist and not technical analysts. The Securities and Exchange Commission recognizes technical analysts by those having satisfied the chartered market technician exam, which is administered by the Market Technicians Association. These analysts study many charts and attempt to draw trends and patterns from them. The charts paint a picture of various events in motion. Based on their finding the analysts make recommendations and predictions.

A chart may simply track a company's share price over time. This can be overlaid with a security index value to see how closely the stock tracks the index and how the stock reacts to index value moves. For example, some stocks are known as defensive stocks and tend to rise when an index is falling in value, whereas other stocks may track the index very closely (although they may lag behind at times).

Along with share price, the chart may track the stock's daily volume. This will tell if there is any correlation between the stock's price move and the number of shares traded on a given day. Let's suppose the volume stays constant as the stock slowly rises in price. The volume begins to pick up as the stock price peaks and continues to increase as the stock price falls. The volume begins to fall off as the stock price levels off and soon starts its slow rise again. If this scenario was to repeat itself over time, the technical analyst would use the sequence of events, along with other statistical information, to project the near-term stock moves.

Let's look at the following charts:

Basic Charts

These charts reflect the history of Zip Corporation stock trading for a month. Chart 1 reflects the obvious fact that at the start of the month Zip

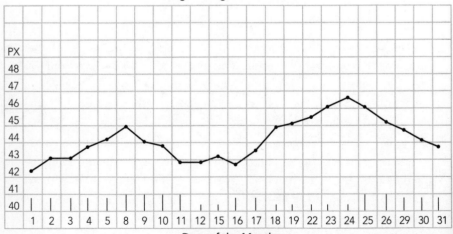

BASIC CHART FOR ZIP
Tracking Closing Price Movement

Days of the Month

BASIC CHART FOR ZIP
Tracking Closing Price Movement with Volume

Days of the Month

Tracking Closing Price Movement for ZIP
with Volume and Stock Index

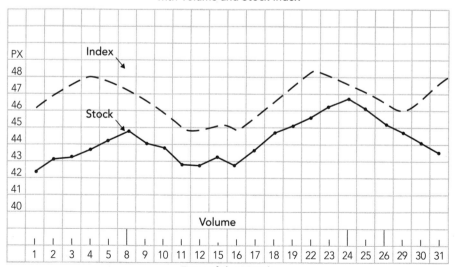

Days of the Month

was trading at $42 per share, reached a high of $46.75, and at the end of the month was trading at almost $44 per share. However, it also shows that the stock is quite volatile, as it is able to move as much as 1 point in a day.

Chart 2 adds to this the fact that the volume picks up considerably around the time the stock takes a drop in price but remains steady or falls when the stock is gaining value. That is valuable knowledge to a trader in that the volume may predict the stock's price movement.

Chart 3 adds to this information the fact that the stock's price and the index value have an interesting relationship: the index tends to rise before the stock has risen in value. Therefore, the analyst can look to the index's movements as an indication of potential stock movements. Many stocks ride with the index up and down, a relationship known as a high beta, or have no relationship at all.

As the charts get more complex, and as other charts add to that complexity, certain traits or characteristics start to emerge. It is these points that the analyst uses to make recommendations.

The following chart tracks Bam Corporation common stock for a month. Notice the pattern. The line of dashes is called a resistance level, and the line of dots is called a support level. The dash line crosses the tip of each price peak, after which the stock falls in value. The dotted line rides below the point where the stock starts to turn and head upward. Based on what you see, would a trader who did not have a position in Bam be more likely to buy the stock or sell it short on the twenty-ninth day of the month?

If all other factors were neutral, the analyst would probably sell short because of the stock's past record of not breaking through the resistance level. However, if the stock did in fact break through the resistance level, the analyst would be busy trying to figure out the next probable resistance level.

Bar Charts

There are other types of charts that are used too. Some analysts use bar charts that show the range for the day and can include where the stock closed, as does the one opposite.

Notice the first two days the stock price is rising in value. On both days the stock closed at the high price. Note on day three that the stock price

Tracking Bam Stock Support and Resistance Levels

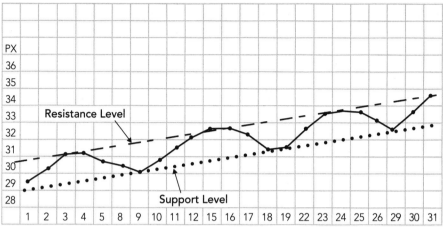

Days of the Month

Bar Chart #1: Daily Price Range with Close of PIPP for one Week

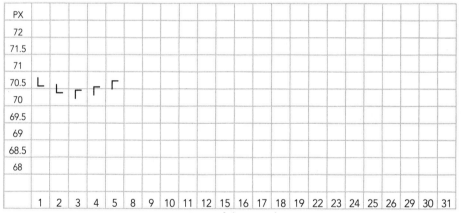

Days of the Month

Key = | Range, − Closing Price

continued to rise but then fell and closed at about middle of the daily range. On day four the price of the stock fell in value and on day five it continued to fall, but later in the day recovered closing at midrange for the day.

If we combine a bar chart showing price range and closing price with

Bar Chart #2: Daily Price Range with Close and Volume for PIPP

PX
72
71.5
71
70.5
70
69.5
69
68.5
68
Volume

Days of the Month: 1 2 3 4 5 8 9 10 11 12 15 16 17 18 19 22 23 24 25 26 29 30 31

one showing trading volume, the chart becomes even more meaningful. Bar chart #2 reveals that the volume increases right before and during a fall in the price but remains lower and constant when the price is stable or increasing.

Point and Figure Charts

Another type of chart is a point and figure. This chart notes moves only when the stock price changes by a predetermined amount. For the following example we will use two-point intervals.

In the first column the stock had a range of 8 points (four boxes representing 2 points each), then from the high box the stock fell in value 4 points. We know this because the highest O is in the same row as the highest X. The stock then rose 6 points, according to the third column, fell two points in the fourth column, then rose 4 points in the fifth column and lost 2 points in the sixth column.

This type of chart is less crowded than some of the other tracking types, as it only records meaningful movements (in this case, 2-point intervals), and therefore is excellent for tracking trends over longer periods of time. However, it does not record time. The stock could have traded in the same two-point range for an hour, a day, a week, a month, et cetera. As it doesn't measure time, it cannot measure volatility.

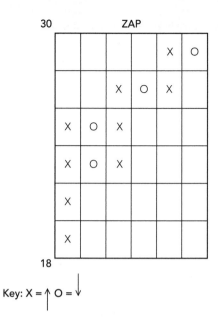

Key: X = ↑ O = ↓

Japanese Candlestick Charts

Yet another type of chart used by technical analysts is the Japanese candlestick chart.

Each candlestick represents a particular period of time. The center section represents the price range of the stock over that period and is color coded to indicate whether the closing price was higher or lower than the opening price.

There is a distinct and important difference between a technical analyst and a chartist. Not all chartists are technical analysts, but all technical analysts use charts. The difference is the quantity of statistical and other technical information that is assembled before an opinion is rendered.

In summary, fundamental research is concerned with the company and its environment, whereas technical research is more interested in the stock's price and its environment. Neither is perfect, but both try to bring intelligence into the thought equation.

A few words on institutional research: Some members of the public believe that institutional research is the "good stuff," whereas the research mentioned above is for everyone else. This is not true. Because of the large security positions held by institutions, slight movements in the value of

Japanese Candlestick PIPP

PX					
72					
71.5					
71			Highest Price		
70.5			Opening or Closing Price, whichever is higher		
70					
69.5			Range		
69					
68.5			Opening or Closing Price, whichever is lower		
68			Lowest Price		
	One Day				

their holdings spell profit or loss for the institution. Changes in the rating of a bond, to be discussed later in the debt section, or a stock will affect the value of the security. As these changes may already be discounted (i.e., taken into consideration) by the market, the adjustment in price when the change actually occurs would affect the institution's portfolio to the degree that the institution may want to swap out one security for another. Also, remember that some institutions are bound by rules and regulations, such as the "prudent man" rule. When the rating places a security at a level where the institution cannot be involved, it must take action (for example, if a bond issue falls below investment grade), whereas a public customer or an institution not bound by these restrictions will just maintain its investment positions. In other words, institutional research focuses on aspects of the market not germane to other investors.

· AMERICAN AND GLOBAL DEPOSITARY RECEIPTS ·

American Depositary Receipts (ADRs)

There are financial markets in other countries where the share quantity and/or local currency do not fit into the American-style marketplace. U.S. banks offer American depositary receipts for those foreign companies that want to raise capital by offering their shares in the U.S. market or wish to have their securities more widely distributed. The issuer deposits a portion of its locally trade shares at the U.S. bank, which in turn issues the "receipts" (shares) against them. The ADRs take the form of the U.S. domestic shares and trade alongside the shares of U.S. companies. Trades in ADR securities are settled through U.S. clearing and settlement facilities and settle in U.S. dollars. These ADRs are, for all intents and purposes, surrogates for the foreign shares that are held in escrow at the U.S. bank. Those purchasing, owning, and selling ADRs come under U.S. rules and regulations.

There are three categories of ADRs. The lowest level is where the issuer cannot meet listing requirements of exchanges and the ADR trades in the over-the-counter market. These are generally very low-priced issues and each ADR share represents several ordinary shares, which by themselves sell at a low price on their domestic market. Next category is small issues that a bank puts together at the request of the issuer to give the issuer and the issuer's products introduction to the U.S. market. These issues can trade on exchanges as well as over the counter. The last category is where a bank acquires a block of the issuer's domestic stock and makes an offering of the converted ADR shares. These ADR shares trade on exchanges and usually have enough depth of market to support active trading.

As the ADR trades are dollar denominated and the ordinary shares trade in their native currency, the currency conversion rate applicable for cash conversion is not applicable between the two security prices. The value of the security, as viewed in respective markets, is what is being converted and not pure currency. Among the reasons for this aberration are such factors as the interest rate differences between the two countries, the economic outlook for the foreign company, the volatility of their currency (either real or perceived), the ease of conversion between the ADR and the ordinary shares and the expenses incurred in accomplishing the conversion. When the concept of converting the shares is addressed, the world of foreign exchange is also brought into play. ADRs trade alongside the domestic issues. Their unit of trading is 100 shares, the same as domestic issues, and they are priced, margined, and settled as if they were domestic issues.

Global Depositary Receipts (GDRs)

Global depositary receipts are similar in purpose to ADRs except that with GDRs an international bank is issuing into a foreign market depositary receipts representing shares of stock issued by a corporation domiciled in a different country (e.g., shares of a U.S. corporation being offered in a European market or a German company's shares being offered in the Japanese market). The shares are issued through the branch network of the international bank. The GDRs take on characteristics of locally traded shares and come under the rules and regulations of the country in which they are traded.

· VOTING TRUST CERTIFICATES (VTCs) ·

The issuance of voting trust certificates is rare. They come about when an individual or group of individuals wants to control a block of votes. The common stockholders assign their voting rights to this individual or group as the trustee under a trust agreement. The trust agreement contains start and termination dates, between which the trustee votes the shareholders' stock. At the end of the agreement, the voting rights revert to the then-existing shareholders. Initially, the trustee takes the common stock to the corporate transfer agent and surrenders the shares in exchange for the voting trust certificates, and at the end of the agreement the process is reversed.

During the life of the VTC, the former common stockholder may sell the securities but must sell them as VTCs and not as common stock. When purchasing the stock, the new shareholder must be careful as to which is being purchased.

The use of VTCs is most often found in cases of corporate bankruptcies. Creditors of the company exchange trust certificates with shareholders so that they can use the votes to protect their investments. Shareholders are willing to do this because the trust has the same basic interest as the shareholders.

The shareholder retains all tax liabilities during the period that the agreement is in force. This includes income tax on applicable distributions and capital gains or losses when positions are closed.

· Voting Rights ·

Common shareholders usually receive one vote per share. When a stock splits up or down, the votes follow the stock. In a two-for-one stock split, for example, the shareholder would have twice as many shares and therefore twice as many votes. In a 10 for 1 reverse split, for every 100 shares owned you now have 10 shares and, therefore, only 10 votes. (Splits are discussed later in this chapter.) However, the one-share-one-vote rule doesn't always apply. Some common stock carries with it the right to only a fractional vote per full share, or even no vote at all.

Standard vs. Cumulative Voting

A twist on the one-share-one-vote approach is cumulative voting. In cumulative voting, while the shareholder has only one vote per share, if he or she is voting on several events, the votes may be accumulated and applied against one event. For example, say the owner of 100 shares of stock has to vote for three of five board of directors positions. In the standard voting procedure, the shareholder would vote his or her 100 shares three times, 100 shares for each candidate of choice. Under cumulative voting, the shareholder could take his or her 300 votes (three times 100 shares) and vote them all for one candidate. Cumulative voting is a way for minority shareholders to obtain some representation on the board of directors.

· Ordinary Shares (Foreign Stocks in Their Domestic Market) ·

With globalization, it is becoming easier and easier to invest in securities traded in foreign markets. Before investing in ordinary shares of a foreign company in its domestic market, it is important for the investor to understand those rules and regulations that affect the trading and ownership of the foreign shares.

While a country may be only too happy to welcome foreign investment, it may be restrictive in releasing the funds on sale of those securities. There may be a time limit before the money can be repatriated. Countries impose this type of restriction to curtail speculative security trading. Even worse, the conversion of the foreign currency back to the customer's domestic currency may be very costly. It may require the intervention of a third (neutral) currency. This process will incur fee after fee after fee. Some countries want and need "hard" currency (British pound sterling, Canadian dollar, euro, Japanese yen, Swiss franc, and U.S. dollar) in order to carry on international commerce. Therefore, they make it nearly impossible for the client to convert from hard currency to the country's own currency or vice versa.

Investing in ordinary shares in foreign markets brings in the possibility of ownership restrictions. Some marketplaces address this through the issuance of class A shares and class B shares. One class will have the right to vote and a voice in the company, and the other will not. An investor may be able to acquire any quantity of the passive shares but be restricted from buying any of the participating shares. Other countries limit the percentage of shares that can be owned by foreigners. The percentage is based on cumulative ownership by foreigners. Investment in the wrong class of stock or in a restricted issue can result in an expensive loss, which will include unwinding the position, commissions, applicable taxes, and potential fines.

The trading and trade settlement rules of the foreign country may differ substantially from those of the client's domestic market. Some countries have mandatory settlement dates. That is, when securities are to be sold, they must be in a certain place at a certain time, or else the transaction is canceled and the seller is fined on top of any losses incurred. The same may hold true for the buy side, where the money, in local currency, must be on deposit at a certain location by a specific time, or else the trade is liquidated, resulting in fines and possible trading loss to the client. In both the purchase and sale scenarios, profits obtained from failure to satisfy the requirements are retained by the governmental authority and not the offender.

Other problems may occur in investing in foreign securities in their domestic market, such as in the case of dividends and similar disbursements. Some countries tax these types of distributions at the point of payment. The United States may have a reciprocal agreement with such a country that frees U.S. citizens from paying taxes to the foreign authority. This type of agreement frees the investor from the burden of double taxation (once by the foreign government and again by the U.S. authorities). However, as the foreign authority may or may not be sufficiently up to date to be able to determine what trade belongs to what client, the U.S. client may be wrongly taxed. The efforts to reclaim the tax may be more costly and time consuming than the payment is worth.

Still other problems involve record keeping. The financial markets in some foreign countries aren't as automated as those in the United States. Therefore, there may be a time lag between when the security is acquired and when it gets posted to the new owner's name and/or account. If a distribution is recorded and/or paid during that period, it may be credited to the former owner. Claiming the payment may be so tedious that it is not worth the time and money.

There are several precautions that an investor interested in doing business in foreign markets ought to take:

1. Do his or her homework to determine if the international investment being considered is something he or she really wants to do. Is it being motivated by need or by some emotional pang, such as the ability to say "I have investments in several foreign markets," when the investor's real need is income and preservation of capital?
2. Find a broker-dealer or bank that has the necessary infrastructure and experience in conducting business in that particular marketplace.
3. Determine what the investor's responsibilities are in meeting the requirements imposed by that marketplace.
4. Check to see if there are any restrictions on the movement of currency.

There are knowledgeable, well-respected institutions that conduct business in these marketplaces every day. They do this for their clients as well as for their own proprietary needs. They understand the requirements, risks, and nuances and can guide a client so that many of the situations described above can be avoided or at least known before entering that marketplace.

· DIVIDENDS AND SPLITS ·

Cash Dividends

Each day, financial services display a stock's current market price. Included is the net change from the previous day's closing price. Occasionally, it appears to be wrong. One who is following that particular stock may say, "That is wrong. It's not up $.50; it's down $.50," referring to the net change from the previous night's close. "The stock closed at $60 last night, and it's now trading at $59.50, so it's down $.50."

The net change is seldom, if ever, wrong. What has happened is that the stock has been involved with some corporate action that caused its official closing price to be adjusted by the marketplace in which it trades. For example: The Zippa Corporation announces a $1.00 per share dividend to owners of its common stock. Let's assume the dividend declaration is made on May 1. This announcement date is known as the declaration date. The company states that it will pay the dividend to those who own the stock on the night of May 15. This date is referred to as the record date. This means that the last day an acquirer of the stock can purchase the stock and still be entitled to the dividend is May 12 for a "regular-way" trade. Currently, equities trade in a three-day cycle, which is known as regular way. If the trade occurred on May 12, the trade would settle on May 15, which is the record date. If the stock was purchased regular way on May 13, that trade would settle after the record date, so the buyer would not be entitled to the dividend. May 13, therefore, becomes the "ex-dividend date." This is the first day a buyer of the stock is not entitled to receive the dividend. The company also sets the day the dividend will be paid, known as the payable date, which in this case let's say is June 1. To review the key dates again:

Declaration date: The day the company announces the dividend and the process begins.

Record date: The night of the date that one must legally own the stock to be entitled to receive the dividend. Security ownership change occurs on the settlement date.

Payable date: The day the dividend distribution is made.

These three dates are set by the corporation. The ex-dividend date, the first day the buyer of the stock is not entitled to receive the dividend, is set by industry convention.

In the discussion of fundamental research earlier in this chapter, we discussed the balance sheet and the fact that assets equal liabilities plus stockholders' equity (net worth). Let's assume Zip company's balance sheet looks like this:

Assets	Liabilities	
Cash: $120,000	**Liabilities:**	$0
	Stockholders' Equity:	
	Common Stock: 10,000 Shares	
	Par Value $10/Share	$100,000
	Retained Earnings:	$20,000
$120,000		$120,000

The company pays a $1.00 per share dividend. As there are 10,000 shares outstanding, the company will pay $10,000 to the common stockholders. After that payment, the company's balance sheet will look like this:

Assets	Liabilities	
Cash: $110,000	**Liabilities:**	$0
	Stockholders' Equity:	
	Common Stock: 10,000 Shares	
	Par Value $10/Share	$100,000
	Retained Earnings:	10,000
$110,000		$110,000

The new balance sheet reveals a $10,000 fall in value and the convention is that the drop in value diminishes the market value of the stock. Therefore, after the close of business of the last regular-way trading day before the record date, the marketplace on which the stock trades reduces the closing price of the stock by the amount of the dividend. In the above example, say Zippa Corporation's common stock closing price was $60 per share. After the close, the price would be adjusted to $59 per share to reflect the pending dividend. When trading opened on the ex-dividend date, the trading day after the last trading day on which a buyer would be entitled to receive the dividend, the stock would open up against the previous night's adjusted close of $59. Therefore, if the stock is trading at $59.50 on the ex-dividend date, it would be up $0.50.

Declaration Date	Last Trade Date for Dividend	Ex-Dividend Date	Record Date		Payable Date
05/01/XX	05/12/XX	05/13/XX	05/15/XX	05/16/XX	06/01/XX
	———————▶ Trade date		3-day cycle ———▶ Settlement date		
		———————▶ Trade date	3-day cycle	———▶ Settlement date	

Declaration, record, and payable dates set by company
Ex-dividend date set by industry convention
The last day the stock can be purchased through the normal trading cycle (trade date plus three days, or "T + 3") is May 12; that trade will settle on the record date of May 15. A trade entered on May 13 will settle on. May 16, the day after record date (the ex-dividend date), so the buyer is not entitled to receive the dividend.

Stock Splits

A company will split its stock for two reasons: to reduce the price of the stock so that more investors can "afford" to buy it and to increase the amount of stock available for the trading (float) in the marketplace.

There is an argument that if the public buys the stock, it will buy the product, and vice versa. Some subscribe to the idea; some do not. In any event, companies that do business directly with the public try to keep their stock's price in a range that will keep the public interested. In addition, if the stock rises one point, the owner will gain $1 on every share owned. Therefore, in a "two-for-one" split, the owner of 100 shares presplit would be earning $200 postsplit on the 200 shares now owned. However, there is an argument that it would take the same effort to move the postsplit stock 1 point as it would to move the presplit stock 2 points.

The second reason for a stock split is that if a company splits its stock, let's say two for one, then a holder of 100 shares would suddenly have 200 shares (and each share would have half the value). When they are sold, the holdings would pour 200 shares into the market instead of the 100 shares that the holder originally purchased. As the holders who were entitled to the split sell their stock, the float in the market increases, giving the company the ability to have more owners of the stock.

The cycle for splits is different from the one for dividends. Because the change in price on the "ex" date is so radical, it is moved to the business day after the payable date, when the actual owner has received the split shares. Unlike cash dividends, stock splits are not taxable as ordinary income. Using the balance sheets from above, let's see what effect a stock split has. Before the split, the company's balance sheet looks like this:

Assets	*Liabilities*	
Cash: $120,000	**Liabilities:**	$0
	Stockholders' Equity:	
	Common Stock: 10,000 Shares	
	Par Value $10/Share	$100,000
	Retained Earnings:	20,000
$120,000		$120,000

After a two-for-one split, the balance sheet looks like this:

Assets	Liabilities	
Cash: $120,000	Liabilities:	$0
	Stockholders' Equity:	
	Common Stock: 20,000 Shares	
	Par Value $5/Share	$100,000
	Retained Earnings:	20,000
$120,000		$120,000

Note that the par value and shares have changed, but nothing else.

Let's assume the stock was trading at $60 per share before the split. As each share becomes two shares, the price will become $30 (2 × $30 = $60). As explained in greater detail below, the cycle for splits is as follows:

Declaration Date	Last Trade Date for Old Stock	Due Bill on Date	Record Date		Distribution (Payable) Date	Ex-Distribution Date
05/01/XX	05/12/XX	05/13/XX	05/15/XX	05/16/XX	06/01/XX	06/02/XX
	Trade date		Settlement date			
		Trade date		Settlement date		

Buyers of the stock on May 12 will be owners on the night of May 15. They have bought the $60 stock and will receive the additional stock on the night of June 1. Those who buy the stock on May 13 and after will still have paid $60 but are actually buying two shares at $30 each. They have bought one share that is currently outstanding and an IOU for an additional share when it is issued (on June 1). Keeping track of the IOUs is done by "due bills" between the client's firm and a central counter party (CCP), such as Depository Trust & Clearing Corporation.

The "due bill on date," used in stock splits date, replaces the ex-dividend date used in cash dividends. The first trading day on which the trades will settle after the record date of stock split is the "due bill on date." The settlement of any trades made from the due bill on date until the payable date will carry due bills. In addition, any securities being moved between financial institutions from the settlement date of the due bill on date, will also carry due bills. While the outstanding shares are being delivered, it is the value of these shares plus the shares to be delivered on payable date that is actually being transacted. Anyone accepting shares of stock during this period without due bills is going to wake up on the ex-distribution date and discover their stock is worth much less. When the due bills are surrendered on the payable date, the shares representing the due bills delivered and the owner of the stock are once again whole.

As shown in the above diagram, both the owners of the stock on the May 12 trade date and those who acquired it after the May 12 trade date will be equal sharewise on June 2.

Stock Dividends

Companies sometimes issue stock dividends to the common stock owners. The stock dividend is not taxable as ordinary income, as are cash dividends. The company "buys" the stock from its retained earnings and issues it. The company's balance sheet totals do not change; it just has more shares outstanding. The purpose is to give the voting stockholders (i.e., common stockholders) something. In the case of a 10 percent stock dividend a client who owns 100 shares that are trading at $80 per share would own 110 shares at $72.727.

Stock dividends 25 percent or less follow the cash dividend methodology. Stock dividends over 25 percent follow the stock split methodology.

· CORPORATE ACTIONS ·

Mergers

In a merger, Company A and Company B merge to form Company C. Company A and Company B cease to exist, although one of their corporate names may continue to be used by the new company. The terms of the merger are negotiated between the management of the two companies. This includes the respective companies' lawyers, accountants, and investment banking firms. Mergers are very seldom made on a share-for-share basis, and this is what makes the merger interesting. For example, it may be decided that for every 1.125 shares of Company A the owner of A shares will receive 1 of the new C shares, whereas $.975 shares of B are worth 1 share of C. As an outcome of the negotiations, it was determined that the value of Company B was greater than the value of Company A. One hundred shares of A would convert to 88.888 shares of C (100/1.125 = 88.888), whereas 100 shares of B would convert to 102.564 shares of C (100/.975 = 102.564).

The industry does not issue script (fractional shares) or any denomination less than a full share. The recipients who are supposed to receive less than a full share will receive cash in lieu of script. The price of the conversion is set as of the close of business of a specific date.

Acquisitions

Similar to a merger, in an acquisition Company A buys Company B and Company B ceases to exist. The company and its name may remain as a subsidiary of Company A or be absorbed into Company A and disappear completely. Here again there will be an exchange of stock. This time, however, only Company B shares will be exchanged, and again fractional shares will be distributed in cash.

Of concern in both mergers and acquisitions is the impact on the companies' balance sheets. In a merger one is concerned about the financial condition of both companies before the merger, the cost of the merger, and the financial condition of the combined company after the merger. In an acquisition, one of the key questions on the table is, how solid is the company being acquired? If it is two struggling companies merging, even with the alleged synergies and cost savings, will the company survive? Does it have a needed product? Does the combination make sense? Is it a merger or acquisition of convenience? In other words, are the two companies joining forces to ward off being taken over by a third company? These questions and others like them will be addressed by research analysts and their opinions documented in their reports. However, one must not exclude what goes under the umbrella of common sense: does it make sense to the investor?

Tender Offers

At times an individual or group may want to acquire a percentage of the common stock of a company. This investment may be passive or aggressive. Passive investments are just what they sound like: the group does not want to interfere with the current management or structure of the company. A tender offer that is aggressive in nature is one where the investor is not satisfied with the way the company is being run and wants to have a voice in its management. This is accomplished by buying enough shares so that the investor can demand to have representation on the board of directors. This in turn could lead eventually to a proxy fight, where common stockholders will be asked to vote for the current board, a modified board, or a new board of directors.

Suppose the Ann Tenna private investment group wants to make a major investment in Holiday Omega Corporation. It wants to acquire 5 percent of the company. The market cannot absorb a purchase of this size, so the investment group decides with its investment adviser to offer a 10 percent premium over the current market price. The stock has been trading around $30 per share for the last two to three years, so an offer is made at $33 per share.

The company has 50,000,000 shares outstanding. Therefore, Ann Tenna wants to acquire 2,500,000 shares at $33 per share for a cost of $82,500,000. It announces the tender offer by stating that it will buy all or part of the tendered shares, up to a maximum of 2,500,000 shares. It also may put a "floor" in, saying "with a minimum of 1,500,000 shares tendered." In other words, Ann Tenna is not interested in acquiring less than 3 percent (1,500,000 shares), but the most it will acquire is 5 percent (2,500,000 shares).

Pat Terrnal owns 12,000 shares of Holiday Omega Corporation and decides to tender them. She notifies her registered representative at her broker-dealer, Stone Forrest and Rivers. The firm in turn submits her request, along with those of other clients, to the agent processing the tender offer. Other broker-dealers, banks, and financial institutions follow the same process. Individuals who are holding the shares themselves will have to submit the shares along with all the required paperwork.

Depending on the total number of shares submitted, Pat may have none of her shares accepted for the tender offer, all of her shares tendered, or a portion of her shares tendered. Let's assume a total of 3,000,000 shares are tendered. The Ann Tenna private investment group will accept five-sixths $(2,500,000/3,000,000 = 25/30 = 5/6)$ of the shares tendered. Of the

12,000 shares that Pat tendered, 10,000 will be accepted and 2,000 will be returned (12,000/6 = 2,000 × 5 = 10,000). Everyone participating in the tender offer will have five-sixths of their submitted shares tendered and receive $33 per share on those accepted shares.

Spin-offs

The opposite of mergers and acquisitions are spin-offs. In this situation companies divest themselves of subsidiaries or other companies. Perhaps the most famous divestiture was when the former American Telephone and Telegraph was split into American Telephone and Telegraph and the seven "baby bells": Ameritech, Bell Atlantic, BellSouth, NYNEX, Southwestern Bell, Pacific Telesis, and US West. Since then, many have merged. But that is another story. The AT&T divestiture was caused by the U.S. Justice Department. Generally, spin-offs result when a company changes its goals or its needs have been satisfied. General Motors (GM) acquired Electronic Data Systems Corporation (EDS) for its technical expertise. After a few years, the need for that source had been satisfied and the world of technology had moved away from GM's needs. GM spun the company off. In this situation the shareholder will receive shares of the spun-off company under a predetermined ratio, which may be share for share. Depending on what percentage of the company's makeup the company being spun off is, the price of the former company's stock may fall. In the case of American Telephone and Telegraph, the price of shares fell dramatically. In the case of GM, it didn't. In most cases, the sum of the price of the spun-off shares and that of the adjusted former company shares may be more than the price of the former combined stock (the sum of the parts is greater than the whole).

As with other corporate actions, an investor has to determine if the divestiture will benefit the original corporation. A question that must be asked is, how did the original company become involved with the company now about to be spun off? Is it an outgrowth from within, an offshoot of the company's current business, or a business it is leaving? Why did the company acquire this business originally, and why does it now want to sell it? Was it acquired as part of a larger acquisition and this part of that acquisition doesn't fit the company's business mix? Did the original company's marketplace change? The answers to these questions will reveal a lot about the company's management decision process.

One of the main questions that has to be asked is, can the spun-off company survive? Where will it get its revenue? If its sole client is the company that just spun it off, why did the company go through all that expense and bother?

There are many reasons for a company to spin off a part of itself. Some are sound; others are not. Profit or loss is the equalizer.

Reverse Splits

There was a TV commercial where an executive, speaking to his staff, says, "Let's put some lipstick on that pig." In a reverse split the shares outstanding consolidate, the par value of the stock increases, and the share price of the remaining stock increases proportionally. The purpose of a reverse split is to take a stock selling at a very low price and, through share consolidation, make the price of the stock rise, so that it appears to have more value as an investment.

Shares of GBG are selling at $.50 per share, and the company has 50,000,000 shares outstanding, with a par value of a $.01 per share. (For all intents and purposes, "par value" does nothing but convert shares to currency on a corporation's balance sheet.) So GBG is carrying the stock value at $500,000 (50,000,000 shares × $.01 = $500,000). The company announces a ten-for-one reverse split. The number of outstanding shares changes from 50,000,000 to 5,000,000, the par value changes from $.01 to $.10, and the value on the balance sheet remains the same (5,000,000 shares × $.10 = $500,000). The owner of what was 100 shares of stock with a par value of $.01 each trading at $0.50 = $50.00, is now the owner of 10 shares of stock with a par value of $.10 trading at $5.00 = $50.00. However, the public is more inclined to invest in a $5 stock than in a $0.50 stock, so the corporation takes on a different appearance to the public.

· SUMMARY ·

Common stock denotes ownership in a corporation and is the voting stock of a company. In the United States, the trading lot, known as a round lot, is 100 shares. Less than 100 shares is referred to as an odd lot. New issues of common stock are brought to market via a negotiated underwriting.

Due to the popularity of this product, information about companies and investment advice is readily available via a number of outlets, from periodicals to television to the Web. Research about the companies falls into two categories, fundamental and technical. Fundamental research is concerned with the company's financials and the management's plans for the company. Technical research is more attuned to market action and the stock's behavior in the marketplace.

Due to the liquidity of U.S. markets, foreign corporations will issue their stock using a U.S. bank as a conduit. The resulting shares are known as American depositary receipts (ADRs). Foreign shares are deposited at the bank, and ADRs are issued against them. The same process in other countries results in a product known as a GDR or Global depositary receipt.

At times, as during a bankruptcy, there may be a need to harness the common stockholders' votes and aim them in a way that will force management to stay fast to a given course. In this case, trust is set up by which common stockholders will exchange their stock for receipts that have all of the properties of the stock but exclude the right to vote. The receipts are known as voting trust certificates. The issue of the VTC retains the right to vote the shares.

Not all common stocks have one vote per share. Some common stocks may not have a vote at all, and others may permit a fraction of a vote per share. The method of voting common shares itself may be different from corporation to corporation. Some corporations allow their shareholders to aggregate their votes and use the aggregated votes in a particular situation, thereby giving them more say in corporate matters. Other companies use the straight share-vote method. The method of voting is covered in the corporation's charter and bylaws.

Many countries refer to their corporations' common stock as ordinary shares. In some of those countries, there may be class A shares and class B shares. One class may have the right to vote and not the other, and/or one may belong to the "family" and the other be traded by the general public.

In the corporate world we find that some corporations pay cash dividends on their common stock, and others may pay stock dividends. Some companies will split their stock to lower the per-share price and get more shares into the public domain. Others may "reverse" split their shares, which will increase the per-share price and reduce the number of shares outstanding. A company may merge, acquire other companies, or spin off parts of itself. Groups or individuals may make tender offer for shares of companies, either for investment or to get involved with the management of the company, or both.

All in all, this is an exiting and dynamic part of the industry.

2

Rights

· INTRODUCTION ·

The issuance of "rights" is mandatory under some companies' corporate charters. The clause in the charter that imposes this requirement is known as the preemptive right clause. It gives then-existing shareholders the "right" to buy additional shares of their existing issue in proportion to what they own. It is a protective measure that ensures that all shareholders are treated equally and that existing shareholders can maintain their percentage ownership of the company without fear of having their share diluted without their knowledge.

Let's suppose that 51 percent of a company is owned by one board member and the other 49 percent by the remaining board members. With the majority shareholder away, what's to prevent the minority shareholders from voting more shares to themselves and becoming the majority shareholders? If the corporate charter does not contain a preemptive right clause, they can do exactly that. With the preemptive clause, the majority shareholder must be given the right to 51 percent of additional issuance of the common class so a coup like this could not happen.

· ISSUANCE ·

The issuance of rights usually requires an infusion of capital. The offering would say, "So many rights and X amount of dollars can subscribe to one new share." The amount of rights needed is determined by the ratio of new shares to old shares. For example: The Loster Corporation has 10,000,000 shares of stock outstanding and wants to issue 1,000,000 additional shares. To ensure that every shareholder's interest is protected, each share of outstanding stock must receive one right. Therefore, 10,000,000 rights will be issued, one per share of outstanding stock. All must be used in the subscription process before the corporation can issue the 1,000,000 new shares. Therefore, the ratio is ten to one; ten rights must be used in the subscription for each new share. The amount of money to be raised is determined by the corporation and its investment banker. Suppose the amount of money the company wants to raise is $80,000,000. All of the rights must be used in the subscription for the company to raise the $80,000,000. If only a portion of the rights is used in subscription, the company will only be able to raise the money represented by those rights.

Those shareowners who do not want to subscribe may sell their rights in the marketplace, where buyers may be waiting to acquire them. To subscribe to the new shares being issued by the company, the buyer must have the exact number of rights needed for the shares being requested. This brings up three scenarios. In the above example, an interested investor needs ten rights to subscribe to a new share. Therefore, someone who owned a number of shares in the company that was not divisible by ten would have an excess of rights. An owner of 125 shares could subscribe to 12 shares and have five rights left. Rights have value. The shareholder may (1) sell the five rights, known as "rounding down," or (2) "round up" by buying the additional rights needed for a thirteenth full share. Someone who does not own the stock at all may buy rights in the marketplace and subscribe to the new shares when the cost of going this route is less than that of buying the actual stock in the open market and paying the broker-dealer commission on the trade. The commission charged on the trade may be more than the commission charged for the rights purchase and the subscription costs.

· Cum Rights and Ex Rights ·

When the rights' offering is announced, it will state the date that a shareholder must be beneficial owner to be entitled to receive the rights. From that date on, and until the rights are actually issued, the stock will trade "cum rights" (with rights). From the right issuance date on, the rights and the common stock will trade separately and the stock would be said to be trading "ex-rights" (without rights). Rights have a very short life span, from three to six months, usually closer to three months.

When the stock begins to trade cum rights, the rights are embedded in the share of stock, as is the value of the right itself. The stock and the right trade as one. On the day after the record date, the price of the cum-rights stock may open up or down in price or have no effect on the value of the stock's price.

The record date is the date in which the common shares of stock have the rights embedded. From that point of time on and up until the time the rights are actually issued, the stock trades "cum rights." Unlike dividends, where the owner of the stock on record date is entitled to the dividend regardless if they sold it after or not, the owner of the stock on the day the rights are issued will be given the rights. Should the shareholder who was the owner of the stock on the record date sell the stock while it is still in the cum rights phase, they sell the rights along with the stock as they are one and the same. Therefore, the rights follow the stock from seller to buyer until they are issued. At that point, the issue date, they separate and trade as two issues.

· Theoretical Value of a Right ·

Rights must have a value for the offering to be successful. Their value is the difference between the market value of the stock and the subscription price, divided by the number of rights needed to subscribe. There are two formulas used. One is for the stock and right trading together, and the other is for the stock after the rights are distributed and are trading on their own.

$$\text{Cum rights (with)} \quad \frac{\text{current market value} \; - \; \text{subscription price}}{\text{number of rights needed to subscribe} \; + \; 1}$$

$$\text{Ex rights (without)} \quad \frac{\text{current market value} \; - \; \text{subscription price}}{\text{number of rights needed to subscribe}}$$

Under the cum-rights formula, one additional right is added to the number of rights needed in subscription to offset the value of the right that is embedded in the stock's current market value. When the common stock begins to trade ex rights, that value will be lost to the common stock, as it will be carried by the newly issued rights.

Let's apply the formulas to the above-mentioned Loster Corporation. With its common stock trading at $85.50 per share, the company wants to add 1,000,000 new shares of common stock to the already outstanding 10,000,000 shares. It has been decided by the corporation's management and its investment banker that the new shares will cost the subscribers $80 per share.

Rights Formula

The computations for the value of a right are based on the following:

Cum rights:

Current market value of a share of stock:	$85.50
Subscription price:	$80.00
Number of rights needed to subscribe:	
10,000,000 shares outstanding divided	
by 1,000,000 new shares:	10
Plus one more share to offset the value of	
the embedded right that is in the stock	1

$$\frac{\$85.50 \; - \; \$80}{10 \text{ rights} \; + \; 1} = \frac{\$5.50}{11} = \$.50$$

If the assumptions above are correct, then when the rights are issued, the stock should lose $.50 in value.

Ex rights:

Current market value of a share of stock: $85.00

Subscription price: $80.00

Number of rights needed to subscribe:

    10,000,000 shares outstanding divided

    by 1,000,000 new shares: 10

$$\frac{\$85.00 \; - \; \$80}{10 \text{ rights}} = \frac{\$5.00}{10} = \$.50$$

The value shown by these formulas is the right's theoretical value. The actual value of the rights will be determined by market forces.

While the rights are "in play," the common stock must stay above the subscription price for the offer to be successful. If it should be equal to or drop in value below the subscription price, the offering is, for all intents and purposes, dead. With the rights worthless and the stock trading at or below the subscription price, no one would subscribe.

Besides being used for subscription purposes, rights offer an attractive trading situation. In the above example, the rights were worth $.50. If the stock rose from $85 per share (ex-rights price) to $90 per share, the rights would double in value:

$$\frac{\$90 \; - \; \$80}{10} = \frac{\$10}{10} = \$1$$

While the stock increased less than 6 percent, the rights doubled in value. In addition, should the stock fall in price and the rights become worthless, the trader cannot lose any more than $.50. Had the trader bought the common stock instead of the rights, the exposure to loss would be much greater. However, the life of a right is very short, whereas the stock will go on as long as the company remains in business.

· TRADING RIGHTS ·

Rights offer an interesting trading opportunity and many times are confused with call stock options. Both appreciate as the underlying issue increases in value, and both expire. There is a major difference in the exercising of the products. When the rights holder subscribes, the issuing corporation receives an infusion of capital vs. the stock being issued, which was the purpose of the rights offering in the first place. When a call option is exercised, the writer of the option delivers shares of stock that are already outstanding vs. payment, and the issuing company receives nothing.

If the right offering is attractive, the price of the rights may go to a slight premium, that is, trade over the theoretical value. Arbitrageurs and traders watch the price of rights very carefully, especially when interest in the rights wanes and they go to a discount. Not everyone who owns the stock would be interested in investing additional money and subscribing to the new shares. Those shareholders who are not interested will sell their rights. If more rights are being sold than bought, the price will fall, possibly below the theoretical value. When it does, arbitrageurs and traders will buy up the discounted rights, subscribe, and sell the common stock, locking in a profit. To accomplish this, the "back office" of the broker-dealer or bank must become involved and take actions that support the transaction. (When we talk about arbitrageurs and traders here and throughout this book, we are referring to professional employees of certain financial institutions, such as broker-dealers, whose job it is to perform this type of trading.)

Assume interest in the subscription does not develop and the rights are selling at $.25 instead of the theoretical value of $.50. An arbitrageur goes into the market and buys 10,000 rights at $.25 per right, for a total cost $2,500, and immediately sells 1,000 shares of stock at $85 per share ($85,000 total). The arbitrageur's firm then subscribes to the 1,000 new shares at $80 per share, for $80,000 plus the $2,500 paid for the rights, for a total cost of $82,500 and a profit of $2,500. If the transaction involved 100,000 rights (out of 10,000,000 rights), the profit would be $25,000, and so on.

Because the arbitrageur has sold stock that has not been issued, the arbitrageur's firm will borrow stock that is currently outstanding and deliver it to the buyer. The lender of the stock will be given the market value of the transaction in the form of cash as collateral against the borrowed stock.

When the "new" shares are issued, the arbitrageur's firm will take the subscribed-to shares and deliver them to the lender, who will return the collateral.

Unfortunately, those shareholders who maintain the common stock in their names and receive the rights directly from the corporation's agent often do not understand what the rights represent, assume they are part of the daily solicitations that they receive in the mail, and toss them out along with other unwanted mail. In so doing, they not only toss their rights to subscribe, but they also are out the money the rights represent. As the company is trying to raise a set amount of capital, the possibility of rights being disposed of is factored into the formula. If 10 percent of the rights are expected to be tossed out, the company will only be able to raise $72,000,000.

1. 10,000,000/10 rights for a new share = 1,000,000 shares
2. 1,000,000 shares × 90 percent = 900,000 shares
3. 900,000 shares × $80 per share = $72,000,000

They could also raise the number of shares they want to issue or find some other vehicle such as debt if the $72,000,000 was insufficient.

During the trading period, rights trade in the same way as common stocks. If the common stock is trading on a particular marketplace, the rights would trade there also. Their settlement cycle and trade clearance process are the same as those of common stock.

· Best Efforts Underwriting ·

At the end of the subscription period, a corporation will hire an underwriting firm to buy up the remaining rights that are in the market and subscribe to the new stock, which the underwriter will sell ("lay off") through its usual channels. This is known as a "standby" underwriting, as the underwriter is "standing by" to clean up whatever hasn't been accounted for. To limit its exposure, the underwriter may enter into a "best-efforts" agreement, which states terms (quantity, price, and marketability) under which the underwriter will act. The corporation may counter with an "all-or-none" agreement, which holds the underwriter to certain specific actions. Whichever is agreed upon, the rights purchased by the underwriter will be used in the subscription and the resulting stock sold into the marketplace. The syndicate manager is said to be "laying off" the stock. Any rights not used in the subscription, either by current stockholders or through a best-efforts underwriting, expire and the shares that they represent cannot be issued. After expiration of the rights, the old shares and the new shares trade as one.

3

Warrants

INCLUDED IN THIS CHAPTER:

- *Issuance*
- *Characteristics*

· ISSUANCE ·

One of the obscure products that we trade is warrants. They come to market attached to preferred stocks and corporate bonds and are known in this form as units. They trade as a unit for a period of time, and then they separate into two products, each trading on its own. The number of warrants included in the unit varies from product to product, and the way warrants are described often add to the confusion. For example, what one may hear described as a $1,000 bond with a warrant to purchase 100 shares of common stock is, in reality, a $1,000 bond and 100 warrants to purchase one share each.

· CHARACTERISTICS ·

A warrant permits its owner to purchase shares of common stock directly from the company over a long period of time. It is structured with an activation price that is higher than the current market price of the converted shares. Therefore, it is only attractive to the investor if the company is a growth-type company. Say the Crabar Corporation's common stock is currently trading at $30 per share. Crabar is a well-managed company, and based on its past results, definitely a growth company. The company needs financing to continue to grow, so it meets with its investment banker to discuss alternatives. The investment banker advises the company to issue twenty-year bonds, and based on where the company fits into the range of debt products, it would have to pay 8 percent interest. The company is looking to borrow $10,000,000. At an 8 percent rate, that is an $800,000 payout annually, or $16,000,000 of interest paid out over the twenty years. The investment bankers recommend that the company package bonds and warrants. With the stock at $30, the warrants are offered with an electing price of $45 per share and can be activated any time over the next twenty years. Based on the attractiveness of the terms of the warrants, the bonds can be offered at 7 percent, saving the company $100,000 per year, or $2,000,000 over twenty years.

With the stock at $30 per share and the warrants being tendered at $45, the warrants do not have any real value. The exception may be to investors who like the company and see the warrants as an inexpensive way of buying into the company at a later date. Suppose the company grows and prospers and over the next few years the company's common stock rises in value above the electing price of the warrant. As Crabar common stock nears the election price of $45, the price of the warrants would begin to appreciate in value also. If the common stock was trading at $50 per share, the once worthless warrants would have a minimal value of $5 per warrant ($50 market value − $45 electing price = $5). We say "minimal value" because there could be an anticipatory amount added on to the price of the warrant. That anticipatory amount, set by the marketplace, is based on the belief that the stock will continue to rise in value and the warrant will increase in value also.

This leads the warrant holder to three possible actions:

1. Sell the warrants and lock in the profit.
2. Hold the warrants and hope for additional appreciation.
3. Elect the warrants and buy the common stock below the current market price, thereby establishing a profit position going into the stock.

While actions 1 and 3 are likely any time the current market price of the common stock is above the warrant's electing price, in most cases, as long as the stock continues to perform nicely, most warrant holders will take action 2 and ride the warrants until they are about to expire. This is the inexpensive way of profiting from the experience. Then they would take action 1 or 3.

It also must be pointed out that the increase in the price of the warrant due to the rise in the price of the stock does not resemble a light switch, as in "on" and "off." The price of the warrant is very low before the electing price of the warrant and the price of the common stock are equal (off) and suddenly shoots up when the price of the common stock passes the electing price (on). In reality, as the price of the common stock approaches the electing price, the demand for the warrant would pick up, first by speculators and arbitrageurs looking for a fast return and then by investors. Therefore, the warrants would gain value in anticipation of the common stock crossing over the warrant's electing price.

During the life of the warrant, it may become an attractive trading vehicle while it is "in the money." (That is, the warrant has value because the electing price of $45 is below the market price of the stock). Say Crabar common stock is trading at $50 per share, the warrants have an electing price of $45, and the warrants have several years of life remaining. The warrants would have an intrinsic value of $5. Should the stock rise in value to $55 during the warrant's life, the warrant would have an intrinsic value of $10, or have doubled, while the stock rose 10 percent. (The term *intrinsic value* is used because the anticipatory value the market places on the warrant cannot be determined but must be considered in the real world.)

Of course, the other side of the coin is that the stock price never reaches the electing price, and the buyer of the unit has overpaid for the interest payment received based on the safety or rating of the bond portion of the unit. The initial unit buyer was willing to give up some amount of interest in return for eventually cashing in the warrants.

The warrant holder does not receive cash dividends or have the right to vote. Stock splits and stock dividends affect the warrant the same way they affect the stockholder. In the case of a two-for-one split, for example, a warrant would become two warrants and the electing price would be halved. In our example above, assuming Crabar's price rose to $60 per share and split two for one, the owner of the common stock would have twice as many shares at $30 per share, whereas the owner of the warrant with an electing price of $45 would have twice as many warrants but at an electing price of $22.50.

Should Crabar become involved in a merger or be acquired, the purchasing power of the warrant would follow the stock. If for every share of Crabar the owner received 0.9 shares of the new company, then the owner of 100 warrants would be able to buy 90 shares of the new company at an equivalent adjusted price.

Warrants are tradable. They are listed on exchanges and also trade over the counter. A round lot is 100 warrants. Warrants that are way out of the money (that is, the electing price of the warrant is higher than the market price of the stock) are priced on the expectation of eventually reaching and passing the electing price. The brighter the future, the more expensive the warrant. However, warrants can also be totally worthless.

Many things can happen to a company during the long life of a warrant. The company can start off strong, then fall into a morass, and then go through a resurgence. All the while, the warrant will track the common stock.

4

Preferred Stock

• CHARACTERISTICS •

I s it a stock or a bond? Stocks denote ownership, but preferred stocks do not carry the voting privilege in corporate matters that common stocks do. Corporate bonds are supposed to pay a regular stream of taxable income; so do preferred stocks. Bonds may contain a conversion feature that permits the security owner to convert the bond into common shares. Some preferred stocks contain this type of conversion feature also. Bond prices are interest-rate sensitive; so are preferred stocks. Common stocks are sold in shares of the company; so are preferred stocks. Bonds are sold as principal loans with maturity. Preferred stocks are not and can remain alive in perpetuity; so does common stock. On some preferred stock, the holders can lose dividend payments if the contracted periodic payments are passed over. Bondholders can start foreclosure procedures if the interest payment obligation is not met. Preferred stockholders cannot, as they are owners and would be foreclosing on themselves. Bonds have a prior claim on assets over common stock in the case of corporate liquidation; so do preferred stocks. (Bonds have a prior claim over preferred stocks in case of corporate liquidation.) So what is a preferred stock?

A preferred stock represents a nonvoting share in the ownership of the corporation. In place of capital appreciation, the preferred stock stresses an income stream in the form of a dividend payout. However, as with bonds, the financial strength of the issuer affects the price. In other words, the surety of the quarterly dividend payment affects the price. The preferred stockholders' dividend is paid before the common stock can receive any dividend. To the issuer it provides an opportunity to raise capital without incurring debt. In others words, the balance sheet is cleaner. To the investor it's another income-producing product to choose from. Depending on the preferred stock's features, there may be a possibility of capital appreciation.

· Dividend Payout Regimen ·

The typical preferred stock is issued with the annual dividend rate displayed in its description. The preferred stock's dividends are paid on a quarterly basis. The rate is presented in either a dollar or percent format. For example: The Zip corporation issues a preferred stock. Its description would look like ZIP $6 pfd. Each share of the issue is supposed to pay $6 per year. A "percent" preferred stock is a little trickier, as it pays a percent of its par value. The preferred stock's par value may be $100 or $50 or whatever the company has set it as at the time of issuance. For all intents and purposes, the par value of a stock does nothing but convert shares to dollars in the stockholders' equity section of the corporation's balance sheet. It does not have a thing to do with the current market value of the stock. If the preferred share is a 6 percent preferred and the par value is $100, the preferred is supposed to pay $6 per share per year. If, however, the preferred is a 6 percent with a $50 par value, it is supposed to pay only $3 per share per year, and so on. Therefore, in a percent preferred, what is seen in the description may not be what the preferred actually pays annually. A broker-dealer or bank can verify the par value by checking its security master or security reference file. The public can do the same by going on the Web and checking the issuer's Web page or looking up the issue in a security source book.

Preferred stocks' dividends are usually paid quarterly. The divided payout policy is usually abbreviated as JAJO (January, April, July, October),

FMAN (February, May, August, November), or MJSD (March, June, September, December). The day of payment will also be stated. As with common stock, the recipient of the dividend must be the owner on the record date, which is also set by the issuer. That could precede the payable date by two or three weeks, and in some cases even more. As we discussed in the chapter on common stock, dividends must be declared and voted on by the board of directors. At the time of an affirmative vote, the board also sets the declaration date, the record date, and payable date. To be entitled to the dividend, the investor must be the legal owner on the night of the record date. As preferred stocks trade in a three-day settlement cycle, the last day that an investor can buy the preferred stock in its usual cycle is three business days before the record date. This is the regular settlement cycle for preferred stocks.

Preferred stocks trade on exchanges and in the over-the-counter markets. A round lot for preferred stock may be 100 shares or 10 shares. This determination is made when the preferred stock begins to trade and is usually a function of the preferred stock offering price. Any quantity less than the round lot size is called an odd lot and only applies to full shares. No fractional shares are offered.

· TYPES OF PREFERRED STOCK ·

Preference, Prior, or First Preferred

A preferred stock with any of these words in its description has prior claim over other preferred stocks for dividends and company assets in the case of liquidation. In the pecking order of default risk, these preferred shares rate higher than other preferred stock that the company may have outstanding. Their dividend is paid before any other equity shares, and they fall right below the payment of interest to debts in the payout cycle.

To make a preferred stock appealing in the market, the corporation may add features to the preferred stock. Some of these features involve the preferred stock's dividend. Others may affect its longevity, while others may affect both. Preferred stocks take earnings away from the pool that is left for the common stock. Dividends, whether they are paid on common or preferred stocks, are after-tax items. Interest paid on debt instruments are before-tax items. That means, for example, that the interest paid on corporate bonds reduces company earnings before the company's income is reported to the tax authorities. This has the effect of lowering the corporation's tax liability. Dividends reduce company earnings after taxes have been deducted from earnings. To the common stockholder, anything that reduces company earnings before those earnings get to the common stockholder for their possible dividend is reducing the amount available to them. Therefore, while features are added to some preferred stocks to make them more attractive to potential buyers, they could very well be taking money out of the common stockholder's pocket. Examples of the impact of some of the features are shown a little later in this chapter. Preferred features under discussion are:

Adjustable rate (Floating rate) / fixed rate
Callable
Convertible / nonconvertible
Cumulative / noncumulative
Participating
Putable
Reverse floating
Straight

In some cases, one or more of these features may appear in a particular preferred stock. For example, a preferred stock may be a cumulative participating convertible preferred or a callable convertible preferred. The issuer and its investment banker want to bring to market an attractive investment product at the lowest dividend cost while minimizing the impact on the common stockholders. It is also possible that the preferred stock offering may contain a clause that states: "If the preferred stockholder has not been paid its dividend X consecutive times, the preferred stockholder shall be granted the right to vote." This is a rare exception to the standard preferred format, but it does exist.

Straight Preferred

The simplest of the preferred stock group is the straight preferred. Some preferred stocks do not have any special features and are priced and traded as if they were bonds. This type of preferred is usually issued by the financially strongest of companies. In trading firms these preferred stocks generally trade alongside long-term corporate bonds. The straight preferred is supposed to pay its dividends quarterly and will be outstanding as long as the company exists. If a dividend on straight preferred stock is omitted by the company, it is lost forever to the holders of the stock; therefore, straight preferred stock is noncumulative preferred stock (see next section).

Cumulative or Noncumulative Preferred

When preferred stock is issued, it may be cumulative or noncumulative preferred. In the case of a cumulative preferred, any dividend or part thereof that is not paid on its payable date must be paid to the preferred shareholders before the common shareholder can receive a dividend, regardless of how long the preferred payment has been delayed. This is an important feature because it blocks the common stockholder from receiving dividends if there are preferred dividends in arrears. In the case of a noncumulative dividend, once a dividend period has passed without payment being made, the preferred dividend is lost, and while the common stockholders cannot receive dividends at that time, they can begin to receive dividends from the next dividend payment period on.

As preferred stocks are interest-rate sensitive, the issuer's track record of dividend payments plays an important part in the pricing of the preferred stock. As with bonds, a $6 preferred is supposed to pay $6 per share per year. If the stock is trading at $100 per share, then its current yield is 6 percent. If suddenly the issuer cannot pay the full amount (say it pays 4 percent, instead of 6 percent) the difference will appear in the preferred stock's price, as the reduction in actual payout from the supposed payout will lower the price of the preferred stock. Someone owning the preferred stock prior to the announcement of the company's inability to meet the $6 requirement would lose principal in the investment as well as income in the dividend. Remember, the preferred stockholder is an owner in the company, not a lender the way a bondholder is. Therefore, the preferred stockholder cannot implement the remedies or take the actions that are afforded the bondholder, such as foreclosure.

If the preferred stock is a noncumulative preferred, the corporation theoretically could deliberately miss a preferred stock payment or two, then at the next period pay the preferred only the payment currently due while awarding the common stockholder a special dividend over and above what the common stockholder usually receives. In the case of a cumulative preferred, the corporation couldn't pay a dividend to the common shareholders before paying the preferred holder the current dividend and all dividends that were in arrears.

While the preferred stock does not have the right to vote, the cumulative preferred stockholder can indirectly put pressure on the common stockholder, who does have the power to vote. If there are preferred stock dividends in arrears, the common stockholders may get annoyed that their cash flow has been curtailed and demand, through their common stock's voting privilege, that the company clean up the preferred stock's dividend backlog so that they can resume receiving their dividend. Not only can't the common stockholders receive dividends because of the preferred stock's dividend arrears, but the value of their investment in the common stock is probably suffering also.

Cumulative preferred stocks may offer an interesting investment opportunity when the company emerges from a financially weak situation, where it has passed over or partially paid its dividends and its finances have now begun to turn around. As the company gets financially stronger, its common stockholders (who vote for the board of directors) are going to want to start to receive dividends. This will push the issuer to pay all and any preferred stock dividends in arrears.

Payment of these owed dividends will increase the preferred stock's yield over the short term, which in turn should cause the price of the preferred to increase. The important questions are what dollar amount of dividends is in arrears, and how long it will take the preferred dividends that are in arrears to be paid down. Those two questions will affect the preferred stock's yield, which in turn will affect its price. The same type of opportunity may exist in the case of a noncumulative preferred where a company has not paid any dividends for an extended period of time and, due to improved or altered financial condition, starts to pay the noncumulative preferred shareholders their dividends. In both cases, the price of the preferred stock will rise in relation to how secure the regular payment of dividend is thought to be. Investors may buy these preferred stocks well in advance of any dividend announcement by the issuer, under the belief that (1) if their assumptions are correct, the back dividends (in the case of the cumulative preferred) and future dividends (in the case of both types of preferred stocks) will be paid, causing the preferred stock's price to rise, or (2) if their assumptions are incorrect, they can sell the stock at a small loss or no loss at all. To benefit from either of these two strategies, one must understand the fortunes of the issuer and anticipate when the issuer will be in a position to commence the payment of missing dividends. Timing of this activity will determine the result. In other words, when there is a general consensus that the company will start to pay the dividends, it may be too late to take action.

Example 1:

Assume that Loster Corporation has one share of $6 preferred and one share of common stock outstanding and pays out all of its earnings. The following charts show the amount earned each year and the dividend paid to the one preferred shareholder and the one common stockholder.

Chart 1
The preferred stock is a $6 noncumulative issue.

Year	Year 1	Year 2	Year 3	Year 4	Year 5	Total
Earnings	$3	$15	$4	$2	$12	$36
Preferred	$3	$6	$4	$2	$6	$21
Common	$0	$9	$0	$0	$6	$15

Note: Over the five previous years, the preferred averaged slightly over $4 per year. It would be priced closer to a $4 preferred of equal financial strength than one truly paying $6 per year.

Chart 2
The preferred stock is a $6 cumulative issue: The dividends not paid to the preferred shareholder accumulate and must be paid with the currently owed dividend before the common may receive its dividend.

Year	Year 1	Year 2	Year 3	Year 4	Year 5	Total
Earnings	$3	$15	$4	$2	$12	$36
Preferred	$3 owes 3	$6 + 3 = $9	$4 owes $2	$2 owes 4 + 2	$6 + 4 + 2 = $12	$30
Common	$0	$6	$0	$0	$0	$6

Year one: The company earned $3 and paid $3 of the $6 owed to the preferred shareholder. The $3 that was not paid is carried into the next year. The common stockholder received nothing.

Year two: The company earned $15. It paid the preferred shareholder the current dividend of $6 plus the $3 that was in arrears from the previous divided period for a total of $9. The common stockholder received the remaining $6 from the $15 earned.

Year three: Earnings for the company were only $4 this year, so it all goes to the preferred shareholder with the $2 being carried into the next year. The common received nothing.

Year four: Earnings were down even further to only $2. The preferred stockholder receives the $2 and $4 is carried over to the next year, along with the $2 being carried over from the previous year for a total of $6 worth of dividends in arrears. The common stockholder received zero again.

Year five: Fortunes change and the company earned $12. It owes $6 for the current year, $2 from year three and $4 from year four, for a total of $12. All of the earnings are distributed to the preferred shareholder and the common stockholder again receives nothing.

Note: In the above example, there are various ways to identify the root of the dividends being paid. The one that was chosen demonstrates more clearly the cumulative feature.

While not a perfect $6 paying instrument, it at least comes close. A more reliable $6 payer would be selling at a higher price.

In the above case, the cumulative feature of the preferred stock cost a common stockholder $9 in dividends over the five years.

Participating Preferred

A participating preferred stock pays its regular dividend and can share in an extra payout when certain stipulated circumstances are present. A corporation that is in a cyclical business may offer a participating preferred. Due to the nature of that business, the company may not be able to pay a level dividend. Instead, the investment banker and company structure the preferred so that it is attractive to the investor and manageable to the common stockholders and the company. In essence, the preferred stockholders and common shareholders will receive their dividend when the company can pay. At the end of the business cycle when the company earnings are at the highest point, the company may announce an extra dividend payment, known as a special dividend. This payment is supposed to compensate, to some extent, for the payments that were small or were missed entirely during the previous period. When the company announces the special dividend, the preferred and common stock will share in the extra dividend in some prearranged ratio. The ratio is established at the time of the preferred stock's offering.

Using the earnings from charts 1 and 2 above, let's assume the common shareholder can earn $2 in dividends per share per year, the preferred shareholder can earn $6 per share per year, and any additional dividend is split equally. And again, the company pays out all of its earning to the one preferred shareholder and the one common stockholder.

Chart 3

Year	Year 1	Year 2	Year 3	Year 4	Year 5	Total
Earning	$3	$15	$4	$2	$12	$36
Preferred	$3	$6 + 3.50	$4	$2	$6 + 2	$26.50
Common	$0	$2 + 3.50	$0	$0	$2 + 2	$9.50

The historical statistics about the issue's payment policy, the income earned by the preferred stock over time, and the timing of the business cycle are all important to the investor's decision process. As there are many participants interested in the company and the preferred stock, the price of the preferred and, depending on the preferred stock's structure, the common stock will likely foretell when the approaching "special dividend" is at hand. Many of those interested are focusing on the return on their investment, which includes the dividend payout and the price appreciation. If this preferred is priced as $4 preferred ($26.50 − $5.50 in special dividends years 2 and 5 = $21.00 / 5 years = $4.20) and is selling at $100 per share, then when the payout rises to $9.50 in year 2 and $8.00 in year 5, the price of the stock will rise to reflect the temporary boost in yield. The price of the preferred will start to rise in anticipation of the special dividend being paid before any formal announcements are made, as those who are following the stock and/or the company will seize on the potential opportunity.

Convertible Preferred

Convertibility of preferred stock as with a convertible bond, is a one-time feature that permits the security owner to convert to another security, usually common stock, at a certain predetermined ratio. In activating the conversion feature, the security owner is giving up the dividend cash flow of the preferred for possible capital appreciation of the common stock, or in the rare cases where the conversion is not to the common stock of the issuer, some desired feature of the other issue.

The ratio of preferred stock to common stock varies from issue to issue. For example, say Loster Motor Corporation $5 convertible preferred is convertible into 2 shares of Loster Motor Corporation common stock. The preferred stock was offered into the marketplace at $100 per share. That is the price it commands due to its dividend rate and the strength of Loster Motor Corporation. At the time of the preferred issuance, Loster Motors common stock is trading at $30 per share. The common stock is selling below parity (2 × $30 = $60). No one will convert the preferred stock into the common shares, and the preferred stock will trade at its value as an income-producing product. As the value of the Loster common stock rises due to the good fortune of the issuer, the stock will approach parity or the point at which the preferred stock value and the converted common stock value are equal. Assuming the preferred is still trading at $100 per share, parity will be reached when the common is trading at $50 (2 × $50 = $100). As the common stock crosses parity, professional traders, called arbitrageurs, will start to buy the preferred and sell the common, locking in the spread between the two securities. For example, say the common stock is trading at $51. They will buy the preferred at $100, convert it into 2 shares of common stock, and sell the common stock, locking in a $2 per share profit.

Proceeds from sale of 2 shares of common stock at $51 each	$102.00
Cost of the 1 share preferred stock	100.00
Profit	$ 2.00

Naturally, they do not arbitrage one share of preferred stock, but a thousand or multiples thereof is a different story. The demand will force the preferred stock's price to rise until it reaches parity with the converted common stock. Therefore, at this point the preferred shareholders, who still own the preferred shares, are receiving the dividend as well as seeing the price of their shares being pulled up in value by the common stock. This is one of the rare instances where the preferred shareowner has the best of both worlds: a bondlike dividend stream and capital appreciation.

All is not so rosy, as some preferred stocks have a "cap." The terms of the preferred may state that the preferred is convertible into X shares of common stock or the number of shares equal to the preferred stocks' par value, whichever is less. The rationale behind this feature is that the preferred stockholder has been receiving a high rate of dividend payment, a rate much higher than that received by the common stockholder. While the preferred shareowner has been earning dividends at a consistent rate with market price stability, it was the common stockholder who participated in the ups and downs of the common stock's price. With the common stock trading below parity, the preferred has been priced based on its dividend payment and yield (as with bonds that trade on the coupon rate and yield). The preferred price has remained fairly stagnant, as long as there haven't been any major changes in the market's current interest rate or the financial strength of the issuer. Therefore, the preferred shareholder shouldn't be entitled to the windfall of the financial rewards that the issuer is finally attaining and should be treated as if it were the holder of a straight preferred.

The difference between the two methods of issuing convertible preferreds is caused by the goal of management. The fixed-convertible preferred would have a tendency to incur a slower conversion process than capped-convertible preferred because there is little for the preferred shareholder to gain by converting. As mentioned earlier, once the converted common stock's value exceeds parity, arbitrageurs will buy the preferred and sell the common stock while converting the preferred shares into common. This process will continue until both issues are back in parity. Because of the demand placed by the arbitrageurs on the preferred stock, which trades in a much thinner market than the common stock, the price will increase. Their selling of the common will have little or no effect on the common stock's price. The preferred shareholder is reaping capital appreciation as well as the preferred stock's dividend. There isn't an incentive for the preferred stockholder to convert. The capped preferred offers a very strong incentive to a convertible preferred stockholder to convert early. As the converted common stock's value exceeds par, the number of shares being converted into common stock diminishes, forcing the preferred shareholders to decide whether they want to be common stockholders and hope for continued capital appreciation or be preferred shareholders and collect the higher-rate dividend.

Assuming the preferred has a par value of $100 and is convertible into 4 shares of common stock, the capped preferred would hold to that ratio as long as the converted 4 shares equaled $100 or less. For example, when the common stock rose in price to $33.33 per share, the preferred would only be convertible into 3 shares of common stock (3 × $33.333 = $100), at a common-stock price of a $50 per common share the preferred would convert into two shares (2 × $50 = $100), and so on.

When a company's common and convertible preferred stock are trading at parity and the company wants to get out of the burden of paying the preferred stock dividend year in and year out, the company may offer the common stockholder an attractive "special" dividend. This usually is in the form of a one-time cash payment. Assuming parity between the two issues, if the convertible preferred shareholders want the special dividend, they will convert their preferred shares into common stock. The preferred shareholder who converts can either continue to own the common shares or sell them after the special dividend has been accounted for and buy some other security. In addition, on the announcement of the special dividend, the demand for the common stock may cause it to rise above parity, and traders and arbitrageurs, who do not want to own either the preferred stock or the common stock, will buy the preferred, convert to the common stock, pick up the dividend, and then sell the common. This may be performed in a one-two-three manner, with the trader or arbitrageur hoping to profit on the slight price discrepancy caused by the common stock being over parity as well as picking up the special dividend. Traders and arbitrageurs are employed by the firms and therefore do not pay commission the way the public does, so their activity can be profitable at a minimal cost.

Preferred Equity Redemption (PERC)

Much like a convertible preferred stock is preferred equity redemption stock, or PERC. This preferred can generally be converted into common stock any time during its life. Unlike a convertible preferred, this type of preferred has a life span and is not perpetual with the company. At the end of the issue's life, either the owner will receive cash or the shares will be converted into underlying issue. The quantity of underlying stock the preferred equity redemption shareholder will receive at conversion may depend on the value of the underlying stock at the time of the mandatory conversion. In other words, the underlying share value is capped.

Callable Preferred

Like callable bonds, some preferred stock may contain a call feature that allows the company to retire the preferred issue. The call feature will be exercised when the company either no longer needs that financing or, more likely, can arrange for the same financing at a lower cost. Remember as noted at the beginning of the bond chapter, rule number one is that no one enjoys paying interest. Companies also do not want to pay dividends to noncommon stockholders (common stockholders vote). If the company can call in the preferred and pay for it by issuing a lower-dividend-paying preferred or a lower-cost debt instrument, the difference between the two preferred payments or the interest/dividend payments will flow into the retained earnings account on the company's balance sheet (a critical financial statement), or some or all of it could be made available for payment to the common stockholder (remember, the common stockholders vote for the management of the corporation).

Many preferred stocks have a waiting period before the call feature can kick in. A preferred stock may be "non-callable for X years." The "X years" is measured from the date the shares were issued, not from the purchase date of the shareholder. The noncallable feature varies from issue to issue. It may be five years, ten years, or whatever the issuer and its investment banker decide. The noncallable clause is instituted for the protection of the investor's interests. An investor may be reluctant to acquire the issue if falling interest rates over the near term could terminate the investment. With the noncallable clause in effect, the investor is assured that the issue will be outstanding for at least that period of time.

Callable preferred stock, like a callable bond, is priced two ways. When the dividend rate is in line with the interest rate associated with securities with similar risk and related characteristics or below the appropriate current rate, the preferred stock will be priced as an interest-rate instrument. When the interest rate falls and it could become economically prudent for the company to replace the callable preferred stock with a lower-cost instrument, it will be priced closer to its call price. The call price is usually found in the instrument's description. If it is not there, it can be found by querying any stock vendor service or looking up the company's year-end report on the Web.

The adage that when interest rates rise, the price of interest-sensitive instruments falls, and vice versa, holds true for noncallable preferred stocks also. When an investor observes that a preferred is paying a higher dividend than securities equal to it in all other attributes that should signal that something is wrong. The "something wrong" is that the market was anticipating the company calling in the issue; the unknown is when. Since the preferred stock is selling below where it should be because of the call feature, other investors may be counting on the higher return for as long as the preferred continues to trade. Once the preferred is called, the dividend payments end and the investor must take the cost of the purchase, less all income received, less the value received at call, to determine if the investment was profitable or not.

EXAMPLE

The prices in the example are assumed for explanatory purposes. They serve to show that even though the buyer of the convertible preferred had a trading loss when the instrument was called in after two years, in effect the buyer was financially better off than he or she would have been had he or she acquired the 6 percent instrument.

8%, callable at 102, *trading at 104*		*6%, noncallable,* *trading at par*	
1. Investor A bought 1,000 shares at $104=	$104,000	Investor B bought 1,000 shares at $100 = $100,000	
Less:			
2. First year's dividends	$8,000		$6,000
3. Second year's dividends	$8,000		$6,000
4. Call / selling price	$102,000	@ $100	$100,000
Net income	$14,000		$12,000

5. $14,000 – $12,000 = $2,000

Note 1: Both preferred stocks have a par value of $100. The 8 percent preferred is to pay $8 per share per year, whereas the 6 percent preferred is to pay $6 per share per year.

Note 2: The 8 percent callable preferred was not a new issue and had been trading for a long period of time.

Note 3: The prices used for the 6 percent assume that interest rate and other factors were the same at the time the investor acquired and sold the issue.

Note 4: Investor A, the owner of the 8 percent callable preferred, earned $2,000 more than Investor B, the owner of the 6 percent noncallable preferred, even after the subtraction of the loss incurred by Investor A when the issue was called.

This example was used to give a holistic view of a transaction. Many times investors and speculators focus on only select parts of the transaction, such as what was paid when the stock was acquired and what was received when it was sold. They neglect to consider additional transactions that occur because of the initial transaction.

A call may be a full call or a partial call. In the case of a full call, the entire issue ceases to exist as of a certain date. The shares of stock are surrendered to the issuer's agent and the call price paid. In a partial call, the quantity being called is announced and then an allocation is made, usually by a lottery, for the desired quantity. Therefore, an investor may have his or her preferred shares entirely called, partially called, or not called at all. At all levels, from the issuer's agent through the custodians that maintain the owners' positions, the allocation methods and application are supervised to ensure fair treatment.

Adjustable (Floating) Rate Preferred (ARP)

The floating rate exists in many debt products, such as corporate notes and mortgages. In preferred stocks, the dividend rate is in effect for a limited period of time, after which it is adjusted to reflect what the rate would be if the issue was being brought to market at that time. It requires all aspects of the appropriate rate decision process to remain constant for the life of the preferred to accomplish its intended goal.

The purpose of a floating-rate feature is to make a long-term, interest-sensitive instrument behave, marketwise, as a short-term, interest-sensitive instrument. As interest rates rise, the value of outstanding fixed-rate interest-rate instruments will decrease because the new instruments being brought to market are paying a higher rate. To make the outstanding fixed-rate instrument competitive with the newly issued one, the price of the outstanding instrument must fall so that it has a competitive yield. (The bond chapter of this book covers this topic in more detail.) Conversely, when interest rates decrease, the value of fixed-income instruments increases, due again to the issuing interest rate of new instruments that are being offered at lower rates. The risk the holder of a long-term instrument faces from the swinging of interest rates is known as market risk. To explain this further, let's look at what would happen if an investor had to sell a fixed-income instrument when the current rates were much higher than the investor's instrument's rate and/or much higher than the going rate was when the investor acquired the instrument. The investor is going to lose principal that he or she invested. Therefore, investors who are more concerned about principal than they are about interest rates will tend to invest in short-term instruments. By following this strategy, regardless of which way interest rates flow, the investor will get his or her investment (principal) back when the short-term instruments mature. The purpose of long-term adjustable-rate instruments is to attract the short-term investor. If the interest rate, in this case the dividend rate, is adjusted to the current equivalent rate, the price of the adjustable-rate preferred should return to the offering price or par.

The risk with this product, and any similar type product, for that matter, is that over time the financial strength of the issuer may diminish, causing the market price to reflect its weaker condition and not return to the level it was before the current rate setting. This decreasing of financial strength may be offset by the issuer increasing the adjustment, but this method is not common. The usual method is to "peg" the preferred rate to another rate (e.g., 200 basis points over LIBOR [London Interbank Offer Rate, used as a base for many debt-type instruments] or 200 basis points over the current U.S. Treasury bill rate). If an instrument is set at 200 basis points over another rate, that equates to a 2 percent point difference. This relationship will continue as long as the instrument is outstanding. If the issuer's financial condition weakens, this will have a negative effect on the pricing of that instrument. A strengthening of the company's financing will cause the issue to rise above its expected level.

Reverse Floating Rate Preferred

The reverse floating rate preferred feature is interesting because it goes against normal processes. The manager of a money fund (a fund composed of short-term instruments) competes with similar funds for the public's investments. As short-term interest rates fall, competition increases as buyers in that segment of the market not only seek out other short-term products but also start to look at longer-term offerings. The reverse floating rate preferred feature can be used to increase the return of a short-term fund.

For example, say Loster Corporation is going to market a preferred stock through its investment banker, Stone Forrest and Rivers (SFR). At the current time, and based on Loster Corporation's financial condition, SFR recommends that Loster Corporation can successfully market a 6 percent adjustable-rate preferred that will contain the following components: At offering, the 6 percent preferred will have a 4 percent regular floating rate preferred and a 2 percent reverse floating rate preferred. The 4 percent preferred will trade at the rate of a 4 percent adjustable-rate preferred with Loster Corporation's level of financial security, but the 2 percent reverse floating rate will trade at a higher price than the conventional-rate preferred because of its unique feature. In this case, the sum of the parts is greater than the whole.

To the Loster Corporation, the issue is a fixed 6 percent preferred stock. To the investing public, there are two separate and distinct products. One is a standard adjustable-rate preferred, whereas the other is the opposite. When the interest rate rises, the adjustable-rate preferred's rate will rise also, and the reverse adjustable-rate preferred will fall. When interest rates fall, the reverse occurs; the adjustable-rate preferred rate will fall, and the reverse adjustable rate will increase. The second is the one of interest to those who manage short-term money. They can buy these securities to augment their portfolios and enhance the returns on their portfolios.

Again, with most investments timing is critical. As interest rates change, so do the prices of these two instruments. A rush to either one of these products will result in a price increase to one and a price decrease to the other. These price changes usually occur before the actual adjustment in interest rates occurs.

Putable Preferred

A call allows the owner to "call in" the underlying product, whereas a put permits the owner to "put out" the product. When it comes to preferred stock, a callable preferred permits the issuer to call in, or retire, the product under certain conditions. As stated above, the two main conditions are time and current financing costs. Therefore, a putable preferred should allow the preferred shareholder to put the preferred back to the issuer under certain conditions. Those conditions should be favorable to the preferred shareholder. While true putable preferred stocks exist, the most popular form is the mandatory put, where the issuer mandates that the preferred stock owner put his or her shares back to the company. This type of put would be exercised when it is to the best advantage of the issuer. To this author, a mandatory "put" looks like, is used like, and has the same effect as a "callable" preferred stock. The difference may be marketing! Those preferred stocks with an actual put, one that allows the preferred shareholder to put the preferred stock back to the issuer when the shareholder wants to, usually have rigid terms, such as time of feature existence, under which the feature can be exercised.

Rule 144A

Preferred stocks are the most interesting of issues because of the variety and combination of features that can exist. Because of their flexibility in structure, they can lend themselves to special situations. Rule 144A of the 1933 Truth in Securities Act made it easier for corporations to issue securities to qualified institutions and select high-net-worth individuals. The basis for this rule is that these investors have had deep investment experience and are savvy enough not to need all the detail, with the *I*s dotted and the *T*s crossed, that a full public offering requires. The flexibility inherent in the preferred-stock structure allows this instrument to be customized so as to satisfy the needs of an acquiring group of these investors.

To qualify under 144A, an investor must be a qualified intuitional buyer (QIB) or a high-net-worth individual. For an institution to qualify, it must own and invest in aggregate, on a discretionary basis, at least $100 million in securities of issuers with which it is not affiliated. The institution can be an insurance company, an investment company registered under the Investment Company Act of 1940, a registered bank, an employee benefit plan (within the meaning of Title I of the Employee Retirement Income Security Act of 1974), or others. High-net-worth individuals must have at least $750,000 managed by a reporting investment adviser, or the investment adviser must believe that the client is worth at least $1,500,000.

The preferred instrument is also used in merchant banking, where sizable investments are made in a company. The merchant banker is willing to accept preferred stock, and the corporation is willing to offer the preferred stock, as it represents a passive investment, not having any voting rights.

· CONCLUSION ·

Preferred stock is a different kind of product. While it does represent ownership, it trades like a bond. It is an interest-rate-driven instrument. It lends itself to many features that attract particular types of investors. The customization that is available makes it a favorite of 144A offerings.

DEBT
PRODUCTS

5

Debt Markets

T he world is made up borrowers and lenders. The borrowers want to borrow money for the least possible cost, and lenders want to lend money at the highest possible return. The phrase equating the two is interest rate.

· INTRODUCTION ·

Let's put down some simple rules to better understand this complex market.

RULE 1 No one likes to pay interest.

RULE 2 An issuer is only obligated to pay off the loan represented by the debt instrument as stipulated in the terms under which the debt was issued. This is known as the deed of trust or indenture.

RULE 3 In the feverish competition for investors' dollars, different products offer different qualities or attributes. These differences may or may not be beneficial to a particular investor, so it behooves that investor to be aware of the existence of these differences before making the investment, not after.

RULE 4 All investments compete for the same investors' dollars, which brings us back to Rule 1: No one likes to pay interest!

· Types of Risk ·

All debt instruments face two primary forms of risk. One is known as credit risk, or the possibility the issuer will not be able to meet its obligations to the loan or debt instruments any time over the life of the debt instrument. The second is market risk, that is, as interest rates fluctuate from day to day, the fluctuation will cause the price of an outstanding debt instrument to change.

Market

(In the following examples, disregard tax liability differences.)

Assume a six-month U.S. Treasury bill is yielding a 3 percent return on your investment. If I am your registered representative, and I tell you we have a twenty-year U.S. Treasury bond for sale that was also yielding 3 percent, would that be a good deal? Under usual circumstances, the answer would be no. The Treasury bill will pay back its face amount in six months, whereas the Treasury bond will pay its face amount in twenty years. From now and for the next twenty years, if you had to sell the bonds, you would receive whatever the market said the bonds were worth, even though the bonds are backed by the full taxing power of the U.S. government. At the time you wanted to sell, the market value of your twenty-year bond would be determined by the then-current interest rate for such an instrument. Therefore, its price might be higher or lower than its value today. This is known as market risk. The next example shows this in more detail.

Let's make up a company, Loster Corporation. It is a large, well-managed, well-financed company. The management meets with its investment banker to raise funds needed for growth. They decide to issue thirty-year bonds (bonds that will mature thirty years from the day of issue). The investment banker tells them that the market will pay "par" for the bonds (that is to say, the market will pay $1 to the company for every $1 of debt) if the bonds pay 7 percent interest.

The company raises the $10,000,000 by issuing 7 percent, thirty-year bonds.

Ten years later, the company, being very successful and needing more money for growth, wants to issue another $10,000,000 worth of bonds, but this time for only twenty years, so that both issues, the original and the new, mature the same day. The investment banker informs the company that interest rates have risen over the ten years, so for the company to be competitive in the marketplace and be accepted at par, the company would have to pay 10 percent interest. The company now has two bond offerings trading in the marketplace, both maturing the same day. One is paying 7 percent interest, the other 10 percent.

As they are both backed by the same creditworthiness and both mature the same day, would they both be trading at par? If the 10 percent bond is commanding par in the market, the 7 percent bond would have to be trading for less. It would be trading at a price that would make its value equivalent to that of the 10 percent bond. That value is called yield to maturity and will be discussed shortly. Therefore, as interest rates rise, fixed-rate bond prices fall.

The company raises its second $10,000,000 by issuing the 10 percent, twenty-year bonds.

Ten years go by and the company wants to expand even more. It wants to raise another $10,000,000 with another bond issue, and according to its plan, the three debt offerings will mature on the same day, so this offering will be for ten-year bonds. The investment banker tells the company that interest rates have fallen in the previous ten years, and based on where the firm stands in the interest-rate pecking order, where the bond stands compared to other offerings, it could issue the bonds with a 7 percent interest rate.

The company issues $10,000,000 in 7 percent ten-year bonds and receives par (a dollar for each dollar of debt).

At this point in time, the company has three bond issues in the marketplace:

The initial 7 percent, thirty-year bond, which has ten years of life remaining

The second offering, a 10 percent, twenty-year bond having ten years of life remaining

The newest offering, a 7 percent, ten-year bond having ten years of life remaining

As the first and last bond offerings both carry a 7 percent coupon rate, mature the same day, and are supported equally by the same financial backing, they both will be trading at par. Unlike appliances, bonds do not depreciate; the fact that the first bond has been trading for twenty years is irrelevant at this point in time. Bonds do not wear out. From the day the third issue of bonds comes into the marketplace until it matures, it is the same as the first bond. For all intents and purposes the two bonds are identical. If both 7 percent bonds are trading at par, what would the bond with the 10 percent coupon be trading at? It would be trading at a premium (above par). Therefore, as interest rates fall, the prices of fixed-rate bonds rise.

To the investor, if there is a reasonable expectation that the money being used for an investment will be needed before the bond matures, it would be prudent to forgive some part of the interest payments and acquire an instrument more aligned to the need.

Credit

Let's say the market determined that the twenty-year Treasury was yielding 5 percent. What would you assume a twenty-year bond issued by a blue-chip, large corporation with a strong financial condition would be yielding? Remember, yield is a function of risk. If your answer to the question is less

than 5 percent, what you are saying is that the corporation is a safer investment than the federal government. As the corporation has a chance of
defaulting over the next twenty years, its bond issue should offer a higher
yield than the equivalent Treasury instrument. A corporation that has a
weaker financial condition than the aforementioned blue-chip company
would have to offer an even higher yield to entice an investor, and so on.
The better the possibility is that the issuer may fold, go out of business, file
for bankruptcy protection, et cetera, the greater the amount of return an
investor would want. This is known as credit risk.

We have demonstrated credit risk and market risk through the instrument's coupon or interest rate. Credit risk and market risk together form
default risk. The bond's price is also affected by these risks and acts as the
equalizer between the debt instrument and the market in general. The
market price or market value of the instrument, together with its coupon
rate or interest payment, form the instrument's yield, or the return on the
investment. We will discuss yield in more detail later on. It is mentioned
here so that the reader doesn't focus on interest rates alone.

Each issue will find its place in the pecking order.

To summarize: Market risk is concerned with the investor's exposure to
changing interest rates during ownership of the debt instrument. Credit
risk is concerned with the financial ability of the issuer to meet the debt's
obligations. The financial condition of the issuer can change over the life of
the debt instrument, thereby increasing or decreasing the risk of ownership. Together, credit risk and market risk are referred to as default risk. No
one enjoys paying interest; people don't, corporations don't, governments
don't, and so on. That is the issuer's or seller's side. On the buyer's side, one
would want to receive the maximum interest income per dollar. The sellers
provide supply, the buyers develop demand, and the equalizer between the
two is price.

The presence of a 6 percent, twenty-year bond trading at 60 percent of
its face value (or $600 per $1,000 of loan), a 15 percent, twenty-year bond
trading at par (or $1,000 for each $1,000 of loan), and a 7 percent, twenty-
year bond trading at par (or $1000 for each $1,000 of loan), all other things
being equal, should shout out to you which bond is the safest investment and which are riskier. Generally speaking, bonds do nothing but pay
interest.

· Bond Ratings ·

Introduction

Assume you are going to hire three employees whose compensation is a direct reflection of their scholastic grade average. One has a 97 percent average, one has a 91 percent average, and one has an 88 percent average. The first two are both A students, since 90 percent to 100 percent is generally considered an A grade, and the third is a B student, as 80 percent to 89 percent is generally considered a B grade. Would you pay the two A students the same salary? What about the B student? An 88 percent average is almost an A. It is also closer to the 91 percent average student's grade than the 91 percent average student is to the student with the 97 percent average. To disburse the compensation fairly, according to the students' grade averages, the student with the 97 percent average should be the highest paid, followed by the student with the 91 percent average and finally the student with the 88 percent average. However, the compensation for the student with the 91 percent average should be much closer to that of the student with the 88 percent average than to that of the 97 percent student.

Bond ratings work the same way. To paraphrase a passage from George Orwell's classic book *Animal Farm:* All bonds with the same rating are equal, but some are more equal than others. There are bonds that are a solid AAA and ones that just made the grade. The solid bonds will yield less than those that just made the grade. Those that just made the AAA rating may be yielding slightly less than the best of the AA-rated bonds, and so on. The yield tells the investor a lot about the particular bond. The reason a AAA-rated bond is yielding about the same as a AA bond is that the slightest negative change in the company's financial picture could have it rated AA.

Standard & Poor's, Moody's, and Fitch are three of the primary bond rating services. Their rating codes are as follows:

Investment-Grade	Standard & Poor's	Moody's	Fitch
Highest quality	AAA	Aaa	AAA
Good quality	AA	Aa	AA
Medium grade	A	A	A

(continued)

Investment-Grade	Standard & Poor's	Moody's	Fitch
Lower medium Grade	BBB	Baa	BBB
Non–Investment-Grade (Degrees of speculation)	BB	Ba	BB
	B	B	B
	CCC	Caa	CCC
	CC	Ca	CC
	C	C	C
			DDD
			DD
			D

Note: Moody's further delineates its ratings using the numerals 1, 2, and 3 (e.g., Ba1, Ba2, Ba3).

Each rating agency has its own means of evaluating bonds. While you won't find one rating agency rating a bond AAA and another rating the same bond B, agencies may differ on a particular issue by one grade level. Also, when one agency changes an issue's grade, the other agencies may not follow immediately or may not follow at all.

To recap where we are at this point: The coupon rate of the bond, that is, the rate that is stated in its description, reflects where the bond sat in the credit-risk analysis at the time of issue. The current price of the debt instrument reflects where the bond sits in the credit analysis currently, as well as where its coupon rate sits in the market-risk analysis based on today's rates. Both of these factors are directly affected by the time remaining to maturity. The application of these two forces makes a difference when applied to a debt instrument with twenty years, ten years, one year, or one day left of life.

· DEBT PRICING POINTS ·

Debt pricing is presented in one of two ways: dollar pricing and basis pricing. Dollar pricing is presented as 10 percent of the actual money value. For example: A $1,000 bond trading at 98 is trading at $980 per $1,000 bond. A $1,000 bond trading at 101 is trading at $1,010 per $1,000 bond. Basis pricing (short for yield-to-maturity basis) represents the yield or percent return the buyer can expect if the bonds are held until they mature. For example: A $1,000 bond priced to yield 7.25 percent will return to the investor 7.25 percent on the money invested at the time of purchase if the bonds are held to their maturity. Yield to maturity is discussed in more detail later in this chapter.

· YIELDS ·

When dealing with pure debt, that is, bonds, notes, et cetera, that have no other features than the payment of interest and a return of principal according to some prearranged payoff schedule, it is important to focus on yield or return on investment (known commonly as ROI) when considering any investment in debt instruments. The two most common yields are the current yield and yield to maturity.

Current

Current yield is computed by dividing the annual interest payment by the cost. For example: A $1,000 bond of the Loster Corporation having an 8 percent coupon maturing in ten years and trading at "90," or 90 percent of its face value, would have a current yield of 8.89 percent—$80 (the annual interest payment) divided by $900 (the cost of the bond), or 8.89 percent.

Yield to Maturity

Yield to maturity is more complex. It takes into account the present value of all cash flows. The present value of all cash flows is what all future payments are worth today. An example of this would be if someone was guaranteed a $10,000 payment a year from now and said that they could use that money today. If someone else offered to "buy" that payment today, they would negotiate a price because if the buyer of the payment paid the full $10,000 today he or she would not have the use of that money for a year, whereas the seller of the payment would have the use of the money, without cost, for the full year. Say the negotiation between the buyer and seller resulted in an agreement for a 5 percent discount, or $500 ($10,000 × .05 = $500). The buyer would pay the seller $9,500 today and collect the $10,000 from the seller when the payment is made a year from now. The $500 is compensation to the buyer for doing without the $10,000 for a year. Another way of saying this is the present value of $10,000 due a year from now is $9,500.

To compute the present value of cash flows, the following formula is used:

$$PV = PO \times \frac{1}{[1+r]^t}$$

PV = present value
PO = payout
r = yield rate
t = number of times the payout occurs

Let's assume a ten-year $1,000 bond with a 7 percent coupon that is priced to yield 8 percent. The 7 percent bond would pay $70 per year, and as most bonds offered in the United States pay their interest obligations twice a year (every six months), this bond's payment will be $35. As the bond is being figured to yield 8 percent, half a year would be 4 percent. Using the above formula, the present value of the first payment would be:

1. $PV = \$35 \times \dfrac{1}{[1 + 0.04]^1}$

2. $1 + .04 = 1.04$

3. $1 / 1.04 = .961538461$

4. $\$35 \times .961538461 = \$33.65$

The present value of the first $35 payment due six months from now is $33.65.

The present value of the next payment would be calculated as follows:

$$PV = 35 \times \frac{1}{[1 + .04]^2}$$

$$.961538461 \times .961538461 = .9246005860$$

$$PV = \$35 \times .9246005860 = \$32.36$$

Based on the above, a $35 payment due six months from now has a present value of $33.65 and a $35 payment due one year from now has a present value of $32.36.

Here is an example of a discounted bond using the present value of cash flows:

$1,000 7 Percent Ten-Year Bond
Priced to Yield 8 Percent

Number of times payout occurs	Payout × Factor	= Present value
• 1	$35 × 0.961538 =	$33.65
• 2	35 × 0.924556 =	32.36
• 3	35 × 0.888996 =	31.11
• 4	35 × 0.854804 =	29.92
• 5	35 × 0.821927 =	28.77
• 6	35 × 0.790314 =	27.66
• 7	35 × 0.759918 =	26.60
• 8	35 × 0.730690 =	25.57
• 9	35 × 0.702506 =	24.59
• 10	35 × 0.676564 =	23.64
• 11	35 × 0.649508 =	22.73
• 12	35 × 0.624597 =	21.86
• 13	35 × 0.600574 =	21.02
• 14	35 × 0.577475 =	20.21
• 15	35 × 0.555264 =	19.43
• 16	35 × 0.533908 =	18.68
• 17	35 × 0.513373 =	17.97
• 18	35 × 0.493628 =	17.28
• 19	35 × 0.474642 =	16.61
• 20	1,035 × 0.456386 =	472.36
• Total		$ 932.02

The "rule of thumb" method is a quick way to approximate yield to maturity. It takes the difference between the current market value and the value at maturity and amortizes (in the case of an instrument that is selling at a discount) or depletes (in the case of an instrument trading at a premium) the difference over the life of the instrument. Next, it takes that annual amount and applies it to the annual interest payment.

This accrual is then applied to the market value, the assumption being that the market value (accounting-wise and not marketwise) is changing by this amount each year, so that at maturity the entire amount of discount or premium has been accounted for. To get an average of this process, the market value is added to the maturity value and divided by two.

1. Value at maturity $1,000.00
    Current value   −932.02

    Difference $ 67.98

2. As the instrument has ten years remaining, the $67.98 is divided by ten, equaling $6.79 annually.

3. To the $6.79 amortized amount we add $70 annual interest, equaling $76.79.

4. The maturity value is added to the current market value and is divided by 2 ($1,000.00 + $932.02 = 1,932.02 / 2 = $966.01) to get a theoretical average value.

$$\frac{1,000\ +\ 932.02}{2} = 966.01$$

The following are theoretical values formed by adding the amortized amounts to the original market value. They do not have any relation to the actual market value of the instrument over its life.

Year	Year
1. 932.02 + 6.79 = 938.81	6. 965.90 + 6.79 = 972.69
2. 938.81 + 6.79 = 945.60	7. 972.69 + 6.79 = 979.48
3. 945.60 + 6.79 = 952.32	8. 979.48 + 6.79 = 986.27
4. 952.32 + 6.79 = 959.11	9. 986.27 + 6.79 = 993.06
5. 959.11 + 6.79 = 965.90*(966.01)	10. 993.06 + 6.79 = 999.85*
	(1,000.00)

Note: The asterisks reflect differences caused by the rounding of figures throughout the process.

The annual adjusted payment of $76.79 is divided by the average theoretical value, which is $966.01, to arrive at the yield to maturity:

$$\frac{\$76.79}{\$966.01} = 7.949\% \text{ or, allowing for rounding, } 8\%$$

Now let's look at a bond trading at premium:

$1,000 7 Percent Ten-Year Bond Priced to Yield 6 Percent

Again, using the formula for the first payment, we calculate as follows:

1. $PV = \$35 \dfrac{1}{[1 + .03]^1}$

2. $1 / 1.03 = .970873786$

3. $\$35 \times .970873786 = \$33.98$

Number of times payout occurs	Payout × Factor = Present value
• 1	$35 × 0.970874 = $33.98
• 2	35 × 0.942596 = 32.99
• 3	35 × 0.915141 = 32.03
• 4	35 × 0.888486 = 31.10
• 5	35 × 0.862608 = 30.19
• 6	35 × 0.837483 = 29.31

(continued)

Number of times payout occurs	Payout × Factor = Present value
• 7	35 × .813091 = 28.46
• 8	35 × .789409 = 27.63
• 9	35 × .766416 = 26.82
• 10	35 × .744093 = 26.04
• 11	35 × .722420 = 25.28
• 12	35 × .701739 = 24.55
• 13	35 × .680950 = 23.83
• 14	35 × .661116 = 23.14
• 15	35 × .641861 = 22.47
• 16	35 × .623661 = 21.83
• 17	35 × .605015 = 21.17
• 18	35 × .587393 = 20.59
• 19	35 × .570285 = 19.96
• 20	1,035 × .553674 = 573.05
• Total	$1,074.42

Now let's apply the "rule of thumb" method from above:

1. $1,074.42
    −1,000.00
    ————
    $74.42

2. $74.42 / 10 = $7.44

3. As this instrument is trading above par, or the actual amount of the loan, the difference is subtracted from the annual interest payment: 70 − 7.44 = $62.56. This is the amortized amount.

4. The market price and the value at maturity are added together and divided by two to obtain the theoretical value: $1,074.42 + 1,000.00 = $2,074.42 / 2 = $1,037.21.

5. The adjusted annual figure of $62.56 is then divided by $1,037.21 to get the yield to maturity, 6.03 percent again, allowing for rounding, 6 percent.

The above mathematical exercises were presented to demonstrate how some debt instruments are priced, how and why their prices change, and the importance of yields.

Yield to Call

Some bonds contain a call feature. This feature permits the issuer to retire the bond prior to its maturity. The purpose and use of this feature will be explained later in this chapter but is brought up here because the feature affects yield calculations. Bonds are usually called in at a slight premium over par (higher than their face value). Therefore, when calculating the yield to call using the rule of thumb method, the call price replaces the maturity value in determining the annual accretion or amortization, and the number of years involved must be adjusted to reflect the call date and not the maturity date.

> **EXAMPLE**
> *A $1,000 Loster Corporation 6% FA twenty-year bond, callable at 102 in the tenth year, is currently trading at 98.*

Using the rule of thumb method:

The yield to call is

$1020	call price
−980	current price
$ 40	

$ 40/10 = $4 per year

$60 interest per year + $4.00 = $64 adjusted interest

$1,020 call price + 980 market price = $2,000

$2,000/2 = $1,000 average value

$64 / $1,000 = 0.064 or 6.4% yield to call

Yield to maturity would be:

$1,000	value at maturity
−980	current price
$ 20	

$ 20/20 = $1 per year

$60 interest per year + $1 = $61 adjusted interest

$1,000 maturity value + 980 market price = $1,980

$1,980/2 = $990 average value

$61 / 990 = .0616 or 6.16% yield to maturity

Therefore, this bond would be quoted to the client as trading at 6.16 basis. That is the worst return the client would receive. If the bonds are called in ten years, the client would receive a better return. However, the client could not do worse than the 6.16 percent yield, so that is what is used.

When quoting the yields of a callable issue to a client, the lesser of the two (yield to maturity or yield to call) must be used because that is what the bondholder would receive if that series of events occurred. If the other series of events occurred, the bondholder would be better off. This method of reporting yield is known in industry jargon as yield to worst. In the above example, the yield to maturity of 6.16 percent would be used.

Yield vs. Price

There is an adverse relationship between yield and price. The more that is paid for a fixed sum, the lower the yield will be. The reverse is true also. For example, a $1,000 6 percent bond is to pay $60 per year in interest ($1,000 × .06 = $60). If the bond is trading at par ($1,000), it will have a current yield of 6 percent ($60 / $1000 = 6 %). If the bond is trading at a price of 105 ($1,050), the current yield will be 5.714 percent ($60 / $1050 = .0571428). If the bond is selling at 110 ($1,100) the current yield will be 5.454 percent ($60 / $1,100 = 0.0545454). Therefore, if a bond is trading at a premium (above par), the current yield and yield to maturity will always be below the coupon or interest rate of the bond. The more expensive the bond's price becomes, the lower the yield.

Conversely, a bond trading at a discount would have a yield higher than the coupon rate. For example, a $1,000 6 percent bond trading at 98 ($980) would have a current yield of 6.122 percent ($60 / $980 = .0612244), whereas a $1,000 6 percent bond trading at 96 ($960) would have a yield of 6.25 percent ($60 / $960 = .062500).

This holds true for current yield and yield to maturity. When computing yield to call, the face amount of the bond must be replaced by the value established in the call feature, known as the call price.

· THE YIELD CURVE ·

The infamous yield curve fluctuates regularly. Two main driving forces are the aforementioned risk factors (credit and market risk) and supply and demand for the instruments.

The risk factors: While U.S. Treasury instruments do not have default risk, they do have market risk. General interest rates change while the particular debt is outstanding, and for that debt to be attractive in the marketplace it must yield a rate that is equivalent to the current rate. As its interest rate is fixed at the time of issue, the market price must absorb the difference. Therefore, while the U.S. Treasury fixed-income debt instrument will pay its obligation at maturity (credit risk), the price of the instrument will not be at par throughout its life (market risk). In addition, to attract investment in longer-term instruments, the buyer would normally expect a higher rate of return than would be received on shorter-term instruments, as payment for not having the use of the funds for a longer period of time. If one was to chart the respective yields over a period of years, one would expect to see an upward curve.

The U.S. Treasury Yield Curve for
October 1 and October 2, 2008

October 2008

Date	1 mo	3 mo	6 mo	1 yr	2 yr	3 yr	5 yr	7 yr	10 yr	20 yr	30 yr
10/01/08	0.66	0.85	1.49	1.72	1.82	2.12	2.87	3.29	3.77	4.33	4.22
10/02/08	0.21	0.63	1.21	1.45	1.62	1.91	2.68	3.13	3.66	4.28	4.16

Let's drill deeper. As we said earlier, yield is a function of price, time, and coupon rate. In the case of current yield, only price and coupon rate are used. Let's assume that the market experts predict that the interest rate will rise over the next few months. Investors would tend to shy away from longer-term debt and invest in short-term instruments, which, when they mature, will allow the investor to reinvest the proceeds in the higher-yielding long-term instruments. The change in demand toward short-term instruments and away from longer-term instruments would cause the prices of short-term instruments to rise (thereby lowering the yield on short-term instruments) and the prices on long-term instruments to fall (thereby raising the yield on long-term instruments). This free-market action is often blamed for predicting interest rate moves. This type of action would cause the yield curve to become steeper, with a greater difference between the yield of the short- and long-term instruments.

Conversely, if the market experts predicted a drop in long-term interest rates over the near future, the demand for longer instruments would rise, so that investors can lock in the higher rate. This switch in demand would cause the price in longer-term instruments to rise (causing the yield to fall), and the resulting drop in demand for short-term instruments would cause their prices to fall (and their yields to rise). There are times when this phenomenon has caused the yield on short-term instruments to be higher than that on long-term instruments. When this occurs, the yield curve is said to be "inverted."

Debt instruments react to interest rate changes differently. Bonds selling at a discount tend to be more volatile than bonds selling at a premium. The same is true with bonds at the beginning of their life cycle compared with bonds near maturity. Bond professionals and credit experts have tools that assist them in measuring the effect that a change in interest rates would have on a particular instrument. One of the tools used is called duration. The term is misleading, as it has nothing to do with the actual life of the instrument. What it does is take into account the amount paid for the bond and the length of time it will take the bond to pay back the cost price from internal cash flows. There are several different methods to compute duration. But without going into the land of Greek letters, let's examine the following.

As stated above, a bond's price is the sum of the present values of all of its cash flows. Therefore, a twenty-year, zero-coupon bond would have a duration of twenty years. A bond with a higher coupon or lower price than another bond would have a shorter duration. When duration is applied to the change in the rate (R) of the present value, the following formula will show which bond has the greater volatility:

$$PV = PO \times \frac{1}{(1 + R)^T}$$

· DEBT INTEREST ·

Bonds pay interest; stocks pay dividends. Stocks never pay interest, and bonds never pay dividends. There is a major difference to the issuer between the two. To the investor they are both forms of income.

Interest is an expense. It appears on the company's profit and loss statements along with other expenses. These expenses are subtracted from revenue to determine whether or not the company made a profit. If the company has made a profit, it pays taxes on the profit and the remainder flows into earnings, from which dividends are paid.

Let's look at two companies that have the same revenue. The Jener-ate Company, which has to pay interest to its bondholders, and the Nicole-N-Dyme Company, which does not have debt but pays the same amount in dividends that Jener-ate pays in interest. Let's assume a tax rate of 50 percent.

	Jener-ate	Nicole-N-Dyme
Sales	$200	$200
Interest expense	100	0
Earnings before taxes	$100	$200
Taxes (50%)	50	100
Earnings after taxes	$ 50	$100
Dividend paid	0	100
Earnings	$50	$0

Notice from the above example that interest on the corporate issue is taxed only at the bondholder's level. The bondholder will have to pay income tax on the bond's interest earned. On the other hand, the dividend paid by the corporation is taxed twice, once at the corporate level and once at the stockholder's.

As stated, bonds pay interest twice a year, in payments six months apart. That is true for the majority of debt. There are exceptions: zero-coupon bonds, adjustable- or floating-rate bonds, and adjustment bonds (used in the recapitalization of a company facing bankruptcy).

Interest Accruals

Most corporate and municipal bonds pay interest every six months. They follow one of the following payment schedules; January/July, February/August, March/September, April/October, May/November, or June/December. Normally, the day of the month is the same for each semiannual payment. An interesting feature of corporate bonds, notes, and municipal bonds, as well as some other issuers' debt, is that the interest is computed on a 360-day year. Under this scenario, every month has thirty days ($30 \times 12 = 360$).

The buyer of a bond pays the seller of the bond interest that has accrued from the last time the bond paid interest, up to but not including the trade's settlement date. For example: Wendy Storm sells a $1,000 6 percent January/July (JJ) bond to Ray Beame for settlement April 6. As the bond paid interest on January 1, Wendy is entitled to the interest up to but not including April 6, the settlement date. On that day, ownership changes to Ray, the buyer. Ray will pay Wendy $15.83 of accrued interest (January 30 days, February 30 days, March 30 days, and April 5 days, for a total of 95 days). The formula for accrued interest is: Principal $\times$ rate $\times$ time $=$ accrued interest. In this example, it is calculated as follows:

$$\frac{\$1,000}{1} \times \frac{6}{100} \times \frac{95}{360} = \text{accrued interest}$$

Multiply the numbers on top across. Then multiply the numbers on the bottom across. Finally divide the bottom answer into the top answer.

$$\frac{1,000 \times 6 \times 95}{1 \times 100 \times 360} = \frac{570,000}{36,000}$$

570,000 divided by 36,000 = $15.83

Let's assume Ray sells the bonds to Sonny Day for settlement June 16. Sonny will pay Ray $27.50 accrued interest (January 30 days, February 30 days, March 30 days, April 30 days, May 30 days. and June 15 days, for a total of 165 days). $1,000 $\times$ 6 $\times$ 165 / 1 $\times$ 100 $\times$ 360 = $27.50. Of the $27.50 Sonny will receive, $15.83 is payback for the accrued interest that

Ray paid Wendy, leaving $11.67 that Ray is entitled to for the period that he owned the bonds.

$$P \times R \times T = \text{accrued interest}$$

$$\frac{1,000}{1} \times \frac{6}{100} \times \frac{165}{360} = 27.50$$

Sonny owns the bonds over the July 1 payment date and receives the full six-month interest payment of $30. As Sonny paid Ray $27.50 of accrued interest, the difference of $2.50 is what Sonny is entitled to for the fifteen days that he owned the bonds:

$$\frac{1,000}{1} \times \frac{6}{100} \times \frac{15}{360} = \frac{90,000}{36,000} = 2.50$$

To recap, the bond pays $60 per year, or $30 every half year.

Wendy received an accrued interest payment from Ray of $15.83. Ray received $27.50 from Sonny and subtracts the $15.83 that he paid Wendy, leaving him with interest he earned of $11.67. Sonny received $30 from the issuer's agent, less the $27.50 that he paid Ray, leaving him with interest he earned of $2.50. The net amount of interest paid during the six months is actually what the issuer will pay on the payable date ($15.85 + $11.67 + $ 2.50 = $30.00).

It is necessary for the buyer to pay the accrued interest to the seller at the time of settlement, as it is the most efficient way of accounting for the interest that is due. The issuer is going to pay the full six months' interest to whoever the registered owner is on the night of record date. The actual payment is made on the payable date; the issuer does not have a way to track who owned the securities during the six-month period, especially since the security's registration is maintained in "street name" and settlement occurs between broker-dealers, banks, and other financial institutions in an electronic fashion.

In the bond market, the record date is the day before the payable date. If the bonds pay interest every April 1 and October 1, whoever is the registered owner on the night of March 31 and/or September 30 is entitled to receive the payment. It is important to differentiate between the registered owner and the beneficial owner, who may or may not be the same. In the case of custodial services, the custodian usually keeps the security in its name as nominee for the benefit of the beneficial (actual) owner. Therefore, it is the registered holder who will receive the interest payment. If the two are one and the same, the correct party has been paid. If they are not, and the security is being held by a custodian in its own name, the custodian will receive the interest payment and forward it to the client, the beneficial owner.

While bonds pay interest every six months, there could be an exception on the first coupon payment. If the bond is initially issued between the payment dates, the coupon payment may be a "long payment" (more than six months) or a "short coupon" (less than six months). Long coupon is known as long payment. Likewise, short coupon is also known as short payment. A January/July payment bond issued in February may well result in the first coupon payment being a short one, only five months instead of the usual six. If the bond was issued in June, the first payment may be the following January, making a long payment of seven months. The first day that interest starts to accrue on a newly issued bond is known as the "dated date."

The term *street name* refers to a form of registration that is readily recognizable and accepted for delivery industry-wide. The industry has made great strides in getting away from the physical pieces of paper known as the stock or bond certificates. Most corporate and municipal securities are maintained by Depository Trust & Clearing Corporation (DTCC) and are registered in its name as nominee. The broker-dealers and banks that maintain securities at the depository keep the records as to which of their clients and which of their proprietary accounts own the securities. Ownership is maintained and controlled by electronic entries between the involved participants.

Here is a simplistic example: Al Luminum has his account and securities at broker-dealer Giant Reckor and Crane. Reelibig Corporation has its account at broker-dealer Stone Forrest and Rivers and maintains its portfolio at First Continental Trust. Al sells $100,000 worth of debt securities through Giant Reckor and Crane, which, on behalf of Al, sells it to Stone Forrest and Rivers, which has an order from its client, Reelibig Corporation, to buy the bonds. On the settlement date, Giant Reckor and Crane makes an electronic entry to move the security out of Al's account and one that instructs DTCC to deliver the bonds to Stone Forrest and Rivers. Upon receipt of the bonds, Stone Forrest and Rivers delivers the bonds to First Continental Bank for the account of Reelibig Corporation. Each of these entries on the participants' books was electronic, and the bonds themselves, which were being maintained by DTCC, never moved either. DTCC moves the bonds between the different participants' accounts electronically. The cash side of the trade followed the reverse steps, and again, it was all done by electronic entries and physical cash never moved.

· DEBT RETIREMENT ·

Corporate bonds are retired procedurally five ways and operationally three ways:

Procedurally	*Operationally*
Maturity	Redemption
Refunding	Refunding
Call	Conversion
Conversion	
Sinking fund	

Procedural Retirement Methods

Maturity

Bonds mature. At maturity the borrower (issuer) must pay the face amount of the loan (the bond) to the lender (bondholder), plus any accrued interest due. The issuer can retire the bonds using its own cash (redemption) or by issuing new debt to pay off the old debt (refunding). The payment of interest, and any other features that bond may have, terminate at maturity.

Refunding

Refunding has two meanings as used here. One is issuing new debt into the public market and using the proceeds to pay off old debt. The other is asking the current bondholders to exchange their debt for new debt.

The former occurs when an issuer issues new debt into the marketplace for the purpose of paying off maturing debt. To the current bondholder, it appears as if the bonds have been redeemed. The current bondholder receives a cash payment for the sum owed, and the obligation of the issuer ceases to exit. However, to the issuer, the new debt obligation replaces the matured obligation and the cycle continues.

The U.S. government does this, for example, on its weekly offering of U.S. Treasury bills. The proceeds for the newly issued Treasury bills are used to pay off the maturing bills. If the government wants to increase its borrowings, it will issue more bills than it is retiring, using some of the proceeds received from the sale of the new bills to pay off the old debt and the excess to fund other projects. If it wants to reduce its borrowing, it will issue fewer bills than it is retiring and make up the shortfall with cash.

On the buy side, some investors roll the proceeds from the maturing bills into the newly issued bills on an ongoing basis. This gives them a constant flow of short-term interest-bearing instruments with very limited risk that they can turn into cash whenever the bills mature or that can, if necessary, be sold into the market at a price close to their face value.

The latter use of the term *refunding* applies to the exchange of bonds between the issuer and the bondholder. The issuer might ask the current bondholders to exchange their bonds, for example, when a noncallable debt instrument carries a high interest obligation compared to current newly issued debt and the bonds have a few years remaining before maturity. The issuer must pay that high rate of interest every year until maturity. The current rate of interest for equivalent newly issued bonds is much lower, as interest rates in general have fallen since the high-interest-paying bonds were originally issued. The bondholders, on the other hand, know either that this high rate of interest income will end soon or that the company has moved from a very weak financial condition to a much stronger one. The issuer offers them a compromise that will pay them a slightly higher rate than the current rate but not as high a rate as their current bonds are paying and will extend the maturity date out for a few more years beyond their current bond's maturity. If the refunding is successful, the company will spread the current annual interest cost over several years, thereby incurring less interest expense each year, and the bondholders will receive less interest each year, but a higher rate than the current rate, for a longer period of time.

For example: A company has a 9 percent bond that only has ten years remaining until it matures. In the current market, the 9 percent bond could be replaced by the company with a 7 percent ten-year bond if it was callable. But it is not. The company makes an offer to the bondholders to replace the bonds with a bond paying a higher rate of interest than the market is currently requiring and extending the maturity for a longer period of time. Suppose the company offered an 8 percent, fifteen-year bond to the bondholders for their 9 percent bond with ten years remaining. Is it worth it?

If they do not accept the offer, the bondholders will keep the $1,000 bond paying 9 percent ($90) per year for ten years, or a total of $900. They could then reinvest the proceeds at maturity (assuming interest rates were stagnant) by purchasing a $1,000 bond paying 6 percent ($60) per year for five years, for a total of $300. This would give them a fifteen-year total of $1,200. Remember, the interest rate when the 9 percent bond matures is unknown now.

If they accept the company's offer, they will receive a $1,000 bond paying 8 percent ($80) per year for fifteen years, or a total of $1,200.

Is it worth it to the company? If its offer is accepted, the company reduces its annual interest expense for the first ten years by $10 per $1,000 bond, or $100,000 per $10,000,000 of debt. That flows directly to the yearly profit and loss statement for the next ten years. For the following five years, it is costing the company $20 more per $1,000 bond, or $200,000 per $10,000,000 of debt. It is not a valid comparison, though, because in the above example the comparison is between a newly issued ten-year bond and a newly issued fifteen-year bond. If a ten-year bond in the current market is paying 7 percent, then, given a normal yield curve, the fifteen-year bond should pay a higher return. The company has locked in an interest rate of 8 percent and is not exposed to rate fluctuations or surprises when the 9 percent bonds finally mature. It also has a lower interest obligation to pay each year for the next ten years. The bondholder has locked in a rate for the next fifteen years. A short-term bondholder would not be interested in the exchange and, depending on when the bonds were originally purchased and the price paid at that time, might sell the bonds at a profit, but to a longer-term bondholder the continuity of the interest payments may be appealing. This is another example of refunding.

Callable

During periods of high interest rates, issuers will bring bonds to market that contain a feature that permits the issuer to retire the offering, either in its entirety or in part, before maturity. This is known as a call feature. For example, say the Loster Corporation has to finance a project to remain competitive. Unfortunately, it will accomplish this by issuing a debt instrument when interest rates are high. This bond is a fixed-income instrument and the company will have to pay the high rate of interest over the life of the bond. During the life of the bond, interest rates may fall enough to make it economically feasible for the company to "call in" the bond and pay for it by issuing a bond with a lower interest rate. If the bond indenture permits the early retiring of the bond by the issuer, the bond is said to be callable.

The Loster Corporation issues its bonds during a high-interest period. It floats a $10,000,000, 9 percent, twenty-year bond. The interest cost to the issuer is $900,000 a year for twenty years, or $18,000,000. By the eighth year, the interest rates have fallen to where Loster Corporation could issue a new twenty-year bond for $10,000,000, paying 7 percent, or $700,000 per year and saving the $200,000 per year for the remaining twelve years—a total savings of $2,400,000. If the bonds are callable, Loster can retire the 9 percent bonds and replace the loan with the 7 percent bonds.

When a bond is callable, the call feature will contain the call price. The price may be at a slight premium or may be at the face amount (par). If there is a premium, the premium will dissipate each year between the first call date and maturity.

For example, on July 1, 2008, the Loster Corporation issued a twenty-year bond. Its description is "$10,000,000 Loster Corporation 9% J J1, 2018/28." The call feature kicks in on July 1, 2018, with a call price of 101. Translation: the Loster Corporation issued a bond evidencing a loan of $10,000,000 that will pay 9 percent per dollar of face value per year. It will pay interest every half year on January 1 and July 1. The bond is callable starting on July 1, 2018. If the bond is called on July 1, 2018, the bond-holder will receive $1,010 (101 percent of $1,000) for every $1,000 of principal owned, and the bond will mature at par on July 1, 2028. If the bond is called on July 1, 2019, it may pay 100.9 percent then, 100.8 percent the next year, and so on until maturity, when it will pay par. The typical bond description will not include the premium paid after the first year. That would be discovered in the data supplied by service vendors.

Because of the call feature, when callable bonds are trading at a premium, they will trade at a lower price than comparable noncallable bonds, all other factors being equal. The price of the noncallable bond is derived from its coupon rate as compared with all other straight bonds. The price of the callable bonds is driven by interest rates but also tempered by the threat of the call and the call price. In a normal situation, the bond is selling at a premium because the new issue of comparable bonds that are first coming to market are commanding lower coupon rates. The issuer will call the bonds in when it can refinance the loan at a substantially lower rate. Therefore, as interest rates fall, the possibility of the outstanding bonds being called increases. The call may be a partial call or a full call. In a partial call, a lottery or allocation is made as to which bonds are called and which bonds continue to exist. As the industry has been dematerializing (doing away with physical paper instruments), the process of allocation in the case of a partial call has been systematized. Depository Trust & Clearing Corporation (DTCC), the main depository in the United States, maintains the financial instruments in its name as nominee and keeps records of the broker-dealers and banks that the instruments belong to. The broker-dealers and banks, in turn, maintain the securities at the depositary and keep their own records as to whom they are representing and so on. Each entity along the way has its own method of assigning the call.

In the case of a full call, the call date sets the last date the bonds will pay interest, so it behooves those involved to make sure their bonds are surrendered in time, so that the issuer will release the proceeds and pay off the loan. Thanks to the dematerialization efforts of the industry, the partial and full call processing procedure operates in a controlled environment.

To the bondholder, the call feature represents an unwanted situation. As stated above, the issuer will call the bonds when it can refinance the loan at a lower rate. In other words, interest rates in general have fallen. When the investor has his or her bonds called, the issuer will pay the required amount, as specified in the bond's indenture, upon retirement of the instrument. If the investor reinvests the funds in similar instruments, he or she will be earning less interest than he or she had been earning previously.

Note: Some bonds have a "put" feature. A true put feature will permit the bondholder to "put" the bonds back to the issuer under certain conditions. The bondholder does not have to exercise the put but can if he or she wants to. However, beware: some bonds have a "mandatory put" feature, where the issuer mandates that the bondholder surrender the bond. The latter is basically a call.

Convertible

From the world of corporate debt we get convertible instruments. These bonds offer the bondholder the ability to convert the bonds to common stock (usually) at a fixed ratio. Besides offering the bondholder a way to convert to equity, they also give the bondholder an opportunity for capital appreciation.

For example: A $1,000 Ripp 7 percent bond is convertible into 25 shares of common stock. If the bonds are trading at par (face value, $1,000), the stock would have to be trading at $40 per share to be equal (25 × $40 = $1,000). The point at which the value of the bond and the value of the converted to security are the same is called parity.

If the price of the stock rises, it may pass parity. Once the converted value of the stock rises past the value of the bond, arbitrageurs (professional traders) will step in to buy the bonds, give conversion instructions to the firm's cashier's department, and sell the common stock. This entire process takes seconds. By purchasing the bonds, the arbitrageurs create demand that causes the bond's price to rise to parity. Therefore, a convertible bond offers its owner the opportunity to receive capital appreciation in addition to the semiannual interest payments. As with all such "opportunities," there is another side. The bond is probably paying a lower interest rate than it would have if it didn't have this feature.

Example:

A $1,000 Ripp 7 percent Cv JJ 20XX is trading at par. The bond will cost the purchaser $1,000. Ripp common stock is trading at $30 and paying a $1-per-share annual dividend. As the bond is convertible into 25 shares, a $1,000 bond would have to be trading at $750 to be at parity, or the stock would have to be trading at $40 per share to be at parity with the current value of the bond. In addition, the bond will pay interest of $70 per year, compared to the stock dividend of $25 (25 shares × $1) per year.

Let's continue. Ripp announces an important development and the stock value rises to $45. Due to the work of arbitrageurs, the price of the bonds will have risen to $1,125 (25 × $45 = $1,125). The bonds would not have risen if it wasn't for the increase in the stock value. Bond prices are affected by current interest rates, life remaining until maturity, the financial strength of the issuer, and seldom by day-to-day developments. It is a fixed-income instrument that will pay interest periodically and the principal of the loan at maturity.

As the stock continues to rise, the price of the bonds will rise also. Regardless of how high the bond price goes, it is still going to pay face value at maturity. Therefore, if it is still trading at a premium as it approaches maturity, because of the conversion feature, more and more of the bonds will be converted into common stock.

Another feature of convertible bonds is that the stock forms a floor under which the price of the bond will not fall. Let's assume our common stock is trading at $37 per share. Twenty-five shares would have a market value of $925. The bonds are trading at par when the Federal Reserve begins a spiral of interest rate increases. As the interest rate rises, bond prices fall, and therefore, the value of Ripp 7 percent bonds will fall also. However, with the stock trading at $37, once the bonds dip below $925, the arbitrageurs will step in, buy the bonds, and bring them back to parity.

The above convertible bond paragraphs have been straightforward. Let's complicate the decision process. Suppose the bonds and the converted value of the stock were approximately the same and the company announced a one-time $3-per-share special dividend in addition to its regular dividend, for a total of $4 per share. Should the bondholder keep the bonds and receive $70 per year or convert them into the stock and receive a one-time total payment of $100 in dividends ($4 × 25 shares = $100) instead of the annual $70-per-year interest payment? Among the factors to be considered are:

1. Does the bondholder want to own the stock? If he or she does not, he or she can do nothing or he or she can have the bonds converted into the stock and pick up the extra payment, sell the stock, and replace converted debt with the same bond issue that was converted or similar bonds. (Remember, there are fees and other costs to do the latter.)
2. How many years are there until the bonds mature? If it's a short time, it may pay to convert and pick up the extra payment. If it's a long time, the decision would be guided by what the current interest rate is for a comparable replacement debt issue.
3. The individual's financial situation and reason for acquiring those particular bonds initially, and other factors all play a roll in the decision process.

Sinking Fund

Some bond issuers use a portion of their net earnings to purchase their bonds on the open market and retire them ahead of schedule. The purchases must be paid out of earnings. Those issuers that engage in this practice are said to be operating a sinking fund. Under the typical sinking fund, the issuer cannot acquire its bonds in the open market if they are trading above par (face value). Therefore, while the bonds are trading at a discount, a buyer of these

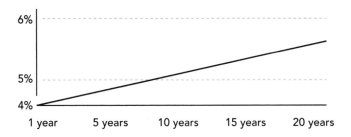

bonds has the opportunity to profit if the "sinker kicks in"—that is, if the company calls the bonds in—as the bond's price will usually increase because of the increased demand. In addition, as stated above, bonds generally trade at the present value of their cash flow, which in turn affects their yield. In the normal interest cycle, the longer the term a debt instrument is outstanding, the greater the yield. Therefore, with a long-term debt that has a sinking fund, should the sinking fund be activated, the buyer would be getting a higher interest rate on a shorter-term instrument.

In the above example, a twenty-year bond is yielding 6 percent, whereas a ten-year bond is yielding 5 percent. Therefore, a buyer of the twenty-year bond who is fortunate enough to sell his or her bonds into the "sinker" when the bond is ten years old has earned a 6 percent yield for ten years, instead of 5 percent.

· CORPORATE BONDS ·

Corporate Debt

Due to the competition in the bond market, issuers try to differentiate their offerings to attract investors. Three such techniques are quarterly paying debt, zero-coupon debt, and floating-rate or adjustable debt. Each is aimed to attract an investor looking for something that best fits their needs.

Quarterly Paying Debt

Quarterly paying debt can be found in the issue of corporate notes, for example. The buyer of these instruments is benefiting from more frequent payments. In the usual every-six-month payout, the company has used the bond interest earned by the bondholder until the payable date. Even though the bondholder earns interest every day that he or she has lent the issuer money, represented by the bond, he or she does not receive the actual cash until the payable date. The quarterly payer cuts the waiting time in half.

Zero-Coupon Bonds

Zero-coupon bonds do not pay interest on a regular basis. They are deeply discounted instruments in which the interest accrues in the price and the bond pays its face value at maturity.

Say Tom Atto wants to put away money for his newborn daughter's education. He decides to purchase a $1,000, eighteen-year Karl Leasing bond discounted at a rate of 6 percent. Using the present value formula, we see that present value (PV) = payout (PO) times 1 over (1 plus the interest rate) to the number of times the event will happen. We are solving for what the present value of $1,000, eighteen years from now is.

$$PO = 1,000 \times \frac{1}{(1+.06)^{18}}$$

A) 1 + .06 multiplied by itself 18 times (once for each year) = 2.854339

B) 1 divided by 2.854339 = .350343810

C) $1,000 × .3503438 = $350.3438

$$PO = \$1,000 \text{ times} \left[\frac{1}{} \right]$$

18 (the bond will pay annual interest 18 times)

—— (1.06) ——

$$PV = PO \times \left[\frac{1}{} \right]$$

18

(1+.06)

Therefore, if Tom bought the $1,000 Karl Leasing bond today at $350.3438 per bond, he would receive $1,000 per bond eighteen years from now.

Three important facts must be presented:

1. Even though Tom never received an interest payment during the time he owned the bond, he still must pay income tax on the amount he would have received if the bond was a regularly paying bond.
2. The .06 (6 percent) used in this equation is the discount rate, not the bond's nominal interest rate. If this was a 7 percent bond and not a zero-coupon bond, in bond parlance one would say "a 7 percent bond priced to yield 6 percent."
3. If Tom was to have to sell the bond before maturity, the value he would receive would depend on the then-prevailing interest rate.

Floating- or Adjustable-Rate Bonds

Floating- or adjustable-rate bonds are a way of making a long-term debt look like a short-term instrument. The issuer or its agent resets the bond's interest rate periodically to reflect the then-going rate. The reset date could occur quarterly or semiannually or at another frequency stated in the instrument's indenture. As long as the issuer retains its financial status, and barring any catastrophe, the instrument's price should return to its original offering price at the reset date. The debt owner, selling the instrument at the time of reset, should be able to recoup the purchase price at the time the debt was first issued. In other words, the floating-rate bond's rate is keyed to a target bond. Let's assume the target bond is a U.S. Treasury bond. At offering, it is deemed that the floating-rate bond will trade at 250 basis points over the equivalent Treasury bond. At offering, the Treasury bond is yielding 4.5 percent, so the floater is priced to yield 7 percent (4.5 percent equals 450 basis points, plus 250 basis points equals 700 basis points, or 7 percent). At the adjustment time, as long as the floating bond issuer is financially able to maintain the 250-basis-point spread, the investor will see the bond return to a price that is close to the original offering price. This is an advantage for the investor who is not sure whether or not he or she will have to sell the bonds prematurely. In investing in these instruments, the investor is attempting to remove the principal invested out of the way of market risk. For example, say Amy Strate purchased a $10,000 face amount of a fixed 7 percent coupon, twenty-year bond at par. Ten years later, interest rates have risen to where Amy's bond would have to yield 8 percent to be competitive in the marketplace. Using the "rule of thumb" method, Amy's bonds would be trading at a price of 93, or be worth $9,300. The calculation is as follows:

1. $10,000
   −9,300
   $ 700

2. $700 / 10 years remaining = $70

3. $700 (annual interest payment) + $70 (annual discounted amount if purchased at $9,300) = $770

4. $10,000 (value at maturity) + $9,300 (current market value) / 2 (to get an average) = $9,650

5. $770 / $9,650 = 7.979%

Amy would have to take a $700 loss if she had to trade out of the positions. If Amy had purchased a twenty-year floating-rate bond, she would receive approximately what she originally paid. However, in place of market risk, Amy would be facing interest-payment risk with the adjustable-rate bond, as the amount of interest payment received at each payment period would depend on the interest rate in force at that time (and could be more or less than expected).

The floating-rate bond also saves the short-term investor time spent selecting a new instrument and the fees charged when purchasing a new instrument every time the short-term instrument that he or she owns matures. While the yield on the twenty-year adjustable-rate instrument may be less (per segment) than the yield on a comparable twenty-year fixed-rate instrument, the investor is spared the market risk of the twenty-year fixed instrument.

There is credit risk with the floating-rate bond, as with any fixed-income debt instrument. If the issuer's finances deteriorate, the 250 basis points will not be enough to bring the price back to the offering price. On the other hand, should the issuer's finances improve, the price may rise to a higher level.

As the floating-rate instrument goes through the different phases of its life, it will take on the characteristics of products with that longevity. For example, the floating-rate instrument under discussion here, when it has no longer than two months of life left, will have a basis point spread commensurate with like instruments. The Treasury bond on which the 250 basis points were initially based also has two months of life left and is yielding the same as if it were a two-month Treasury bill (short-term instrument). The floating-rate bond is trading as if it were a short-term corporate debt (commercial paper).

Security Behind Corporate Bonds

Collateral Trust Bonds

Corporations raise money through the debt market by issuing debt supported by different types of collateral. Young companies may issue debt backed by the common stock of other companies and/or other assets pledged by the management or main shareholders of the fledgling company. In case of default, the bondholders can lay claim to the underlying assets. This type of bond is known as a *collateral trust bond*. Issuing this type of bond instead of one backed by the assets of the issuing company, makes the company's debt less risky, and therefore the debt can be floated with a much lower interest cost. (Remember rule #1: no one likes to pay interest.)

Mortgage Bonds

Corporations also issue bonds backed by their real estate, factories, office buildings, warehouses, et cetera, known as *mortgage bonds*. These bonds are not to be confused with mortgage-backed securities, which are discussed in a different part of this book. Those are pooled mortgages that pay back principal and interest during their life. These bonds follow the standard format of bonds, paying interest periodically and principal at the end of their life. In addition, the mortgage bond is financing real estate, equipment, or other assets used by the issuing corporation in its business. As the bonds are secured by property, each bond's indenture will state whether it is an open-ended or close-ended offering. This is important, as it relates to the coverage of the debt. With an open-ended offering, the corporation can issue additional bonds against the same property that will have a claim equal to that of this issue. With a close-ended offering, all subsequent bonds' claims on the assets will be junior to that of the one being offered. Coverage of the debt has a direct result on what the bondholder would receive in case of bankruptcy and what the bond's rating would be.

Equipment Trust Bonds

Bonds secured by the rolling stock of a company, such as transportation vehicles or computer hardware and the like, are known as *equipment trust bonds*. While the bonds are secured by equipment, different structures are employed as to who is responsible for the maintenance and care of the equipment. The indentures of some equipment trust bonds call for the appointment of a trustee to act on behalf of the bondholders. Others leave the responsibility for care and maintenance to the issuing company.

While mortgage bonds and equipment trust bonds are backed by tangible assets, the liquidity of those assets must be considered. A factory may be carried on a company's books for several million dollars, but what would the structure be worth if the company ceased to exist? Who else could use the factory, and how quickly could it be renovated to accommodate another company? While assets carried on the company books are depreciated to reflect wear and tear, the remaining value of a nondepreciated asset is not indicative of its current value.

Debenture Bonds

Companies that have the financial wherewithal can issue bonds that are backed by nothing but the good name and financial strength of the issuer. These are known as *debenture bonds*. In case of default, the holders of these bonds fall in line with general creditors. The ability of the issuer to meet its obligations can be sorted out by checking the rating services and checking the bond's yield against those of similar issued bonds.

Adjustment Bonds

Adjustment bonds are issued when a company is facing bankruptcy and is working with its creditors to restructure the company's capitalization. If the company fails, the creditors will receive only a small portion of their investment, if anything at all. The plan is to set up a structure that will give the company a chance of surviving. Existing bondholders will be given the adjustment bonds in exchange for the bonds they own. The adjustment bonds will differ from the debt they are replacing in their longevity and/or interest rate. This will give the company a better chance of meeting its payment obligations. If the restructuring is successful, the creditors will be able to get a better return on their investment.

Receiver's Certificates

Receiver's certificates are issued by a receiver in the case of bankruptcy. The proceeds are used to allow a company to finish an operating cycle and thereby repay more of its obligations or to protect the company's assets during the bankruptcy proceedings. The receiver's certificate is a lien on the assets of the company and takes precedence over all other creditors' obligations.

Covered Bonds

Covered bonds are a corporate-type bond that is "covered" either by cash flows from a project or by a group of assets that the investor has recourse to in case the issuer fails. They are issued by banks and the debt remains on the bank's books and appears on its financial statements (e.g., the bank's balance sheet). They remain as direct obligations of the issuer. The fact that they are backed by a group of assets should not confuse these issues with asset-backed securities, which are not carried on the issuer's books; instead, the pool of debt is sold to a special-purpose vehicle (SPV) that securitizes and then sells them.

Covered bonds are usually overcollateralized, affording investors additional security. The loans backing the bonds are dedicated to the bonds. This permits the investor the opportunity to examine the quality of the loans the covered bond comprises. During the life of the bond, nonperforming mortgages or other debts (those in default) are removed from the collateral and performing mortgages replace them. As these are on the bank's books, it is perceived that the banks will be more prudent in making loans than they were previously.

Junk Bonds

There are circumstances where financially weak companies that have few or no real assets will offer bonds that are backed by nothing. Issuers whose finances have deteriorated to a point where the ability of the issuer to live up to the obligation becomes questionable fall into this group also. These bonds are usually not rated or are rated very low by the ratings services and come under the general rubric of *junk bonds*.

· CORPORATE NOTES ·

While corporate bonds are issued with duration from ten to thirty years, companies issue intermediate term debt called *corporate notes*. These instruments are issued from one year to ten years in duration. Except for the time span, they have the same characteristics as bonds. Those that pay interest, pay it twice a year. On some the interest payment is set at issuance; on others, the interest rate is adjusted during the life.

Corporations also issue short-term debt called *commercial paper*. This instrument is discussed in the money-market section.

· TAXABLE AND NONTAXABLE INTEREST ·

The interest paid on corporate bonds is considered taxable income at the federal, state, and maybe even local levels. The interest on U.S. Treasury debt is only taxed at the federal level. The interest on most municipal debt is free from federal, state, and local taxes if the owner resides within the state of issuance and therefore is referred to as triple tax free. However, there are municipal bond issues that do not qualify for the tax exemption and are treated as corporate bonds and are therefore fully taxable. The interest paid on bonds issued by the Commonwealth of Puerto Rico is triple tax free regardless of where the owner resides.

· MUNICIPAL BONDS ·

Municipal Issuance

Municipal bonds are issued by state and local governments to fund various activities. They are best known as tax-free instruments, which is not always true. Many municipal bonds are as taxable as corporate bonds. The determining factor is how the proceeds from the issue are to be used. Generally, if the proceeds from the offering are for schools, hospitals, or toll roads, the interest paid on the bonds is not taxable. If the beneficiary of the proceeds is a small group or if the issue doesn't benefit the public at large, the interest paid will be taxable. A shopping mall or an industrial park could fall into this category.

Competitive Underwriting

Municipal bonds are offered under a competitive underwriting. Broker-dealers and banks form independent syndicates. Once the original group is formed, it meets to discuss and agree on the terms it is going to offer to the municipality. Sometimes the municipality dictates the terms it is looking for, but generally it gives the potential underwriters a framework to move in. The different syndicates offer their bids for the new issue, and the municipality accepts the one that best suits its needs. If it is not satisfied with the terms, it may ask the syndicates to resubmit the terms. This may result in some of the potential underwriters dropping out and new syndicates being formed. After the winning bids have been selected, the distribution follows the process used for corporate securities. Some of the underwriters whose syndicate bids were not accepted may become part of the selling group with the winning underwriters and assist in the distribution. It must be remembered that the tax-free interest feature of most municipal bonds while being applicable to federal income tax is only applicable for residents of the state of issue on state and local taxes. Other buyers are subject to state and local taxes applicable in the state in which they reside. Therefore, the underwriters would have clients residing in the state where the municipality wants to float the debt, as these bonds would be attractive to them.

Serial Offering

Unlike corporate bonds and U.S. government bonds, municipal bonds are generally issued in serial form. While the issue may be large, the offering will contain a series of different bonds. A corporate or U.S. government offering is issued in "bullet" form; the entire issue is one security.

An example of a bullet offering is "$100,000,000 Loster Motor Corp 6% FA 20XX" (twenty-year bond).

An example of a serial offering is:

Total offering:
"$100,000,000 Dairy Falls FA GO" (general obligation bond)

> *Component bonds:*
> | | |
> |---|---|
> | $5,000,000 6% ten-year yielding | 6% |
> | $5,000,000 6% eleven-year yielding | 6.05% |
> | $5,000,000 6% twelve-year yielding | 6.075% |
> | $5,000,000 6% thirteen-year yielding | 6.10% |
> | $5,000,000 6.05% fourteen-year yielding | 6.10% |
> | $10,000,000 6.05% fifteen-year yielding | 6.125% |
> | $10,000,000 6.05% sixteen-year yielding | 6.175% |
> | $10,000,000 6.05% seventeen-year yielding | 6.20% |
> | $10,000,000 6.10% eighteen-year yielding | 6.20% |
> | $10,000,000 6.10% nineteen-year yielding | 6.25% |
> | $25,000,000 6.15% twenty-year yielding | 6.25% |

As the last maturing bond issue is larger than any of the previous ones, this type of serial offering is known as a balloon maturity. It is due to this type of offering that there are millions of municipal bonds outstanding. Since each issue is small in size, the issues themselves are not as tradable as corporate or government debt, which is issued in bullet form. In other words, the life of a municipal bond is, as it comes to market, bought and over its life pieces of it float back to the market and are resold.

Let's say Bill Melaiter wants to invest $10,000 in municipal bonds. He selects the $10,000 worth of Dairy Falls GO 6.15 percent that just became available on the market. Someone who owned $10,000 worth of this bond, which is part of the $25,000,000 that was originally sold to the public, has decided to sell that piece and Bill bought it. Later that day he mentions the purchase to Shelly Fish, who is also interested in buying municipal bonds. As Bill bought the only $10,000 piece of Dairy Falls GO 6.15 percent that was in the market at that moment, Shelly would have to choose a different municipal bond.

Typically, when investors want to acquire a municipal bond, they give their brokers or agents parameters. For example, Bill from the previous paragraph, who we will assume resides in Illinois, would say something like "I am looking for a municipal bond from Illinois, investment grade, going out twenty years." The agent would then read a list of bonds that qualify or satisfy Bill's requirements and it would sound something like this:

"I have: 25,000 Chicago GO's 5.5% of 20XU yielding 5.50, 10,000 State of Illinois Toll Road 5.75% of 20XU yielding 5.60, 15,000 Kankakee High School District 5.45% of 20XX yielding 5.53, 100,000 Cook County Illinois Public Works 5.25% of 20XU," and so on. Bill would choose from this list. The more restrictions Bill puts on his requirements, the shorter will be the response list from the agent. When Shelly calls later in the day, the agent will tell her what bonds are available at that time that satisfy her needs or requirements.

Tax-Free and Taxable Municipal Bonds

When transacting in municipal bonds, the agent seldom states the dollar prices but does announce the yield to maturity. The reason is that if the prices were given, the next question from the client would probably be "What's my yield?" So, to be expedient, the price step is dropped.

Many people are under the misconception that the tax status of many of these bonds is an exemption intended to lure wealthy people into purchasing them. That simply isn't true! Go back to the beginning of the section on debt instruments, when we said, "No one likes to pay interest." The fact that interest on municipal securities MAY be free from federal, state, and local taxes benefits the resident taxpayer, not the "wealthy" bond buyer. If a municipal bond was as taxable as a corporate bond, it would have to pay a rate competitive with that of the corporate debt. That means that the residents of the municipality issuing that debt would have to pay more taxes to make up the difference.

Let's assume the federal and state and local income taxes total 35 percent. The owner of a 6 percent corporate bond would be left with 3.9 percent of the payout after taxes (100% − 35% = 65%, and 6% × 65% = 3.9%), or for every $60 of interest the corporation paid, the bondholder would get to keep $39 ($60 × 65% = $39). As the municipal instrument that we are studying is triple tax free, it can carry a coupon of 3.9 percent to be competitive:

Corporate Bond

$1,000 principal amount paying 6%:	$60
Less taxes of 35%:	−21
Total:	$39

Municipal Bond

$1,000 principal amount paying 3.9%: $39

Less taxes of 0%:   0

Total: $39

The $21 difference is saved by the taxpaying public!!

The debt market is huge, and the number of participants from all walks of life is also huge. Many investors own municipal bonds for the wrong reasons: "If I own municipal bonds, people will think I am rich" or "If I own municipal bonds, I won't have to pay taxes on the interest." The decision to purchase municipal bonds or the risk-equivalent corporate bonds should be based on "what is left in my pocket after all taxes are paid."

Also, people should not use the arbitrary rate based on the total or gross income. The rate that is relevant is the tax bracket that they are in when they compute their annual income taxes. (which is gross income less deductions.)

Let's look at a hypothetical situation. When Scott Chensoda figures his tax liability for federal, state, and local taxes, it totals 25 percent. Let's assume that the highest rate is 38 percent. Scott is looking to purchase investment-grade bonds with a duration of fifteen years. He focuses on two bonds of equal rating, one corporate, the other municipal. He can acquire an 8 percent corporate bond or a 6.5 percent municipal bond for about the same cost. As to interest income, which one would be the better purchase? The 8 percent bond would pay $80 per $1,000 per year, less the tax liability of 25 percent, leaving him with $60 per year (100% − 25% = 75%, and $80 × 75% = $60). The municipal bond would pay $65 per year, leaving Scott with $65 per $1,000. Even though Scott is not in the highest income tax bracket, a municipal bond would have been a better purchase, interest-wise, for Scott.

In a stagnant world, Scott would be better off with the municipal bond. In the real world, however, the $5-per-$1,000 penalty that Scott would be incurring by buying the corporate bond may be worth it to Scott, as the value of having the use of the $80 per $1,000 until taxes are due may outweigh the tax-free benefit of the $65.

In other words, the corporate bond would pay $40 per $1,000 twice during the calendar year, for a total of $80 per $1,000. As Scott will pay his income tax in April of the following year, he could use the interest payment until the taxes due date. On the other hand, Scott may not want to face April of the following year knowing he owes $20 per $1,000 bond in taxes and therefore would be only too happy to receive $32.50 in interest twice a year, for a total of $65, and not have any tax liability the following April on the interest received.

Types of Municipal Bond Offerings

Municipal bonds are offered in two major categories, general-obligations and revenue bonds. General-obligation bonds require an approval vote of the public before they can be issued. Revenue bonds require a feasibility study to be prepared and approval by the appropriate governing board. General obligation (GO) bonds are supported by the creditworthiness and full taxing power of the issuing authority. Revenue bonds are backed by and interest paid semiannually, as well as principal paid at the end of the bond from the project that the funds were intended for, such as a toll road or bridge.

Some municipal bonds are backed by two sources and are known as double-barrel bonds. This could occur if the state and federal governments are jointly funding a project or when two municipal jurisdictions are funding a project that they both will use, such as a school.

General Obligations

General-obligation bonds are used to fund the general operating expenses of the municipality. General obligations are generally secured by income, sales, and excise taxes, et cetera. Localities usually fund themselves through ad valorem taxes, which are based on the value of assets such as real estate.

In studying the issuance of or investment in GO bonds, the demographics of the source of the issue are of major importance. While GO bonds are issued to support a municipality's ability to operate, one must determine if the locality is healthy and vibrant or slipping into decay. Are the funds being used to build schools, roads, or waterworks, which are all signs of a growth area, are they being used to refund the status quo, or are they being issued to cover deficits caused by a shrinking tax base? Is the general population of the area growing, and what is the average age of the populace? Of importance also is the attentiveness of the issuer to its financial responsibilities, insofar as the budget is concerned. Does it have a revenue surplus or a deficit over recent years? All of these and other related factors play into the quality of the debt issue.

Revenue Bonds

Revenue bonds have a different set of criteria to be judged by. These include the appropriateness of the project. If the bonds are issued to build a toll road, how is the local population getting around currently? Is the municipality issuing the bonds to refurbish a bridge that no one uses? Are they to fund a huge airport facility where a much smaller one would more than accommodate the need? Many such projects are in the news on a regular basis. In the case of the secondary trading of this type of bond, of importance to the perspective investor is the number of times the net revenue covers the debt costs. This will show how secure the interest and principal payments of the bonds are. In reviewing an existing revenue bond, the interested party should compute gross annual income from the project, then subtract annual operations and maintenance expenses. This will produce the net revenue. Then divide net revenue by annual debt costs. The result is the times net revenue covers the debt.

EXAMPLE

A toll road generates $10,000,000 of revenue, its cost of operation and maintenance is $5,000,000, and the cost to service the debt (which includes the interest that must be paid) is $2,000,000.

Revenue	$10,000,000
Less operating/maintenance cost	5,000,000
Net revenue	$5,000,000

Net revenue of $5,000,000 divided by debt service of $2,000,000 equals 2.5. Thus, the net revenue of the toll road covers the debt expense two and a half times. As a result of this computation, one can see if the project provides a revenue stream or is operating a deficit that must be funded.

The investor should ascertain whether certain legal requirements are part of the deed of trust or in the official statement—such items as agreement to keep rates at a level that is sufficient to cover costs, that proper maintenance will be performed on a regularly scheduled basis, that adequate insurance will be provided, and that generally accepted accounting principles and practices (such as regular financial reports and the employment of outside accountants) will be employed.

Insured Municipal Bonds

Broker-dealers and banks may take a bond issue or group of bonds and have them insured against default. Two of the main insurers are MBIA (Municipal Bond Insurance Association) and AMBAC (American Municipal Bond Assurance Corporation). With this insurance, the bond will become AAA rated, whereas without it, the rating would be much lower. Let's take a BBB-rated bond selling for 95 percent of face value. The equivalent AAA-rated bond is trading at par (100 percent of face). A financial institution buys the BBB-rated bonds, has them insured, pays the insurance fee, and sells them as AAA-rated bonds. The insurer will evaluate the bond offering and determine its risk before setting the cost of the insurance. The financial institution will obtain this insurance when the cost of the insurance and the internal operating and legal expenses are less than the spread between the bond as a BBB-rated instrument and the same bond as a AAA-rated instrument.

· MUNICIPAL NOTES ·

Types of Municipal Note Offerings

Short-term municipal instruments have a duration as long as two years. They are known as BANs, TANs, RANs, and PNs.

Bond Anticipation Notes (BANs)
Bond Anticipation Notes (BANs) are issued as interim funding pending the issuance of bonds. One purpose that they serve is when interest rates are expected to fall in the not-too-distant future and a state or municipality has to raise money. Rather than issue longer-term instruments now and be

compelled to pay a higher rate of interest for the duration of the instrument, the state or municipality will issue BANs. The issuance of this instrument will carry the municipality over until a later period when the expected interest rate will be lower and the bonds could be issued at a lower cost. Another purpose is when a bond offering is awaiting final approval and weather or other extenuating factors require the project to begin immediately.

Tax Anticipation Notes (TANs)

These are issued in anticipation of receiving taxes, such as sales taxes, and other fees. When the tax collections occur, the notes are paid off.

Revenue Anticipation Notes (RANs)

They are another form of interim funding and are issued in anticipation of collecting tolls from bridges, toll roads, and other revenue-producing properties. Upon collection of the fees, the notes are retired.

Project Notes (PNs)

PNs are used as temporary funding in the construction of hospitals, schools, and the like. The notes are issued as the funds are required for the project. When the project is completed, bonds are issued, the proceeds of which pay off the notes.

· UNITED STATES TREASURY INSTRUMENTS ·

Treasury Bonds and Notes

United States Treasury debt is the direct obligation of the federal government. Long-term debt instruments, with ten to thirty years from day of issuance to date of maturity, are called bonds; those that have from one to ten years until maturity are referred to as notes; and short-term ones, with one year or less from date of issuance, are called bills. It's important to note that as the instrument ages, it takes on the trading characteristics of shorter-term instruments but not their name. Therefore, when researching

Treasury notes, for example, one will find Treasury bonds that have between one year and ten years remaining until maturity.

The interest paid on Treasury instruments is taxable by the federal government but not by state and local governments. They are brought to market through a scheduled auction. Interest calculation for Treasury bonds and notes is on an actual-days-over-actual-days basis, with each day of the year accounted for. U.S. Treasury bills are discounted instruments, with the interest subtracted from the face or principal amount and the face or principal amount paid at maturity. The interest for Treasury bills is calculated on an actual-days-over-360-day basis. Treasury bonds and notes trade at dollar prices; bills trade at basis process.

The following is the interest computation for U.S. Treasury bonds and notes. Methodology = Actual/Actual.

Assume Jimmy Oppen purchases a $100,000 Treasury instrument with January/July 1st payment dates and a 4 percent coupon rate traded for settlement April 16th. As interest accrues up to but not including the settlement date, the interest accrual would be:

$$
\begin{array}{ll}
\text{January} & = 31 \text{ days} \\
\text{February} & = 28 \text{ days (leap year 29 days is used)} \\
\text{March} & = 31 \text{ days} \\
\text{April} & = 15 \text{ days} \\
\hline
& 105 \text{ days}
\end{array}
$$

As there are 181 days from January 1 up to but not including July 1 and as interest is being calculated for half a year (coupon rate of 4 percent / 2 = 2 percent):

$$
\text{Principal} \times \text{Rate} \times \text{Time}
$$
$$
\frac{\$100,000}{1} \times \frac{2}{100} \times \frac{105}{181} = \$1,160.22
$$

Multiplying the top row across = 21,000,000
Multiplying the bottom row across = 18,100
Dividing the bottom row answer into the top row answer = $1,160.22

For leap year, the divisor would be 182.

The second half of the year would use a divisor of 184 days. Nonleap year = 181 days + 184 days = 365 days. As with corporate and municipal bonds, the Treasury instrument will pay the same amount of interest for each half of the year. In this case the interest payment would be $4,000 per annum, or $2,000 per half year.

$$\text{Principal} \times \text{Rate} \times \text{Time}$$

$$\frac{\$100,000}{1} \times \frac{2}{100} \times \frac{181}{181} = \$2,000.00$$

$$\text{Principal} \times \text{Rate} \times \text{Time}$$

$$\frac{\$100,000}{1} \times \frac{2}{100} \times \frac{184}{184} = \$2,000.00$$

Treasury Bills

United States Treasury bills are discounted instruments traded on a discounted-yield basis.

EXAMPLE

Ms. Amy Strate purchases a $100,000 Treasury bill with ninety days remaining until maturity. The bills are discounted at a rate of 4 percent. What will Amy pay?

$$\text{Principal} \times \text{Rate} \times \text{Time} = \text{Discounted interest}$$

1. $\dfrac{\$100,000}{1} \times \dfrac{4}{100} \times \dfrac{90}{360} =$

Multiplying the top row across:

2. $100,000 \times 4 \times 90 = 36,000,000$

Dividing answer by the bottom row:

3. $36,000,000 / 36,000 = $1,000

Subtracting answer from face amount:

4. $100,000 − $1,000 = $99,000

Thus, Amy would pay $99,000 for the "T" bill today and at maturity would receive $100,000. The $1,000 difference is the interest Amy earned.

Note: Unlike a nondiscounted instrument, where the accrual of interest is apart from the price, in discounted instruments, the interest is included in the price. As interest rates rise, the price of the instrument will fall, as with any other interest-rate-sensitive instrument, but as the interest is being calculated as part of the price, the real price may be distorted.

EXAMPLE

Amy bought the bill discounted at a rate of 4 percent. Let's assume that forty-five days later, Amy has to sell the bills, and because interest rates have risen dramatically must sell them at the discounted rate of 5 percent.

1. 90 days − 45 days = 45 days

2. 100,000 × .05 × 45 days = $225,000

3. 225,000 / 360 = $625

4. $100,000 − $625 = $99,375

Thus, Amy would receive $99,375.

However! Amy did not earn a $375 profit. Accrued in the price is the interest that Amy earned. She would have earned $1,000 had she held the bills the full ninety days. As she was the owner for half the time, she is entitled to $500 interest and must pay federal income taxes on that income. When the $500 earned interest is added to the price Amy paid, Amy should have received $99,500 on the sale. As she received $99,375, we see that Amy had a trading loss of $125 ($99,000 + 500 = $99,500, and $99,500 − $99,375 = $125).

Because bills are discounted instruments, they are traded on a discounted-yield basis. As with any instrument that is traded on a yield basis, the quote would look strange, as the bid would be higher than the offer. The higher the yield, the lower the price. Therefore, the higher bid price means the dollar price is lower than the offer.

EXAMPLE

A 182-day (six-month) U.S. Treasury bill is quoted = Bid 3.10 – Offer 3.00

A $1,000,000 U.S. Treasury bill is discounted to yield 3 percent for 182 days, and another $1,000,000 bill is discounted to yield 3.10 percent for the same period. Let's compare the two.

Discounted to yield 3 percent:

1. $1,000,000 × 3 / 100 × 182 / 360

2. Eliminate unnecessary zeros: $10,000 × 3 / 1 × 182 / 360

3. Reduce fractions to lowest common denominator: $10,000 × 3 / 1 × 91/180 = $2,730,000

4. Multiply numerators: $10,000 × 3 × 91

5. Divide by denominator: $2,730,000 / 180 = $15,166.66

6. Subtract from face value: $1,000,000 – $15,166.66 = $984,833.34

Discounted to yield 3.10 percent:

1. $1,000,000 × 3.1 / 100 × 182 / 360

2. Eliminate unnecessary zeros: $10,000 × 3.1 / 1 × 182 / 360

3. Reduce fractions to lowest common denominator: $10,000 × 3.1 / 1 × 91 / 180 = $2,821,000

4. Multiply numerators: $10,000 × 3.1 × 91

5. Divide by denominator: $2,821,000 / 180 = 15,672.22

6. Subtract from face value: $1,000,000 – 15,672.22 = $984,327.77

Thus, the dollar equivalent of the two discounted yields converted into their dollar amount would be:

bid 98.43 – offer 98.43

The aforementioned yields are discounted yields, not the effective yield that a buyer or seller would receive. That is because the computation was based on the maturity amount ($1,000,000) and not what was actually paid or received. A buyer who paid the offering dollar price of $984,900 would have an effective current yield of 3.080 percent (15,166.66 discounted amount, divided by $984,833.34 actual cost, times two to annualize the amount).

Cash Management Bills

Besides Treasury bills, the Federal Reserve also issues cash management bills (CMBs), which are short-term instruments used by the government as an interim step until regular funding can be put in place.

U.S. Treasury Bill Auction Schedule.

Bills	Auction	Day	Settlement
CMB	vary	vary	vary
4-week (1-month)	weekly	Tuesday	Thursday
13-week (3-month)	weekly	Monday	Thursday
26-week (6-month)	weekly	Monday	Thursday
52-week (1-year)	monthly	Tuesday	Thursday

United States Treasury notes and bonds follow the methodology of standard bonds. They are dollar priced; in other words, they are priced as a percent of their face value. The minimum price movement is 1/32, except in the case of a tight and active market, in which case the movement may be to 1/64. They pay interest every six months, and their principal is paid back at the end of their life. They are quoted as whole numbers, for example: A quote of 98.08 $-$ 98.16 $= 98\,^{08}/_{32} - 98\,^{16}/_{32} = 98\,\frac{1}{4} - 98\,\frac{1}{2} =$ a bid of 98.25 $-$ an offer of 98.50.

Treasury Inflation-Protected Bonds (TIPs)

One of the negative aspects of buying bonds is the loss of purchasing power over time. In other words, $1,000 twenty years from now would buy considerably less than $1,000 would buy today due to inflation. The U.S. Treasury offers TIPs (Treasury inflation-protected securities) bonds to compensate for this. The coupon payment and principal amount are increased by changes in the consumer price index (CPI). While the coupon rate remains the same, the payment will increase as the underlying principal increases.

Treasury Debt Auction Schedule

U.S. Treasury Note Auction Schedule

Notes	Auction	Settlement
2-year	Every month on the third or fourth Wednesday	End of month
3-year	Not offered at this writing	
5-year	Every month on the third or fourth Thursday	End of month
10-year	Feb., May, Aug., Nov. (historically), plus Mar., June, Sept., Dec. (at this writing), during the second week of the month	15th of the month

Note: The announced date of the auction is usually two or three days before the offering date.

U.S. Treasury Bond Auction Schedule

Bonds	Auction	Settlement
20-year	Not offered at this writing	
30-year	Feb., Aug. (historically), plus May, Nov. (at this writing), during the second week of the month	15th of the month

U.S. Treasury TIPs Auction Schedule

TIPs	Auction	Settlement
5-year	Apr. (historically), plus Oct. (at this writing), during the last week of the month	Last business day of the month

(continued)

TIPs	Auction	Settlement
10-year	Jan., July (historically), plus Apr., Oct. (at this writing), during the second week of the month	15th of the month
20-year	Jan. (historically), plus July (at this writing), during the last week of the month	Last business day of the month
30-year	Not offered at this writing	

Treasury Derivative Product

Separate Trading of Registered Interest and Principal of Securities (STRIPS)

STRIPS (separate trading of registered interest and principal of securities) are Treasury bonds that are "stripped" by a financial institution into two types of instruments. The principal-only portion acts as if it were a zero-coupon bond without coupon payments every six months, but the buyer is paying a discounted amount based on the present value of future cash flows and at maturity will receive the face amount of debt. The difference is the interest earned on the investment. The formula is discussed in the yield section of debt markets.

PV = present value
PO = payout
r = applicable current rate
T = number of times payout occurs (annualized)

$$PV = PO \, \frac{1}{(1+r)^t}$$

EXAMPLE
For a $10,000 U.S. Treasury bond maturing in thirty years, discounted at a rate of 5 percent:

$$PV = \$10,000 \ \frac{1}{(1+.05)^{30}}$$

$$PV = \$10,000 \ \frac{1}{4.321942375}$$

$PV = \$10,000 \times .23137744866$

$PV = \$2,313.77$

An investor who buys a thirty-year principal-only certificate would pay $2,313.77 and receive $10,000 thirty years from now.

The same application would apply to each interest payment. The buyer of the interest portion will pay the present value of each interest payment to be received. While the amount being paid is based on the coupon rate, the present value is based on the rate used in the formula by which the coupon payment is discounted. The buyer pays one total amount for the future payments purchased.

· MORTGAGE-BACKED SECURITIES ·

To understand mortgage-backed securities, one must first understand mortgages. Unlike bonds, mortgages do not mature. Instead, they deplete. Each payment made by the mortgagee pays the interest on the mortgage's outstanding principal for that period, and the remainder is applied to paying down the loan principal. In the case of fixed-payment mortgages, in which the interest rate doesn't change, the first payments are mostly interest, but over time, as the principal erodes, a greater percentage of the payments go to principal and less to interest.

With the monthly payments being fixed, the percentage going to interest on outstanding principal decreases as outstanding principal decreases, allowing a greater percentage of each monthly payment to be applied toward the outstanding principal.

After a bank has granted a mortgage, it may either put it in its portfolio or sell it. If it sells the individual mortgage to an investor, the investor has purchased a "whole loan." The bank or representative servicing entity will

Dramatized Chart of the Effect of Payments
30-Year Fixed-Rate Mortgage

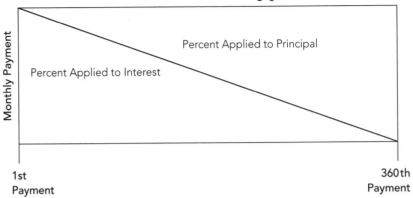

collect the monthly payments from the mortgagee and, after deducting a servicing fee, pass the payment on to the mortgage holder. The mortgage holder, besides receiving the benefits, also receives all the liabilities. This includes forfeiture on the part of the homeowner. To diffuse this risk, issuers began to pool the mortgages and issue securities against the pool, selling the whole pool or pieces of the pool in the marketplace.

Government National Mortgage Association (GNMA)

The Government National Mortgage Association, which is a division of the Department of Housing and Urban Development (HUD), began pooling government-guaranteed or insured mortgages in 1970. These instruments, known as pass-throughs, contain mortgages insured by the Federal Housing Administration (FHA) or guaranteed by the Veterans Administration (VA) and the Rural Housing Service (RHS). GNMA guarantees the prompt payment of principal and interest to the pass-through holder but does not guarantee the mortgages themselves.

As stated above, mortgages do not mature, but the principal depletes over time. The owner of a GNMA pass-through security receives principal and interest periodically, usually monthly. Simply phrased, the homeowner of a single-family home pays the monthly mortgage payment, which contains interest and principal, to the mortgage service company.

The mortgage service company, in turn, deducts a fee for its work, and the remainder of the payment passes through to the GNMA mortgage pool owner.

The standard GNMA mortgage is a thirty-year mortgage. Pools can contain up to one hundred mortgages. The product that is known as GNMA I contains issues from the same source, with all mortgages having the same coupon rate and the same expected termination time. While all the mortgages in the pool are to be paid off in the same period, in reality that is not the case. People can refinance their homes or sell their homes and move elsewhere during this thirty-year period. The demographics of the area will give insight as to how long, on average, the mortgages will be in force. This "average life" estimate affects the pricing of the pool and is known as weighted average maturity (WAM). It is this calculated weighted average maturity that is used in the calculation of the GNMA I's price.

A GNMA II can contain mortgage pools from several issuers within a permissible range of interest rates and expiration dates. As the size of the mortgages and their respective interest rates can affect the average coupon payments between different GNMA IIs, the products will trade based on the weighted average coupon rate (WAC). This does not exist in GNMA Is, as all the mortgages are at the same interest rate.

The homeowners to whom the mortgages were issued have the same rights as any other mortgage holder. They can refinance their homes by paying off their existing mortgage with a new mortgage. The funds used to retire the original mortgage will flow to the pool owners and be included as part of their regular interest and principal payment. The principal payment portion of the payout would include the regular pay-down or return of principal, as well as a prepayment section that would include the proceeds from the paid-off mortgage. The homeowner may refinance to obtain a lower rate or to cash in on his or her equity for a child's education. He or she may pay off the mortgage because he or she is moving to a new location. Once the mortgage is paid off, it ceases to exist in the pool. If the home is refinanced, the new mortgage will not replace in the original pool the one that was terminated prematurely. If there is a new qualifying mortgage, it will be placed into a pool that is being formed.

Though not specified in the mortgage-backed security's description, the mortgages have a built in "call" feature. The homeowner can retire the mortgage whenever he or she wants to. Therefore, what is the possibility of one hundred new homeowners whose thirty-year mortgages are packaged on a new GNMA pool still living in those houses thirty years from now, and those that do still having their original mortgages? If you think it is possible, it would mean that no one moved to a bigger or smaller home, relocated to another town, city, state, or country, or had the need to refinance.

Now it becomes interesting (to me, and, I hope, to you). We established earlier that market risk plays an important part in pricing. Therefore, the longer a debt is outstanding, the greater the chances of its being exposed to adverse market conditions. Add the present value of future cash flows, then apply this to the life of the mortgages, where any homeowner can terminate at any time, and it gets to be very complicated. Where applicable, the pricing of these instruments is based on a weighted average maturity (WAM) or based on previous offerings in the same geographical area.

Using computer models, market makers and other participants set parameters, such as the demographics of the area where the dwellings that the mortgages will be issued on are located, the history of previous pools from the issuer, the local economy, main employers, the average age of the home buyers, the economic outlook, and more. Based on this data, the price is set.

Let's look at two hypothetical pools of mortgages. One emanates from a retirement area where the average age of the home buyer is between fifty-five and sixty-five years. The other emanates from an area where the majority of home buyers are in their late twenties or early thirties, working in the computer software industry. Barring any dramatic change in the interest rates or the economy in general, the members of the group whose primary employer is the software industry will be terminating their mortgages much sooner than those of the retirement group. Those involved with software will be relocating to new jobs, upgrading or downgrading their homes, et cetera, whereas the retirement group will be more stationary. The mortgage pool of the software group will fall in with other intermediate-term debt and follow its yield curve, whereas the retirement group pool will belong to the long-term debt market. Between these two extremes is the rest of the mortgage-backed-bond world.

Let's refer back to an earlier part of the book, where yields and yield curves were discussed. It was stated that in a normal yield curve, the longer out a bond goes, the higher the interest cost it will incur. These factors are taken into account when the market prices these pools of mortgages. A mortgage pool that is expected to be outstanding for a longer period of time should be priced to yield more than one with a much shorter life expectancy. But what if the assumption is proven to be wrong over a period of time? Suppose some unexpected occurrence causes the mortgages that are supposed to be paid off over a long period of time to be paid off at a much faster rate. A sudden or more drastic decrease in the interest rates could cause this to happen. The buyer of this pool received a rate of return based on a long-term instrument, when in reality it owned a shorter-term instrument. Conversely, what if we assume that on average these mortgages will be outstanding for eight to twelve years, and the demographics of the area changes, causing the mortgages to be outstanding for fifteen to eighteen years? The owner of this pool of mortgages is receiving a return on its investment based on a shorter-term instrument when in fact it owns a longer-term instrument. While the shortening of a debt's life can occur with callable debt and debt that has a sinking-fund clause, those instruments are expected to remain outstanding until their maturity. In the case of mortgage-backed issues, the mortgagees can choose to retire their mortgages almost at will. Based on expected "average life" the pricing of mortgage-backed issues involves one of the few instruments that can remain outstanding longer than anticipated. As with other debt instruments, mortgage-backed securities pay interest. Unlike most other instruments, most pay interest on a monthly basis. And unlike most other instruments, they return their principal (deplete) over time and not at the end of the instrument's life (maturity). These payments also come through to the mortgage-backed security owner periodically.

To determine the amount of principal outstanding at any one time, the industry turns to factor tables that are produced monthly by one of the industry utilities. The factor tables show the particular pool by its number, the original pool's principal amount, and the pool's current outstanding principal amount. For example, to determine the amount of interest and principal being received, take last month's outstanding principal balance, multiply it by the coupon rate of the instrument, multiply the answer by thirty days, and then divide the result by 360 days. For example, assume a pool of mortgages contains $3,745,369.68 of outstanding principal on 6 percent mortgages. The interest to be received is $18,726.85 ($3,745,369.68 × .06 × 30 / 360 = $18,726.85). To calculate the amount of principal being returned, using the factor table, subtract the current outstanding principal value for that pool from the previous month's balance. The difference is the principal to be received. For example, assume the above-mentioned pool had an original value of $4,000,654.23. Assume last month's factor was .9361893. Multiply the original pool value by the factor to obtain last month's outstanding value of $3,745,369.68. Then take this month's factor and repeat the process. Assume a factor of .9326875 ($4,000,654.23 × .9326875 = $3,731,360.19). The difference of $14,009.49 is the amount of principal being returned. A shortcut to this process is to take the original pool principal value and multiply it by the difference between the two factors (here, .9361893 − .9326875 = .0035018). Then multiply, $4,000,654.23 by .0035018. The result is $14,009.49, the amount of principal to be received. If the entire pool is not owned, take the original value of the portion owned and multiply it by the factor in force for the previous period. That will produce the actual principal outstanding at that time. Then take the factor for current month and repeat the process. To determine the amount of principal being returned, multiply the original value of the piece owned by the difference between last month's and this month's factors, as we did above.

To Be Announced (TBAs)

GNMA pass-throughs come to market through the efforts of a mortgage banker. From the time the mortgage banker assembles a pool of approved GNMA mortgages until the time homeowners take possession of their homes and begin the monthly payment of their mortgages, the mortgage banker is at credit risk. As the mortgage banker is not in business to take that type of risk, the pending pool of mortgages is sold to a GNMA dealer. This pending pool is known as a TBA, which stands for "to be announced." What is to be announced is the unique number that GNMA will assign to the particular pool of mortgages. The dealer does not pay for the pool until the mortgage banker can deliver certificates (transmitted electronically) representing the pool of live mortgages. So into the negotiated price goes the GNMA dealer's opinion as to which direction interest rates are going to go over the time the TBA is outstanding. The product then begins to trade as an interest-rate instrument. All that is known at this time is the size of the pool, the coupon rate, the delivery date, the type of mortgages, and the fact that these are thirty-year mortgages. The GNMA dealer mixes this pool with other pools having the same nomenclature. Therefore, those trading the TBA are making decisions based on the coupon rate and the delivery date of an actual pool of mortgage.

While the TBA is trading, the approved pools are being activated as people are moving into their homes. As they do, the mortgage banker is taking their mortgages to an escrow bank for financing. When all the pending mortgages in the pool are in force, the mortgage banker takes the mortgages and places them into a pool. Then the mortgage banker takes proof of the live pools to GNMA, which assigns the unique pool number (the assigned number is what is "to be announced"). The GNMA certificates with the newly assigned pool number are delivered electronically to the GNMA dealer's clearing bank. The GNMA dealer pays the mortgage banker the agreed to price on the actual principal outstanding. The principal outstanding will be slightly different from the original contracted amount, as some of the homeowners have begun to pay down their mortgages. The mortgage banker takes the proceeds from the sale and pays off the loans taken from the escrow bank.

Some clients trade in and out of positions while the product is in the TBA state. These individuals are engaged in interest-rate change trading. Depending on the financial status of the client and the policies of the financial institution, clients' trading profits are held until the TBA pools are delivered. Client losses are collected immediately in some cases, and in other cases the losses are collected when the TBA pools are delivered. Settlement of trading profits or losses that occurred during the TBA trading period are addressed at the end of the TBA trading cycle, when the mortgage-backed securities are delivered, because that is the first time actual money changes hands between buyers and sellers. Prior to this period, money adjustments are bookkeeping-type entries. Not only are the GNMA dealers trading with their clients, they are also trading with other GNMA dealers and broker-dealers. Each participant will net its trading activity during the period to one figure. Each GNMA dealer will settle each net figure with its individual customers. The money owed to the client by the mortgage-backed security dealer and broker-dealers is included in the final settlement money at Mortgage-Backed Securities Division (MBSD) of the Fixed Income Clearing Corporation (FICC). Losses incurred by clients are collected from the clients at that time also. Some clients may have to settle the losses immediately if their finances are such that they present a potential risk to the mortgage-backed securities broker-dealer or the firm's experience with the client is limited. Another important consideration that the firm takes into account is the amount of client assets the firm is carrying in the client's accounts at the firm.

Still other clients of the financial institutions may own the TBA or be short (owe) the TBA. As the TBA transactions are not tied to any one pool, the deliverer of the pool has flexibility as to what can be delivered. At the writing of this book, delivery of up to three pools per $1,000,000 of principal (as long as two of the pools do not reach the bottom threshold) are good delivery. The allowable threshold has been decreasing over the years as more and more product becomes available. The threshold is necessary because the instruments pay down the principal. It would be virtually impossible to deliver the exact amount required by the trading contract, as is done with other securities. The threshold currently is $+/-.01$ percent (or 0.0001). A million-dollar trade can be settled by delivery of GNMAs whose outstanding principal is as low as $999,900 ($1,000,000 × .0001 = $100, $1,000,000 − $100 = $999,900) or as high as $1,000,100 ($1,000,000 × .0001 = $100, $1,000,000 + $100 = $1,000,100).

This may appear confusing, but with other instruments, the principal contracted for what is delivered for the agreed-to price. For example, "$100,000 U.S. Treasury 5% FA 20XX @ 96" would cost $96,000 ($100,000 × .96 = $96,000,) or "100 shares of ZAPP @ $35.50" would cost $3,550 (100 × $35.50 = $3,550). Mortgage-backed securities are different; the cost of "$1,000,000 GNMA 6% of 20XX @ 97" would depend on the amount of principal being delivered. Assume Pool 131313X is being delivered and has $999,955.30 of principal currently outstanding. This amount of principal is within the threshold limits ($1,000,000 +/− 0.01 percent = $1,000,100.00 − $999,900.00) and is therefore good for delivery. The buyer would pay the seller $969,956.64 ($999,955.30 × .97 = $969,956.64). In the same manner, the deliverer could deliver up to three pools, as long as two of the pools did not reach the bottom threshold. An example of good deliveries:

Trade of $1,000,000

Pool #	Principal
167843X =	$356,421.63
254381X =	487,513.54
187345X =	155,989.31
	$999,924.48

This would satisfy the terms of the trade:

Pool #	Principal
177823X =	$515,521.63
125488X =	484,413.54
	$999,935.17

As these two pools satisfy the bottom threshold, a third pool may not be included. If a single pool satisfies the bottom threshold, no additional pools may be added.

The role of the Mortgage-Backed Securities Division of the Fixed Income Clearing Corporation is the same as that of other industry clearing corporations. It is to expedite settlement. This is accomplished by:

1. Making certain that for every buy trade there is an equal and opposite sell trade
2. Rolling the previous day's balances into the new day
3. Netting each member firm's daily trades and previous balances into a single new position
4. At the end of the TBA cycle, issuing receive instructions to the member firms that are net buyers and delivery instructions to those member firms that are net sellers

· Asset-Backed Securities ·

Structure of a REMIC, CDO, CBO, or CMO

The product that we just discussed is known as a pass-through security. Each owner of the pool receives a proportional amount of the payments, depending on the amount owned. The coupon rate is usually fixed and varies only in amount depending on the amount of principal outstanding at that time. These payments of principal and interest occur from day one until the final day that the instruments exist. The products we are looking at now are also a pool of debt, but they distribute interest and principal differently. They are of the Collateral Mortgage Obligation, or CMO-type, of pool.

Comparison of Pass Through to CMO

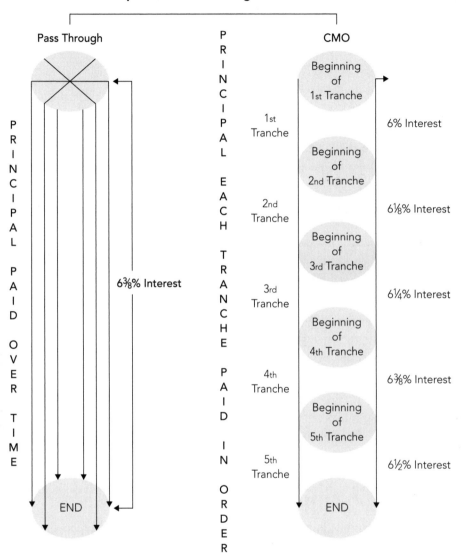

The pool is divided into sections called tranches. In a sequentially paying pool, the tranches are stacked on top of one another. Each tranche is treated as a separate debt, with the first tranche receiving principal payments before the others. When the first tranche is paid down, the next tranche begins to receive principal payments, and so on. Each tranche has an expected end date. However, prepayments of the debt carried in the pool may cause the tranche to retire early.

Interest rates are set based on the length of time the tranche is expected to be outstanding. The longer the longevity of the tranche is, the higher the interest payment will be. Sometimes, the structure will include a zero-coupon tranche known as a Z tranche.

Note: In the tranche-type security, all principal payments are directed to the first tranche, and when it is paid down, the principal payoffs will be directed to the next tranche, and so on. Each tranche will pay a different rate of interest, usually going from lowest for short-term to highest for long-term. There may be a zero-coupon tranche included, which is known as the Z tranche. Principal payments are made sequentially. In the pass-through, principal payments are continuously made to all holders of the pass-through (aka pass-thru) until the debt in the pool is paid off. The interest rate is continuous throughout the life of the product.

Real Estate Mortgage Investment Conduits (REMICs)

REMICs came into existence through the Tax Reform Act of 1986. Under this act, qualified residential and commercial mortgages are pooled and placed in a trust, securitized, and sold to the public. The structure of the securities is of the CMO type, having tranches, rather than the pass-through form. The Act removed the double taxation from these types of instruments by eliminating tax at the issuer level, leaving only the tax at the investor level.

Collateralized Debt Obligations (CDOs)

A CDO is composed of several different types of debt. These include corporate bonds, real estate investment trusts, mortgage-backed securities, secondary mortgages, and so on. Due to the possibility that each pool may have a different mixture of debt, it is sometimes difficult to assess value or compare one CDO against another. Sometimes the term *CDO* is used as an umbrella phrase to cover many types of collateralized debt, such as collateralized loan obligations (CLOs), collateralized bond obligations (CBOs), collateralized insurance obligations (CIOs) and collateralized mortgage obligations (CMOs).

CDOs are structured so that the tranches have different risk elements. The risk elements are based on the debt instruments the pool comprises.

There are tranches that are rated AAA, representing the minimum risk. Riskier tranches then follow, and finally nonrated tranches, representing the greatest risk, are last. Naturally, the amount of interest paid is in relation to the tranche, with the nonrated tranche offering the highest interest rate.

The process by which these instruments and other asset-backed securities are issued is that a financial institution acquires assets and sells them to a special-purpose entity (or vehicle) (SPE or SPV). The special-purpose vehicle (or entity) is created by an underwriter to package the component parts of soon-to-be-collateralized obligation and issue the securitized shares. It is set up as a "triple-A" company, as it buys the debt and sells shares in itself. The buyers of the CDO are equity holders, not debt holders.

Structured investment vehicles (SIVs) are entities that borrow money by issuing shorter-term instruments (at shorter-term interest rates) and buying long-term issues, such as asset-backed securities, which pay a higher rate of interest, and profiting off the spread. The rates used by the short-term instruments are based on such rates as LIBOR (London Inter-Bank Offered Rate) or the T bill rate. The instrument is issued in tranches, usually with a senior tranche, which is triple-A rated, and a junior tranche, which is usually not rated. Some may have a mezzanine tranche, which may carry a rating of A by the agencies.

The terms of the CDO will state what actions the asset manager is permitted to perform. As the assets in the CDO mature, the asset manager usually will reinvest the proceeds in other assets of equal quality. The asset manager may be permitted to trade out an asset whose quality is failing and replace it with a stronger asset. This will be done to maintain the integrity of the tranche.

Collateralized Bond Obligations (CBOs)

These securitized products consist of corporate junk bonds that are pooled and sold as a CMO-type instrument. Because the default risk is spread over the entire pool, the instrument is reclassified as investment grade.

Collateralized Mortgage Obligations (CMOs)

Unlike other participants in the collateralized obligation group, CMOs are not all brought to market through special-purpose entities. Those CMOs that contain insured or guaranteed mortgages that are issued by the Federal Home Loan Mortgage Corporation (FHLMC, aka Freddie Mac) and the

Federal National Mortgage Association (FNMA, aka Fannie Mae) do not. Fannie Mae and Freddie Mac are GSEs (government-sponsored enterprises) and are empowered by an act of Congress. They pool mortgages from their portfolios and sell the pools into the market through dealers in a manner similar to that used for GNMAs discussed above.

Auction-Rate Securities (ARS)

Auction-rate securities (ARS) are intermediate or long-term municipal or corporate debt or preferred securities in which interest or dividends are reset periodically through the auction process. The auction process is conducted every seven, fourteen, twenty-one, or twenty-eight days, and the instruments are issued at par. However, due to the resetting of the payment rates, ARS are traded and priced as short-term instruments. Typically, bidders enter the market with the lowest interest rate they are willing to accept (the highest price they are willing to pay). The rates are set through a process known as a Dutch auction. In a Dutch auction, the bid rates are selected in ascending order and totaled until bid rates equal the amount of supply. Then all bidders pay the equalizing bid, known as the clearing rate. The bids representing lower rates are filled at the clearing-rate price, and bids that were submitted at the clearing bid's price are prorated. Those making bids with higher rates (lower prices) receive nothing. The clearing rate of interest or dividend is paid for the next period. As is usual with debt instruments, the lower the interest payment rate against par, the higher the price, and conversely, the higher the interest payment rate against par, the lower the price.

ARS trade in a marketplace that may not be liquid. Even though the interest rate is supposed to reflect the current market rates, dealers may be reluctant to take on positions or contra parties may not be available. Therefore, the owners of these instruments may get locked in or have to offer an exorbitant interest rate (accept a low price) to sell them. An issuer must hire an auction agent as a manager and broker-dealers to add liquidity. The agent's job is to gather all the orders, separate buy from sell, determine the amount to be sold, sort the buy orders by ascending rates (keeping track of the totals), and finally, determine the clearing rate.

Only broker-dealers selected by the issuer can accept orders. The orders that are permitted are:

Buyers: bid orders at a rate

Sellers: sell order irrespective of the clearing rate

Hold order with a rate (if the rate requirement is satisfied, the security is sold)

Hold order (owner does not want to sell regardless of rate)

It must be noted that the securities that trade in the auction are different from money-market instruments and from floating- (adjustable-) rate instruments brought to market from issuers. Money-market securities are short-term instruments of one year or less and must be paid off at maturity. Whether the issuer uses its own cash (redemption) or issues a new instrument into the market, the proceeds of which are used to pay off the maturing instrument (refunding), isn't any concern of the owner of the maturing instrument. The loan ceases and the owner is to be paid at maturity. In the case of securities issued as floating- (adjustable-) rate instruments, the terms and time interval of the instrument's adjustments are stated at the time of issuance and follow the instrument throughout its life. This includes the standards to which the rates are adjusted, such as U.S. Treasury bill, LIBOR, federal funds, et cetera, which will be used to set the instrument's new rate. As this information is known, the liquidity of the instrument should not change, or if it does it should follow the trend of that financial product segment of the market. Auction-rate securities are dependent on market participants for the new rate and for liquidity. The rate setting is not the responsibility of the issuer, nor is it set against any standard; instead, it is a result of the auction process. Therefore, broker-dealers and banks do not have to participate or support the market. If the auction fails, sellers may not find a market to trade in and may be locked in to their position.

· MONEY-MARKET SECURITIES ·

A money-market instrument in any security issued is for a period of one year or less. It includes U.S. Treasury bills, commercial paper, certificates of deposit, banker's acceptances, Repos, eurodollar deposits, and Federal notes.

U.S. Treasury Bills

United States Treasury bills are issued in four-week, thirteen-week, twenty-six-week, and fifty-two-week offerings. The four-, thirteen-, and twenty-six-week bills are auctioned every week and the fifty-two-week bill monthly (every four weeks). The auction for the first three offerings is held on a Monday, and the one-year bill is auctioned on a Tuesday. All are discounted instruments, which means the interest is subtracted from the face amount at the time of purchase and at maturity the instrument pays the face amount. The difference between the purchase price paid and the face amount received is the interest earned.

As explained above in the discussion of U.S. Treasury instruments, these are discounted instruments. The discounted rate is applied to the face amount of the instrument and the result subtracted from the face amount to arrive at the purchase price. As the purchase price is derived from the computation using the face value, the actual (or effective) yield will be slightly higher than the discounted yield. It should be noted that the effective yield or expected return on investment (ROI) would only be obtained if the instrument is held until maturity. Selling the instrument before then will affect the ROI because of the profit or loss on the closeout trade.

Treasury bills are accepted in lieu of cash in many business arrangements. When a company must maintain a minimum money balance at another company, the company will usually deposit Treasury bills instead of cash. By doing this, the depositing company is earning interest instead of having dead cash lying on deposit somewhere.

Bills are offered by Dutch auction, in which the highest bids are filled first, then on down until the total of accepted bids equals the offered amount. That is the price that all the accepted bids will pay. If there are more bids at that price than remaining supply, the supply will be prorated to the bid's quantity.

Cash Management Bills

These bills are short-term (measured in days) instruments issued by the U.S. Treasury. They are offered through auction in the same manner as Treasury bills.

Banker's Acceptances

These are used in international trade. They usually involve an importer, an exporter, their respective banks, and three documents: (1) a letter of credit,

(2) a bill of lading (or other such document), and (3) a time draft. Banker's acceptances are a way of assuring payment against delivery.

1. A letter of Credit (LOC) is issued by a bank for a client. The recipient of the LOC is assured of payment because the LOC is guaranteed by the bank's credit and not the debtor's. As loans are needed, the recipient, with the debtor's permission, will draw down the needed funds. When the funds needed are less than what has been lent, the overage is returned to the bank. Interest is charged only on what is lent. The debtor pays a fee for the letter.
2. A bill of lading is a contract between an exporter and a transportation company stating the terms under which the goods will be delivered. It is also proof that the goods have left the exporter's facilities.
3. A time draft is issued when payment is required in a couple of days. The amount stated on the draft is due to be paid on the stated day.

The importer secures a LOC from the importer's bank and sends it to the exporter. When the shipment begins its route, the exporter takes the LOC and the bill of lading, or other such documents, to the exporter's bank, which pays the exporter the amount owed less a discount. The exporter's bank sends this documentation, along with a time draft, to the importer's bank, which stamps it "accepted," converting the time draft into a banker's acceptance, which is sold into the marketplace. The money received from the sale of the banker's acceptance flows back to the exporter's bank to cover the payment made to the exporter. The receipt of the goods and payment should coincide with the maturity of the banker's acceptance. The importer makes payment upon the receipt of the goods, which are used to pay off the banker's acceptance.

Banker's acceptances are issued as discounted instruments for periods of 90 days but can range from overnight to 180 days.

Commercial Paper

This is short-term, unsecured debt issued by corporations, with a maturity of up to 270 days being the norm. It is usually issued as discounted paper.

Creditworthy companies borrow short-term funds at the prime rate and turn to this market for additional funding at prime or better rates. The minimum denomination is $100,000. Most commercial paper is issued by financing companies. It constitutes an unsecured loan.

The "paper" is either bank placed or dealer sold. Banks that are holding clients' cash awaiting investment will call issuers to determine which will issue commercial paper at the best rate and timing to meet their clients' needs. Once a deal is made, the banks "take down" the paper and hold it until maturity. At maturity they retire it, collecting its face value, which includes the accrued interest, from the issuing corporation. Commercial paper dealers will buy the paper from the issuer and sell it to their own clients, as well as into the marketplace. As these are discounted instruments, the dealers must acquire the paper at a higher discount rate so that they can sell it at a competitive discount rate that the banks are offering their clients. The paper that is sold moves from the broker-dealer's clearing bank to the agent bank of the purchaser.

Commercial paper is rated, but differently from longer-term instruments. The rating for commercial paper is based solely on default risk. Under Standard & Poor's rating system, an A−1+ rating for commercial paper is equivalent to a AAA to AA− bond, an A−1 commercial-paper rating is equivalent to an A+ to A longer-term debt rating, an A−2 rating is equivalent to a longer-term corporate debt's A−to BBB rating, and so on.

Finally, as long as the commercial paper is outstanding for 270 days or less, it does not have to be registered with the Securities and Exchange Commission, making it a very cost-effective way for companies to raise funding.

Asset-Backed Commercial Paper (ABCP)

Similar in concept to commercial paper, these instruments are secured by receivables due to companies. ABCPs can be outstanding from 90 to 180 days. They differ from asset-backed securities in the longevity of the instrument, known as the tenor. The product is formed when corporations sell their clients' receivables to a bank (usually at a discount) to raise cash, rather than waiting for the receivables to come due. It is normal practice for a business to deliver goods and services, bill the client the amount owed, and await payment. This period between billing and payment forms the "receivable." The bank sells the receivables to a special-purpose vehicle (SPV), which pools them, forming the ABCP, and sells the ABCP into the marketplace. In many cases the bank or other large institution sets up its own SPV and is expected to support the issue by providing liquidity. Some ABCPs are issuers fully supported by issuers, while others are only partially supported.

For example: First Continental Bank acquires receivables from Patgeo Corporation. Kernet Limited, and other companies are being carried on the books of Patgeo as assets as they have made loans against them. Under the banking laws, they must set aside reserves for these loans, which are carried on their balance sheets. The bank sets up an SPV, which will act as a conduit for these loans, pool the receivables, and sell the ABCPs into the market. This activity removes the loans from the bank's balance sheet, which in turn frees up the reserves.

Some issuers of ABCPs derive their supply of receivables from one source. Others obtain their supply from several sources. This affects the issuance of the ABCP. The ones originated from a single source are known as single originator; the others are known as multiple originator. In the case of a multiple originator, all of the originators are expected to support the offering.

Certificates of Deposit

When we refer to certificates of deposit (CDs) here, we are referring to "jumbo" CDs of $100,000 at a minimum. These CDs are fungible and are traded against the CDs of smaller size that one sees advertised in bank windows. CDs represent unsecured loans of commercial banks and range in duration from fourteen days to more than year; some are even issued for up to five years. The most popular are the one- to three-month. CDs are insured, up to a point, against default by the Federal Deposit Insurance Corporation, the same agency that insures savings accounts. At the writing of this book, individual-owned CDs are insured up to $100,000, jointly owned CDs to $200,000, and CDs in IRAs up to $250,000. The insurance covers the account, not the CD.

While most of the CDs are issued with a fixed rate of interest, some of the longer-term instruments can be issued with a variable rate. The terms of interest period vary from CD to CD. A longer-term CD may even have a call feature permitting the issuer to retire the CD before its intended maturity.

· CONCLUSION ·

Debt instruments are one of the most interesting segments of the marketplace. All aspects of the financial world are involved with these products. They are either borrowers, investors, or both. Each comes to the market to seek out the situation that best fits it. Their nuances separate one instrument from another, which causes price differences. The different tax implications stemming from the issuer and the instrument's reflection of the yield curve all converge to make for an interesting product.

6

Foreign Exchange

INCLUDED IN THIS CHAPTER:

- *Understanding Foreign Exchange*
- *Methods of Trading Foreign Exchange*
- *The Foreign Exchange "Market"*
- *Conclusion*

· UNDERSTANDING FOREIGN EXCHANGE ·

Foreign exchange is the conversion of one currency into another. The rate of exchange changes from moment to moment. The fluctuations are more apparent when one travels outside one's home country on business or pleasure. When people say that it's very expensive to visit a particular country or that it is relatively cheap there, they are referring to that country's cost and prices as compared with the visitor's domestic currency.

To better understand the relationship and language of foreign exchange, one only has to look at the domestic stock market for the base. Say common shares of the Divad Corporation are trading at $30 per share. They rise in value to $60 per share, and that is how we explain it: "The stock rose in value." Couldn't we also say that the dollar lost value against the Divad shares? Once, we needed $30 to buy one share, and now we need $60. The commodity is common shares of Divad Corporation; the currency is the dollar. It sounds strange, but we could also say that at one time $30 would purchase one share of Divad Corporation, but now it buys only half a share.

Let's take this concept into the real world. An American has gone to visit

England several times over the past few years. On the American's first trip abroad, the exchange rate for the dollar was $1.40 to one British pound sterling (£). Upon returning, the American tried to determine the cost of the trip.

• Hotel, five nights at £250 per night	£1,250
• Food, five days at £50 per day	250
• Taxis	100
• Entertainment	300
Total	£1,900
	× $1.40
	$ 2,660

On the American's last trip to England, the exchange rate was $1.90 to £1. Coincidentally, the American experienced the same expenses as the first trip.

• Hotel, five nights at £250 per night	£1,250
• Food, five days at £50 per day	250
• Taxis	100
• Entertainment	300
Total	£1,900
	× $ 1.90
	$ 3,610

The prices in England remained constant, but it cost the American approximately $1,000 more for the same services.

Therefore, did the dollar rise or fall against the pound? Conversely, did the pound rise or fall against the dollar?

If the dollar is the currency and the pound is the commodity, the dollar fell against the pound, as $1.90 was needed at the end to buy £1, whereas at the beginning $1.40 would accomplish the same purchase.

If the pound is the currency and the dollar is the commodity, then the pound rose against the dollar, as it was at £0.71 (£1.00/$1.40) per $1 during the first trip and at £0.53 (£1.00/$1.90) per $1 during the second one.

Let's take this into the commercial sector, ignoring tariffs, shipping costs, et cetera. At the current time, the conversion rate is £1 to $1.40. Both England and America are producing a product called widgets. The English made widgets to sell in London for £10 each. The Americans made widgets to sell in New York for $14 each. Therefore, with the conversion rate of £1 to $1.40, it doesn't matter whether a customer acquires a British-made widget or an American-made widget, as it would cost the same in either country.

If the conversion rate became £1 to $1.90, which country would be in a better position to export widgets?

An American would be able to acquire an American-made widget for $14 or an English-made widget for $19 (£1 = $1.90).

An Englishman would be able to purchase an English-made widget for £10 or an American-made widget for £7.39. The calculation is £1 is to $1.90 as $1.40 is to X.

$$\frac{£1.00}{X} \quad - \quad \frac{\$1.90}{\$1.40}$$

$$\frac{£1.00}{X} \quad \times \quad \frac{\$1.90}{\$1.40}$$

$$1.90\,X = 1.40$$

$$X = £0.739.$$

$$10 \times .739 = 7.390$$

As the value of a currency falls, the country with falling currency is in a better position to export its products, all other factors being equal. As the price for the English-made widget in England is £10 and the price for the American-made widget in England is £7.39, we could also refer to the exchange rate in terms of price. The price for an American to buy an American-made widget is still $14.00, but the price to buy a British-made widget in America is now £19.00. The price to buy a British pound was $1.40, and the price is now $1.90.

The exchange may also affect our personal lives even if we never leave the country. Suppose Ellie Phant works for a domestic company that manufactures wholesale parts that are used in the assembly of many products. The parts cost $3.00 to manufacture, and Ellie's employer sells them for $3.25 to $4, depending on quantity. The company acquires the supplies used in the manufacture of these parts from a local company. Suppose a foreign company offers to sell these same supplies for 25 percent less. After testing the foreign supplies, Ellie's company determines that they are as good as the domestically produced supplies. If the company buys the foreign-produced parts and continues to sell its manufactured products at the same prices, it will increase its profits and with the increased profits will be able to give Ellie a raise in salary. (Good for Ellie!) However, what would happen if a foreign company that manufactures the same product as Ellie's company, of equal quality, begins to offer its product in the United States for $2.75–$3.25, depending on quantity? It can do this profitably because its costs are lower than the equivalent costs in the United States and it has a "favorable" rate of currency exchange. Ellie's company's customers, seeing the opportunity of acquiring the part for less and by keeping its price the same, can increase their profits. The company begins buying the foreign parts instead of Ellie's company's products. Ellie's company begins to drop its prices but finds out it can't compete with the foreign company and eventually goes out of business, at which point Ellie becomes unemployed. No one is immune to or sheltered from foreign competition, and with it foreign exchange.

· Methods of Trading Foreign Exchange ·

Foreign exchange can be transacted five ways:

1. Spot market
2. Forward market
3. Option market
4. Future market
5. Swap market

Spot Market

The spot market involves buying the foreign currency today for delivery two days from the trade date (today). The settlement date is known as the value day. The participants exchange currency, and they own the foreign currency. The rate of exchange has been set, and the buyer owns the underlying currency. The disadvantage to the spot market is that it is time dependent. The longer in advance the foreign currency is owned, the longer is the time period that the buyer of the foreign currency is without the use of the buyer's own domestic currency.

Forward Market

The forward market sets the rate at which currency will be converted at a later date. This appears to be the best solution for the typical commercial transaction. The rate is locked in, the buyer still has use of its domestic currency, and the forward market being as liquid as it is, the buyer usually has the opportunity to unwind the position and establish a new position if warranted. Timing is very important in the trading in and out of the forward positions, as it can result in losses if not timed correctly. Typical businesses are in the commodity world, not the finance world, so they usually eradicate themselves from (stay out of) currency masterminding.

Currency Options

The option market comes in two varieties. One is known as the listed market, where options trade in an exchange environment and have rigid predetermined requirements. The other is known as the OTC (over-the-counter) option environment, where options are custom made between buyer (holder) and seller (writer). Both forms of options require the buyer to pay the seller a premium, which could be expensive in comparison to the currency risk that the buyer is trying to avoid.

The Philadelphia Stock Exchange is one of the exchanges that trade currency options. Among the products offered are puts and calls on 10,000 Australian dollars, 10,000 British pounds, 10,000 Canadian dollars, 10,000 euros, 1,000,000 Japanese yen, and 10,000 Swiss francs. The options are in the European form, meaning they are only exercisable at the end of their life. The options expire the Saturday after the third Friday of the expiration month. The benefits are that the options are guaranteed by the Options Clearing Corporation and that markets are liquid. The downside is that the quantity is fixed, the options are only exercisable at the end of their life, and, as mentioned above, the premium to buy the option may negate its purpose.

Currency Futures

Futures are forwards that trade in an exchange environment. The specifications are fixed by the exchange. Unlike options, futures do not expire but become deliverable at the end of their life. And unlike options, futures do not require the payment of a premium. However, futures contracts do require the deposit of margin, which becomes part of the settlement money on delivery. Due to the structure of the futures contract, the markets are liquid, making it easy to enter into and close out positions.

Currency futures trade on the Chicago Mercantile Exchange (CME). The products offered are futures on 62,500 British pounds, 100,000 Canadian dollars, 125,000 euros, 12,500,000 Japanese yen, and 125,000 Swiss francs. Options are offered on these futures, the deliverable being one future contract on the underlying contract, except on the last day of future trading, when currency is used for settlement as the future no longer exists.

Cross-currency futures are also offered on the CME. These include 200,000 Australian dollars settled in Canadian dollars.

With globalization, the need for and use of the foreign exchange markets has intensified. Many products that we use every day are imported. Even those that are made in this country probably contain components that were made abroad. The exporters of these products eventually will need to use their domestic currency. Somewhere in the currency trail, conversion out of the U.S. dollar has to occur.

For example, factory workers in some foreign town or city can't go to their local food store and pay for their goods in dollars; they need rupees, kroner, lire, euros, pesos, won, et cetera. When the conversion occurs depends on the negotiation between the buyer (importer) and the seller (exporter). Is the importer going to pay for the product in the native currency or the foreign currency? If payment is made in the native currency, then the exporter must do the conversion. If the importer is going to pay in the foreign currency, then it will be responsible for the conversion.

It is important to note that to either party, the other party's currency is a foreign currency, and the ratio between the two currencies is constantly changing. The negotiation being conducted today decides what currency the payment will be made in when the product is delivered tomorrow, next week, next month, et cetera. Who made a better deal time will tell.

Whoever is going to go to the bank and arrange for the conversion faces a dilemma; when? If the importer buys the foreign currency today, the rate of exchange has been locked, but the importer no longer has use of the domestic funds in the day-to-day activities and operation of the company. The decision to buy the foreign funds now carries with it a "lack of availability" cost in addition currency-rate risk. What if, during the period between the contract signing and delivery, the importer falls short and has to borrow funds to use in its day-to-day operation, thereby incurring the additional expense of interest on the borrowed funds? What if the foreign currency weakens between the two dates? The importer would have paid less for the foreign goods had the importer waited, thereby increasing the profit opportunity. However, the foreign currency could rise, too, costing the importer more than originally planned. If the exporter is the one performing the exchange, should it wait until receipt of the physical payment from the importer, or should it enter into a forward contract, locking in a rate today that will be used to convert the currency when it is received? Either decision could be beneficial or detrimental to the outcome of the transaction to the exporter.

· The Foreign Exchange "Market" ·

There isn't a physical exchange, per se, where the currency trades. The major currencies, Australian dollars (AUD, $), British pounds sterling (GBP, £), Canadian dollars (CAD, $) euros (EUR, €), Hong Kong dollars (HKD), Japanese yen (JPY, ¥), Swiss francs (CHF), and U.S. dollars (USD, $) trade twenty-four hours a day, literally around the world. Foreign exchange dealers "pass" their position books to colleagues or associates located in the different market centers. Say the currency-trading firm of Stone Forrest and Rivers has currency-trading locations in New York, London, and Tokyo. When the trading day ends in London, the London traders send their positions and the positions that they are monitoring for the Tokyo office traders to the New York office, with trading instructions as to what action to take if specific events occur. At the end of the New York trading day, the New York traders send their positions, the London traders' positions, and the Tokyo traders' positions, to Tokyo for the start of its trading day. Finally, at the end of the Tokyo trading day, all of the books move to

London and the cycle continues. Therefore, while a particular currency center may be closed, its currency positions are being monitored by traders located at other centers. Based on the instructions given by the traders at the closed center, the active traders will either take trading action or contact the trader whose instructions have been elected by market activity.

Banks and money brokers trade in those currencies that aren't the hard currencies and do not trade in open markets primarily to satisfy their clients' settlement needs for international trade and the tourist trade. Some countries have restrictions on the movement of their currencies outside their borders. Trades that settle in these countries' currencies usually settle in those countries.

The rate of exchange for today is called the spot rate. Buying or selling currency in the spot market requires an exchange of the actual currency two business days from the trade date. Currency can also be acquired for later delivery; the exchange rate for these transactions is referred to as the forward rate. Depending on the currency, most forward-rate transactions are for under a year. If the forward rate of a particular currency is higher than the spot rate, it is said to be at a premium; if the forward rate is less than the spot rate, it is said to be at a discount.

The usual trade in foreign exchange is against one's own currency, for example, a German company going to its German bank to buy British pounds for settlement of a commercial contract. There are, however, transactions where neither currency is the home-based currency, such as a German company going to its bank to buy Swiss francs and paying for them in British pounds. This is known as a cross-currency transaction.

Effect of Interest Rates

Interest rates play an important part in the ever-changing exchange rates. Let's assume that the three-month forward rate in Japan is 0.89 percent and the rate in America 4.78 percent. If one looked at the forward rates of the two currencies, one would see that the dollar is increasing in value from the spot market to the three-month forward market and that the yen is losing value for the same time span. The reason is that if you invested yen in the dollar market, you would exit the transaction with more yen than if had you left them invested at the yen rate.

This can be seen best by looking at the interest rate futures. Say the euro interest rate falls between the dollar and the yen. Therefore, on a given day, against 100 euros then:

	1 month	3 months	6 months
euro/dollar future	95.32	95.61	95.77
euro/yen future	99.155	99.135	99.120

Also, because the interest rate in Japan is so low, the future is trading at almost 100, or par.

The forward market does not predict where the exchange rate will be at the delivery time of the contact. It is simply an allocation of the difference between the interest rates of two currencies. The actual rate at that time will be determined by the activities mentioned above. Businesses use the forward rate as a hedge against the eventual purchase of the foreign currency.

EXAMPLE

Centurion Corporation has imported $100,000 (or ¥11,427,000) worth of parts from a Japanese manufacturer, to be paid in Japanese yen (¥) upon delivery three months from now. The question is, does Centurion buy the yen now, three months from now, or through a three-month forward contract? Centurion should consider the following:

1. If Centurion buys the yen today, the company will be without the use of $100,000 for three months.

2. If Centurion waits to buy the yen, the company is exposed to market risk for the next three months. As the yen and the dollar fluctuate in the market, it may cost Centurion more than it initially would have cost, or it may cost less. But Centurion is not in the market to trade risk.

3. Centurion could buy a three-month forward contract, locking in the rate, and at the end of the three months cash in the forward rate and use the proceeds toward paying for the goods. Centurion

could also unwind the forward during its life, if it sees the rate going in its favor, and buy the currency at the end of the three months, to its benefit.

The decision could mean profit or loss to Centurion. At today's rate of ¥114.27 to the dollar, the parts would cost ¥11,427,000. Centurion expects to make a net profit, after all expenses, of $2,000, or, based on today's rate ¥228,540.

What would happen if Centurion waited the three months and discovered that the yen had risen to ¥112 to the dollar? Centurion still must pay ¥11,427,000. Centurion would have to pay $102,026.79 to purchase the ¥11,427,000. The calculation is 112.00 is to 1 as 114.27 is to X.

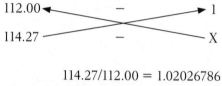

$$114.27/112.00 = 1.02026786$$
$$1.02026786 \times \$100,000 = 102,026.79$$

As a result of the dollar falling against the yen (or the yen rising against the dollar), Centurion must use more dollars to acquire the necessary amount of yen. The additional $2,026.79 wipes out the anticipated profit Centurion was expecting to earn.

· CONCLUSION ·

For those who do not need to travel abroad and/or do not come in contact with the currency conversion often, remember: The currency being used to pay for the "other" currency is the "cash." The other currency is the commodity.

7

Mutual Funds

· INTRODUCTION ·

Welcome to the world of mutual funds. The product we will be discussing is known as an open-end mutual fund. The purpose of a particular fund is to utilize pooled money in an attempt to achieve specific goals. The shares of these funds are bought and sold by investors against the fund. The fund makes a continuous offering of its shares and stands ready to redeem them. There isn't any secondary market. Mutual funds do not trade on exchanges or in the over-the-counter market. Their price is determined by the net asset value of their portfolio at the end of the trading day, plus, in some cases, a sales charge.

· Types of Funds ·

There are other forms of funds that operate under the name *mutual funds*. They include closed-end mutual funds, joint ventures, and unit investment trusts.

Closed-End Mutual Funds

A closed-end mutual fund sets a target amount of capital that it wants to raise. While it is in the accumulation stage, it operates the same way as an open-end mutual fund, buying and selling its shares directly against the public. The price of the shares is set by the fund's "net asset value" (the value of its portfolio and cash awaiting investment minus operating expenses divided by the number of shares outstanding). When the predetermined level of investment is reached, the fund closes and begins to trade the same way as shares of common stock. Its share price is determined by supply and demand in the marketplace, and not by net asset value. The price reflects the market's current opinion of the shares and through it, of the fund itself. The net asset value of an open-end mutual fund is priced once a day, after the markets have closed, and is based on the value of the fund's underlying portfolio. The closed-end fund's shares trade in the secondary marketplace and are traded between buyers and sellers and not with the fund itself. The mutual fund itself is not involved with these transactions, just as a corporation is not involved with the trading of its shares in the secondary market. Closed-end funds can trade on stock exchanges or over the counter and follow the general practices and processes of common stock.

Joint Ventures

A joint venture is another form of mutual fund. Participants in a joint venture pool their collateral in an attempt to achieve a one-time event. Once the result of the effort has been determined, either successfully or in failure, the venture ceases to exist. The consortium of participants composing the joint venture may continue and form new joint ventures over time. An example of this type of fund is an oil-drilling venture. The funds provided to the venture by the participants are used to pay the expenses involved in the exploration and the sinking of the well. If the well is successful, the participants will reap the profits; if not, all or most of the investment is lost. If the joint venture is successful, the venture may continue for many years. Corporations enter into joint ventures to accomplish a common interest and to share the expenses involved in development or other costs. The venture may have many investors. Sometimes these investors band together and form a consortium whose purpose is to seek out interesting opportunities, which they may invest in.

Unit Investment Trusts

Unit investment trusts are another form of mutual fund. Here, funds are pooled to acquire a portfolio of securities. Unlike a typical mutual fund, the securities in the portfolio are not traded. Except under certain circumstances, the initial instruments remain in the portfolio until the trust expires. Among the exceptions are the premature calling in of a bond, where the proceeds are reinvested, or where the quality of an issue falls below the required level dictated by the trust. The expiration date of a trust is set at the time of issuance. A bond investment trust's expiration usually coincides with the maturity of the components of the debt portfolio. The advantage of a unit investment trust over a mutual fund is that the unit owners know what securities are in the portfolio at all times and can follow their performance in the market. Mutual fund portfolios are adjusted and/or traded regularly, as the investment manager seeks to improve the return on investment (ROI). The positions being maintained are reported periodically. Unlike an open-end mutual fund, there is a secondary market for investors to buy or sell the units.

Actually, any time funds or collateral are pooled for a common purpose, that purpose by definition can be a form of mutual fund. We will continue with the form of mutual fund most recognizable by the public.

Open-End Mutual Funds

As stated earlier, open-end mutual funds sell their shares to the public and stand ready to buy their shares back at any time. Therefore, there isn't any secondary trading of these securities. Their market value is determined by the fund's net asset value. This value is arrived at by the following formula:

$$\text{value of the portfolio} + \text{money awaiting investment} - \text{expenses} \div$$
$$\text{number of shares outstanding}$$

To determine the value per share, the fund must wait for the markets to close. As such, open-end mutual funds are priced once a day. Orders received after the pricing has been completed are filled at the next day's computed closing prices. Therefore, it doesn't make sense to trade mutual funds in and out of position during the trading day. If one owns shares of a fund and the securities in its portfolio rise in price dramatically during the day and fall back to where they started at the end of that day, one cannot take advantage of the midday increase in the fund's value. There is a twenty-four-hour lag time between pricings.

When quoting a mutual fund, if the offer is higher than the bid, the difference between the two is the front-end-load sales charge. For example, a fund quote with a bid of $25 and an offer of $26.25 would signify a sales charge of 4.8 percent ($1.25 / $26.25 = 4.8%). Funds that do not have a front-end-load sales charge will show only one price, or the bid and offer will be the same.

(Recently, regulators discovered cases where institutional clients were given the better of the old or new price. Those involved were heavily fined by the Securities and Exchange Commission.)

Because the fund buys and sells its shares directly from and to the client, the sale of its shares is considered to be a new issue and must be accompanied by a prospectus. The prospectus issued by a mutual fund company is a very readable document. It describes the fund's purpose, its management, its advisers, its shares outstanding, its portfolio at the time of printing, and other important points. Funds also issue a profile document that is an abbreviated version of the prospectus. The profile highlights the fund's purpose, management, distributor, and fees.

In addition to the particular fund's prospectus, the major mutual fund companies have a master prospectus that informs the reader of all the funds offered by the company. The abbreviated version, the fund's master profile, is usually available also. The funds are listed in order, from riskiest to safest. Each fund that is listed is accompanied by a brief description of its purpose and goal. The document is usually referred to as the fund family.

Mutual funds run the gamut of financial products. Some are very general and diversify their investments, while others are very specific, investing in certain product types or countries or industries. Still others are very aggressive, taking risks. The following paragraphs reflect on the wide range of mutual fund products available.

Balanced Funds

Balanced funds invest in the market at large and can diversify their portfolios in accordance with their prospectuses. A corporate balanced fund will invest in stock and corporate debt issues. If permitted in the prospectus, balanced funds may even employ option strategies.

Equity Funds

Equity funds invest primarily in common stock, which can be blue chip, growth, income producing, high risk, indexed to follow a specific stock index, domestic and/or foreign issues, common stock, and/or preferred stock, and they may use options either to increase income by selling them against owned positions or as a more aggressive approach to a potential situation.

Bond Funds

Bond funds include government, municipal, and corporate debt products. These may be further differentiated by risk level (e.g., investment grade, high yield), long- and/or short-term debt, specific products within a group, such as select municipal bonds (e.g., State of Massachusetts municipal bond fund), or domestically issued or foreign-issued debt. The foreign-issued security funds may contain only sovereign debt or sovereign debt and other debt issued within those countries (i.e., issued by companies domiciled in those countries). A sovereign debt fund may be composed of Brady bonds, which drastically changes the risk factor. (Brady bonds are U.S. government zero-coupon debt instruments that back some sovereign debt of emerging countries. The United States stopped issuing them in the 1990s.

If there is turmoil in the foreign country, so that the foreign government is unable or unwilling to honor the debt instrument and the sovereign debt defaults, the bondholder receives U.S. Treasury debt.

Regardless of the issuer of the debt, the investor must consider the bond fund composition. Is it made up of long-term, medium-term, and/or short-term debt or a combination of the same? It is important at this juncture to understand that as bonds age, they change their trading pattern; a long-term bond will become a medium-term bond, which will become a short-term bond as time passes. The fund's prospectus will explain what trading action the fund will or won't take as the bonds in its portfolio age. The result will have an effect on the portfolio's turnover rate and could cause unwanted taxable events to occur as a result of the profit or loss of the transaction closing out the position.

Foreign Funds

The mutual fund company may invest by country, region, industry, major financial centers, indexes or emerging markets. The fund will invest in securities that are issued in the relevant country or area and are eligible for the fund's agenda. The fund usually does the conversion from the native currency into dollars, and the fund share prices are quoted in dollars. It should be noted that these funds contain two additional types of risk besides credit and market risk. They are currency risk and government intervention risk.

Currency risk, discussed in more detail in the section on foreign exchange, is the risk caused by the relationship between the U.S. dollar and the native currency of the relevant country or another major currency (if the fund is denominated in that currency). As the dollar rises or falls against the other currency, there will be an effect on the income earned and the profit or loss from the fund share transaction.

Another concern is intervention by foreign governments. Actions such as freezing foreign (to them) assets, nationalizing segments of their commercial industries, or changing their tax codes all have an impact on the experience outcome to the foreign share investor.

Index Funds

They replicate the performance of indexes, such as the well known Standard & Poor's 500 Index and Dow Jones Industrial Index, or specific industry indexes, sector indexes, and so on. Bond indexes vary by longevity, country of origin, product class within country (e.g., municipal or government), and degree of risk.

Some index funds are "share weighted," and others are "price weighted." A "market value share-weighted" index is one weighting the market value of all of the included companies' shares, either outstanding or listed on a particular marketplace. The Standard & Poor's 500 index is a market-value-weighted index. Therefore, the company with the largest dollar amount of total shares will have the greatest impact on the index value. The price-weighted index is based on the share's price, with all companies' shares being equal in number (e.g., 100 shares for each company) regardless of the number of shares the company has outstanding. The Dow Jones Industrial Index is an example of a price-weighted index. In this type of index, the company that has the highest price per share will have the greatest impact on the index.

When investing in index funds, it is also relevant to understand how the index operates mechanically. In the case of a stock index, does the index adjust the component stocks' prices to reflect dividend payments? How does it handle stock splits? Is there a minimum dollar amount of capital required for a company's stock to remain in the index? In the case of a bond index, is there a standard or rating the bond must maintain to remain in the index? Is there a longevity requirement? What action does the fund take in case of default? Some of the fund's actions could result in a taxable event to the fund shareholder.

Derivative Funds

These specialize in options and other derivatives by employing strategies aimed at maximizing profits while accepting varying degrees of risk. Some of the strategies that they employ are derived from computer risk models. Included in these funds are the asset-backed securities group and the pooling and securitizing of the debt.

Fund of Funds

This is a fund that invests in hedge funds and is open to qualified investors only. Hedge funds operate pooled collateral and through an investment manager have much more latitude in permissible investments than the regulated investment manager.

Mutual funds may also be categorized by terms such as *growth*, *income* or *preservation of capital*, *high risk*, et cetera. These terms are usually applied in addition to the terms discussed above. For example, a "high-yield long-term corporate bond fund" is a fund that invests in subinvestment-grade bonds with a longevity of more than ten years. A U.S. government bond fund may not own a single dollar's worth of U.S. Treasury debt but invest in other government securities, such as agencies.

· MUTUAL FUND COMPANY ·

Mutual funds usually comprise a management company that includes a board of directors, investment advisers, a custodian, and a transfer agent. At least 75 percent of the board of directors must not be directly affiliated with the fund. The board oversees the activity of the fund and makes sure its investments and policies are maintained in accordance with the charter of the fund. The management runs the fund operationally from day to day, acting on the recommendations of the advisers and marketing and selling the shares of the fund.

The investment advisers keep the management apprised of what is happening in the economy, in the marketplace, and in the products that are used by the fund. They recommend strategies to be employed and issues to dispose of. Their ability to remain as investment managers of the fund is directly related to their performance.

The custodian, usually a bank, is responsible for the safekeeping of the fund's portfolio. In addition to keeping up-to-date records, the custodian is responsible for servicing the assets it is holding. If the fund is a bond fund, the custodian must collect the correct amount of interest when paid by the issuer. It must pay or receive the correct amount of interest involved with each transaction and settle transactions promptly. The custodian must respond to issuers' calls when bonds are retired prematurely and surrender bonds to the issuers' agents in a timely fashion when they mature. Failure of the custodian to take the last two actions will cost the fund income, as the issuer will stop paying interest at a specific date and the fund will not have received the principal due on the retiring debt so that it can be reinvested. In the case of a stock fund, the custodian is responsible for the collection of dividends due, as well as response to corporate actions such as mergers, acquisitions, tender offers, splits, reverse splits, spin-offs, et cetera. Regardless of the type of issue in the fund's portfolio, the custodian must service it on a timely basis.

The transfer agent is concerned with the shares of the fund itself. It is responsible for the issuance of new shares when bought by clients and the cancellation of outstanding shares when surrendered (sold) by the clients. It is responsible for keeping the registered owners' records up to date, as well as distributing dividends and capital gains as instructed by the fund's management. The recording of fund share ownership is now electronic. Mutual funds have not issued physical shares (shares in paper form) in decades. All positions are maintained in statement form and reported to the registered holder on a quarterly or monthly basis, depending on activity.

The transfer agent maintains a record of the shares' registered owners, not necessarily the actual (beneficial) owners. If the client transacts mutual fund business through a broker-dealer, the broker-dealer may maintain the shares of the fund in the name of the client (beneficial owner) or in its own name (as nominee). The decision as to how the shares are registered is dependent on the business mix of the broker-dealer, the relationship between the broker-dealer and the particular fund, and whether the client is using mutual fund shares to support a margin account.

Investment Company Act of 1940

Mutual funds are registered with the Securities and Exchange Commission and operate under the Investment Company Act of 1940. The Act does the following:

1. Dictates how the fund is to calculate the current net asset value and requires that the updated value be available the next business day;
2. States that 75 percent of the board of directors must be disinterested members, or if the fund has a three-member board, two must be disinterested members;
3. Establishes the criteria for determining whether a person qualifies as a disinterested member;

4. Mandates the timely filing of reports;
5. Sets the requirements for timeliness and accuracy of the information contained in sales material;
6. Sets forth the requirements for custodial services;
7. States that capital gains distributions cannot occur more than once per taxpayer year and dividends should be distributed in the period received;
8. Contains other provisions aimed at protecting the investing public.

The Act was passed after numerous reports of abuses by the funds and their sales representatives. For example, performance charts depicting past performance were not drawn to scale, skewing the relationship between profitable periods, which were exaggerated, and unprofitable periods, which were minimized, or not using up-to-date information in their presentations. For example, the fund would use an out-of-date chart to show they were profitable even though the last profitable year was a few years previous.

Requiring outside board members and defining the role of a custodian went a long way in protecting the public against the shenanigans that were perpetrated by unscrupulous funds.

· Mutual Fund Sales ·

Mutual fund shares are sold several ways. Once upon a time, mutual funds were sold as either load funds (those with sales charges, sold through financial institutions such as brokerage firms and banks) or no-load funds (sold directly by subscription to the fund). The sales charge was used to compensate stockbrokers and other sellers of the fund.

Custodial Services

With the introduction of IRAs, the public began using mutual funds as a convenient investment vehicle. At the same time, broker-dealers and other financial institutions were trying to be the hub of their clients' financial activity. Until then, most clients had maintained separate accounts. They would have accounts containing their security investments at broker-dealers, their savings and checking accounts at banks, and their mutual fund accounts at the respective mutual funds. As the clients transacted business, they had to move funds from one location to another. To simplify matters, broker-dealers began offering money funds, in which clients could invest cash balances that were in their brokerage accounts and earn interest, rather than having to withdraw the cash from their brokerage accounts and deposit it in their savings account at the bank, only to reverse the process when they acquired securities. With balances in the money-market funds, the broker-dealer or other financial institution would simply move the funds between accounts, a seamless process as far as the client was concerned. Some broker-dealers began offering their own mutual funds and the shares of other mutual funds, which they would maintain on their books rather than pass the position off to the fund itself and lose control of the asset.

Today, through an industry service run by the Depository Trust & Clearing Corporation called Fund/SERV, the broker-dealer determines how it wants to carry the mutual fund positions of its clients. The broker-dealer can pass the position to the fund, so that the fund maintains an account for the client or maintain the positions of the clients and have the fund maintain an account for the broker-dealer.

EXAMPLE
The fund maintains the client's position. Client buys $10,000 worth of Le Sabre Fund.

Customer   Broker-dealer   Mutual fund

Dinah Myte ⟶   SFR   ⟶ Le Sabre Fund

Dinah's account at SFR = $0
Dinah's account at Le Sabre Fund = $10,000
SFR's account at Le Sabre Fund = $0

EXAMPLE
The broker-dealer maintains the client's position. Client buys $10,000 worth of Le Sabre Fund.

Dinah Myte ⟶   SFR

SFR   ⟶ Le Sabre Fund

Dinah's account at SFR = $10,000
Dinah's account at Le Sabre Fund = $0
SFR's account at Le Sabre Fund = $10,000

The difference is which company Dinah can transact her mutual fund business with. In the case where the broker-dealer is maintaining the mutual fund position on its books, the client cannot do business directly with the fund unless she opens a separate account that the mutual fund will carry on its books. That account would not include the position at the broker-dealer. In addition, the client would have to notify each entity of the other accounts in order to be entitled to sales charge discounts, which are applied based on the total amount that the client owns. The same is true for any other accounts the client may have that reflect ownership in that fund. This notification of the total amount owned turned out to be a major problem about a year ago, when it was discovered that clients had been overcharged sales fees because their total position per fund was spread between two or more entities that did not communicate with each other. Nor did the client volunteer this information to the share-acquiring institution. In the case where the broker-dealer passes the transaction information to the fund, the client is free to conduct business with either one.

Sales Charges

As the popularity of mutual funds being used for IRAs grew, the individual funds fought for the clients' investment dollars. No-load funds, which generally had higher operating fees, introduced "12b-1 fees" (fees that permit the use of the fund's assets for marketing) to be used for the marketing and selling of their shares. This fee became part of the operating fee, making some "no-loads" more expensive to own on a year-to-year basis than the typical front-end load, which charged lower operating fees.

Front-End Load

Front-end-load funds were sold through financial institutions such as broker-dealers. The sales charge was used to compensate the financial institution for selling the shares, but the charge would diminish as the size of the investment grew. For example, the Le Sabre Fund's break-point sales chart might look like this:

Investment	Sales Charge
$0−$24,999.99	4.0%
$25,000−$49,999.99	3.8%
$50,000−$74,999.99	3.6%
$75,000−$99,999.99	3.4%
$100,000−$124,999.99	3.2%

↓   ↓

Break-Point Sales The point at which the sales charge lowers is called the break point. An investor investing $100,000 would be charged 3.2 percent. If an investor chose the "rights of accumulation" option (an option that permits a lower sales charge as the fund shares are accumulated) and invested $10,000 each year, the investor would be charged 4 percent on each of the first two years' investments ($10,000 × 2 = $20,000), then 4 percent on the first $4,999.99 of the third year's $10,000 investment (total account investment is $24,999.99) and 3.8 percent on the second $5,000.01 (for a total of $30,000), and so on.

Rights of Accumulation Rights of accumulation caused the problem mentioned above, where investors had their investment in one fund located in several different financial institutions and the total amount was not in a centralized location. Each institution charged the rate applicable to the investment it was holding. When the investment was totaled, it was discovered that the clients had been overcharged.

Letter of Intent Front-end-load mutual funds offer investors other options besides rights of accumulation. Some funds offer a "letter of intent" option, which is a thirteen-month agreement. The investor decides what sum of money he or she wants to invest over the thirteen months. Each investment made during this period is charged at the rate applicable to the total amount. If the investor fails to reach that total by the end of the period, the sales charge is adjusted to the rate appropriate for the amount actually invested.

Voluntary and Contractual Plan There are two other plans; one referred to as the voluntary plan and the other the contractual plan. The voluntary plan is set for a period of time during which the investor attempts to reach a predetermined goal. This is similar to the letter of intent option, but the commitment is for years, not months. Each deposit that the investor makes to the fund is charged the rate based on the total agreed to. If the investor fails to reach the goal, the rate charged is adjusted to reflect the appropriate rate for that size investment.

The sales charge in a contractual plan acts in a similar way to the sales charge in an insurance policy purchase. The sales charge is based on the total commitment, with the greatest portion taken in the first few years. A typical contractual plan might have the following load: Up to 64 percent of the total sales charge (based on the contracted amount) is deducted during the first four years, with no more than 20 percent of the total sales charge deducted in any one year, and the remaining 45 percent is deducted over the next nine years. The sales charge is collected regardless of the amount of investment actually made. The investor has an opportunity to cancel the plan at the end of the first eighteen months for a fee, plus any loss in market value.

Back-End Load

Back-end-load funds have become popular. In the case of these funds, sales charges are not imposed at the time of the investment, but a sales charge is imposed when the shares are sold. In addition, unlike front-end-load funds, there aren't any "break points" by which the sales charge lowers as the amount invested increases. The sales charge is based on the total amount in the fund at the time of sale. Therefore, if the investment management of the fund is successful and the amount of actual investment grows due to increases in the value of the investments, the sales charge will be at a lower percentage rate but based on a larger amount. Due to the popularity of this type of fund, it would appear investors don't mind paying a higher dollar amount if the performance is there.

ABC Funds

ABC funds were a way funds could appeal to mass investors. These funds offer investors a choice of ways to acquire the fund. Again, it is up to the investors to determine which of the choices best suit them, considering, for example:

1. How long do they intend to own that particular fund?
2. How large an investment are they making?
3. Are they making a one-time investment or periodic investments?
4. What are the fees, charges, et cetera?
5. What alternatives or programs does the fund offer?

"A" shares are front-end loaded and, as such, generally have lower operating fees. Being front end loaded, they offer the investor break points in the sales charges as well as rights of accumulation and other options. The sales charge is subtracted at the time of the investment directly from the investment. Therefore, only the remaining portion of the investment is available for the acquisition of fund shares. These shares are designed for the longer-term investor, who will benefit from having paid the sales charge and not be bothered with it when shares are liquidated. In addition, the savings on the lower operational fee will accumulate.

"B" shares are back-end loaded. No sales charge is assessed at the time of purchase, so 100 percent of the investment is used to acquire fund shares. The charge is levied upon share liquidation without the benefit of break points. The sales charge could diminish over time. The annual 12b-1 fee is generally higher than that imposed on the A shares and the C shares. After a period of time, eight to ten years, the B shares can be converted to A shares. This will benefit the clients, as the operating fees are less.

"C" shares do not have up-front fees but may carry a small back-end load charge that may be removed if shares of the fund are held for a predetermined period of time. These shares are not eventually converted into A shares, so they do not participate in break-point sales charges and the owner of the shares continues to pay a higher overall operating fee than the A share owner, but the rate is not as high as B share owner pays. Due to the small back-end sales charge, this version may be best suited for the short-term investor.

· FAMILY OF FUNDS ·

Larger funds offer their shareholders a "family of funds." The term has two meanings. First is that the family is comprised of several funds of the same company that the investor can go in and out of for only a service fee after payment of the appropriate initial sales charge. As the different funds have their individual sales charge schedules, a switch-out of a lower-sales-charge mutual fund into a fund with a higher requirement will cause an additional sales charge to be imposed. The family of funds may not include all of the funds under the mutual fund company's umbrella. Investing in those funds that are not covered by the "family" will constitute a new commitment and therefore result in new expenses. This is true even if the funds for the investment are coming from a different mutual fund of the same mutual fund company. The "family of funds" never includes the mutual funds of another mutual fund company.

In its second meaning, *family of funds* can also be referred to as "funds family" and refers to all the funds offered by the parent company. Our made-up Le Sabre Fund could offer all different types of funds, such as sector funds, derivative funds, debt funds, international funds, and so on. That is the Le Sabre Fund family. Within the Le Sabre Fund Family there will be a selection of funds, which could include a long-term, investment-grade bond fund, a general or balanced fund, and a common-stock growth fund, for example, that will allow the investor to switch in and out between them for a processing fee. This, too, would be referred to as the family of funds. To clarify this further, imagine a family. There are parents and children. That is the family. The term *family* can also include grandparents, great uncles, great aunts, uncles, aunts, and cousins (first, second, third, et cetera).

Again, in switching between funds in the fund family, if sales charges are imposed, then when switching from a lower-load fund to a higher-load fund, the investor would be charged the difference.

· DIVIDENDS AND CAPITAL GAINS ·

Bonds pay interest; stocks pay dividends! Bonds never pay dividends; stocks never pay interest. As mutual funds sell shares of themselves, when they make a distribution they distribute dividends. This includes not only stock funds but also bond funds, money-market funds, and any other fund distributing earnings. The dividends are from the income earned by the fund's portfolio. These are usually paid to the shareholder monthly. The other distribution that a mutual fund will make is capital gains. This is paid from the net profits the fund has earned in trading its portfolio. The distributions are made once per year. Regardless of the length of time that the shares are owned, the capital gains distribution to the mutual fund share-owner will be treated as long-term capital gains for tax purposes.

Many share owners leave their dividends and/or capital gains in their mutual-fund accounts. The fund will take the distribution and acquire more shares. As there isn't any physical certificate, the fund will make bookkeeping entries out to four decimal places and acquire fractional shares. For this process, it doesn't matter whether the shares are in the beneficial owner's name or the name of a financial institution for the benefit of the actual owner; the distribution and subsequent acquisition will be posted to the share owner's account. Many investors see this as a painless way of accumulating wealth over time.

There is a strategy in mutual-fund investing known as dollar averaging. Since the funds permit partial shares in an account, the theory goes that a client investing the same amount of money on a preset schedule will accumulate more shares of the fund over a period of time than the investor that requires a set amount of shares with each purchase. As the fund's share price falls, the client will be acquiring more shares, and when the price rises would be acquiring less shares. However, with the inclusion of fractional shares, the sum of the parts (each investment) will be greater than the whole.

· Conclusion ·

As investment in mutual funds continues to grow, the financial industry will find new investment opportunities. Other products will come along to challenge the mutual fund industry for investors' dollars. One such product is already here, in the form of exchange-traded funds, or ETFs. These instruments are discussed in their own section. Investors must be cognizant of the investments being made and whether or not a particular opportunity is right for them. The market is very careful in balancing risk and reward. Therefore, especially in the case of mutual funds, with all of their products and all of their sales tools, investors must do their homework.

8

Option Products

· INTRODUCTION ·

Options are a tool, and a tool in the hands of a novice can be an accident waiting to happen. This may seem cruel, but it is true. An option is, simply put, a contract that allows the buyer (owner) certain privileges for a period of time. Once that time has passed, the owner loses all privileges. The seller of the option has nothing to do unless the option is exercised by the option owner. At the end of the contract's life, if it is not exercised, the contract expires and the writer is freed from any further obligation. For the privilege, the buyer pays the seller a premium.

Options are a derivative product. The product it represents is known as the underlying. The size or amount of the underlying product covered by the option is specified in the contract. In the case of common-stock options, it generally is one round lot (100 shares); an index option uses $100 X, a percentage of the index value, for example.

There are only two forms of this contract. One allows the owner the privilege of buying the underlying, that is to say *call* it in. The other gives its owner the privilege of selling, that it to say to *put* it out. The writer or seller of the contract is obligated to perform the terms of the contract *only* when the owner exercises the privilege during the agreed-to time period.

Let us suppose you were trying to sell your home. I came to look at it and wanted to buy it. However, I wasn't sure that I could get the money together for thirty days. There are several steps we could take at this time. We could do nothing; that is, if another buyer came in and could buy the house during the thirty-day period, you would be free to sell it. You could promise not to sell it for that period and hold it for me, which would be foolish on your part, or we could enter into a contract, for a fee, that would restrict you from selling the house to anyone else, regardless of what price they were willing to pay for it, until the thirty-day period had expired. I could contact you any time during the thirty-day period and say that I was ready to purchase the house. If you responded by saying that you were sorry but you had sold the house to someone else, I would seek legal action against you for violation of the contract. If, on the other hand, I contacted you during the thirty-day period and told you that I didn't want the house, we would need another contract voiding the first one. Let's assume that I contacted you on the thirty-first day and said I wanted to buy the house. You would be within your rights to tell me that you had sold it to someone else, as the original contract between us would have expired the previous day. Actually, as soon as the contract expired, you could refuse to sell me the house for whatever reason you could think of. That is the same way financial options function.

· STRUCTURE OF AN OPTION ·

The structure of an option has the following components:

1. Type (put or call)
2. Underlying issue (trading lot of security, index, currency, et cetera) that the option is issued on

3. Expiration date (the last day of life for the contract)
4. Strike or exercise price (the value to be exchanged upon exercise)

Putting it all together, the following is an example of an equity-listed option:

Type	Underlying	Expiration Date	Exercise Price
Call	ZAP	Oct	40

Translation: This is a listed call option that permits its owner to call in (buy) 100 shares (a trading lot in the United States) of the common stock of Zappa Corp (ZAP) any time he or she wants up until the Saturday after the third Friday of the expiration month (October) and pay $40 a share. Listed (exchange-traded) standard equity options all expire on the same day of the expiration month, and their exercise prices are regimented. The terms of an over-the-counter option are negotiated. Therefore, an over-the-counter option can expire on any day and contain any exercise price that was negotiated between parties.

· EQUITY OPTIONS ·

Call

If an option is stated as "Call RAM Oct 60," the buyer (aka holder, owner, taker) of this option has the privilege to call in (buy) 100 shares of the Ram Corporation common stock any time he or she wants up to the day in October that the option expires. For this privilege the call buyer will pay a premium to a seller. Upon exercise, the buyer will pay $6,000 plus any other fees charged by the buyer's financial institution and will own 100 shares of the Ram Corporation common stock. As this is an exchange-traded option, the buyer can go back into the market and sell the option without the knowledge or consent of the original counterparty. If the option becomes worthless because of the price movement of Ram, the owner will allow it to expire.

The seller (aka writer, granter) of the call option "Call RAM Oct 60" will collect a premium for granting the option. That premium is for the writer to keep. If a buyer does not exercise the option, the writer must do nothing else. If, however, the buyer decides to exercise the call option, the writer must deliver 100 shares of RAM through his or her financial institution to the buyer's financial institution, which in turn will deliver them into the buyer's account. As stated above, upon exercise of the call option, the buyer will pay $6,000 plus the appropriate fees, which would follow the reverse route of the stock, with the fees being kept by the buyer's financial institution. The writer's financial institution would receive the $6,000 upon delivery of the stock and subtract its fees for services rendered. The remainder would be booked to the seller's account. During the period that the writer has position, he or she can go to the appropriate exchange and buy the same option from someone else and close the position out, without knowledge or consent of the buyer.

Put

If an option is stated as *"Put WIP Jul 40,"* the buyer of this option has bought the privilege to sell 100 shares of the Wipper Corporation common stock any time he or she wants to, up to the last day the contract is valid, by exercising the option. If the buyer decides to exercise the put option, he or she will deliver the 100 shares of WIP and receive $4,000 less any fees charged by the option buyer's financial institution. For this privilege the put buyer will pay a premium to the seller. As with the call option, the buyer can also go back into the market and sell the put, closing out the position. If the put should become worthless at the end of its life, due to the price movement of the underlying security, the owner will simply let it expire.

The grantor, seller or writer of the *"Put WIP Jul 40"* option will collect a premium for selling the option. If the buyer does not exercise the option, the writer needs to do nothing. If the buyer of the put does exercise the option, the option buyer will deliver 100 shares of Wipper to the seller's financial institution, which in turn will deliver it into the seller's (writer's) account. The writer will pay $4,000 plus the appropriate fees for the shares of stock. The money, less the fees, which will be kept by writer's financial institution, will follow the reverse route of the stock. As with all of the above, the writer can go back into the market and buy the put option, which would close out the position. If the option is worthless at the expiration time, the writer has to do nothing.

It is important to note that a buyer of an option, be it a put or call, can never lose more than the cost of the option, plus fees charged by the financial institution. The writer, on the other hand, can face risk of loss many times greater than the premium received.

Let's look at the option itself as it relates to the underlying security.

The exercise price of the call option on Ram is 60. That translates to $6,000 (100 shares × 60). If Ram common stock was trading below $60, the owner of the option would not exercise it. Why call in stock at $60 per share if it could be bought in the open market for less? Because of the relationship between the exercise price of the option and the underlying security value, the option is said to be "out of the money." In other words, the holder would take a loss if he decided to exercise it, so the writer does not have to be concerned about being exercised against. The writer hopes the relationship stays that way, so that the option will expire worthless. Therefore, the option is "out of the money" for the owner and seller of the option.

On the other hand, if Ram common stock was trading above $60 per share, the buyer of the call option could exercise it. The buyer would call in the common shares of Ram at $60 per share, which would be less expensive than buying the same security in the open market. That relationship between the exercise price of the option and the market value of the underlying security causes the option to be "in the money." The option is said to be "in the money" for the buyer, and since it can be profitably exercised by the buyer, the option is "in the money" for the seller.

If the exercise price of the option was the same as the price of the underlying security, the option would be said to be "at the money."

Remember, we are looking at a relationship between the exercise price of the option and the value of the underlying security. That relationship is the same, whether it is the buyer or the seller looking at it.

Let's track a put option:

In a put option, the option is said to be in the money if the market price of the underlying security is below the exercise price of the option. An owner of the option could purchase the underlying security at the lower price of the two and "put" it out at the exercise price of the option. If the market price of the underlying security is higher than the exercise price of the option, no one would buy the stock at the higher price and put it out at the lower price. In that situation, the option is "out of the money."

Let's track a put option:

A simple way of figuring out the status of an option is to ask yourself, "If I was given this option as a present, would I exercise it?" If the answer is

Call RAM October 60

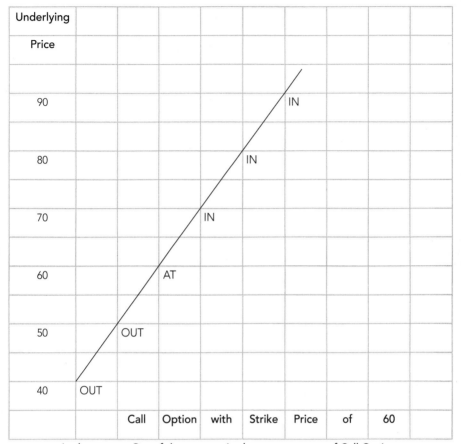

Underlying										
Price										
90						IN				
80					IN					
70				IN						
60			AT							
50		OUT								
40	OUT									
		Call	Option	with	Strike	Price	of	60		

In the money, Out of the money, At the money status of Call Option

yes, the option is in the money. If the answer is no, then the option is out of the money.

The option contract transaction, like all such transactions, requires an exchange of assets. The buyer must pay the seller for the privileges offered in the contract. This payment is known as the option premium. The premium is composed of two parts, intrinsic value and time value.

Intrinsic value is synonymous with *in the money.* It represents a value that equalizes the difference between the strike price of the option and the underlying security's value. For example, a call option with a strike price of 60 would be in the money by 10 points if the underlying security was

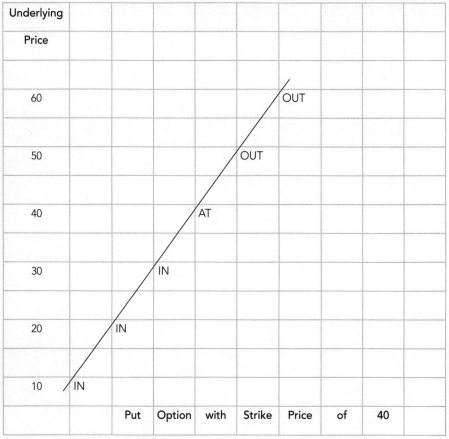

Put WIP July 40

In the money, Out of the money, At the money status of a Put Option

trading at $70 per share. To explain this another way, if you were given the $60-strike-price call option as a gift, and the underlying security was trading at $70 per share, you could call in the underlying security (100 shares of stock) and pay $6,000 (100 shares × $60), immediately sell the 100 shares at the current market price of $70 per share, and earn a 10-point profit, less fees and other expenses. Therefore, the minimum price anyone would sell the option for is 10 points, because that is the buyer's and seller's break-even point.

Staying with the above-mentioned $60-strike-price call option, if the underlying stock was trading below $60, the option would be out of the money and therefore wouldn't have any intrinsic value.

The second part of the premium is called time value. How much time has the option left before expiration? Consider how volatile the underlying security has been (known as historic volatility) and how volatile it is at the current time (implied volatility) and you will have an indication of how much the underlying security can move up and/or down between today and the day the option expires.

Let's look at two companies: the WIP company, which manufactures saddles, bridles, and whips, and the ZAP company, which is working on a new wonder drug that could cure a life-threatening disease. While both companies are financially sound, which company would tend to have more price movement in its common stock? The ZAP company's common stock is more attractive for possible long-term capital appreciation than the WIP company's. The ZAP company also offers more risk of loss than does the WIP company. Therefore, if both companies' common stock were trading at the same price, an at-the-money option on ZAP common stock would be selling at a higher price than an at-the-money option on the WIP company's common stock.

It should be noted that time is your friend if you are a buyer of options and your enemy if you are the seller (writer) of the options. If you are buying options, you want as much time as possible to allow the anticipated event to happen, so time is your friend. When you sell (write) an option, you want to limit your exposure to that event happening, so time is the enemy. However, time is money, and the longer an option has until expiration, the more time value it will usually have in its premium. Somewhere between time and cost should be a happy medium. If not, it may be better to find some other opportunity to trade.

The importance of the above is that if the buyer looks at market sentiment, sometimes the cost of buying an additional thirty or more days of time may be trivial, so the next-expiration option may be worth the investment. At other times the spread between the two option prices may negate the advantage. The reverse is true for the seller of an option; sometimes the price difference between an option and one out for thirty days more isn't worth the additional exposure. Better to "take the money and run." In other words, collect the premium of the shorter-term option and deal with that risk, rather than selling the longer-term option for a slightly higher premium and incurring the risk and exposure for an additional period of time.

We will now consider the concept of breakeven, profit, and loss.

In options, the premium and all other expenses (commission, et cetera) must be taken into account to calculate the buyer's pure profit or loss. In addition, the cost of "unwinding" (getting out of the position) must be taken into consideration. For the writer, all costs are subtracted from the premium to get the net received. However, the cost of closing out the position must be calculated and added to the figure to get the true breakeven.

In the following example, we will assume a commission of $50 to get into the position and $50 to get out of it. Mr. Mike Rafone buys two calls at $6. The total cost, $1,200 (2 × 6 × 100) plus $100 "round turn" commission, equals $1,300. The options would have to be trading at $6\frac{1}{2}$ for Mike to break even. The chart would look like this:

Option premium	Profit/loss	−6½	−1	−½	+/−0	+½	+1	+1½
8								•
7½							•	
7						•		
6½					•			
6				•				
5½			•					
0		•						
+Profit	−Loss	−6½	−1	−½	+/−0	+½	+1	+1½

If the premium was zero at the end of the option's life, Mike might just let the call option expire and save the second $50 commission. That decision would depend on any one of several independent events. Also, if Mike exercised the option instead of closing it out, the commission charged would be based on the commission structure charged by Mike's firm on the underlying 100 shares.

On the other hand, if Maxine Emumms (Max) sold two put options for $2\frac{3}{4}$ points, she would net $5\frac{1}{2}$ points (2 × $275 = $550 − $50 = $500). If the option premiums fell to zero and the option expired worthless, Max would net $500. If, during the life of the option, Max decided to reacquire the option, she would have to pay the other $50 commission, plus the cost of the closeout option. Finally, if an exercise by an owner should be assigned to her, she should have to receive the underlying vs. payment, besides the cost of acquiring the underlying, she would have to contend with the commission cost associated with the underlying product.

The chart below depicts Max's profit or loss outcome per option. She sold the puts for a net of 2½ points per option. If the option was trading at 4 points, she would have an unrealized loss of 1½ points. If they were worthless, she would have an unrealized profit of 2½ points.

Option premium	Profit/ loss	−1½	−1	−½	+/−0	+½	+1	+2½
4			•					
3½				•				
3					•			
2½						•		
2							•	
1½								•
0								
+Profit	−Loss							

Many studies have been done on the behavior and pricing of options. Perhaps the most well known is the Black and Scholes model. These studies and models can be found in some option-specific textbooks, which go into more detail beyond the scope of this book.

The following chart depicts the optimal results of an option position, both the maximum profit and the maximum loss.

Long (Bought) Call Option	Written (Sold) Call Option
Maximum profit:	Maximum profit:
infinity minus strike price plus premium plus acquisition expenses	premium minus cost of selling option (option expires worthless)
Maximum loss:	Maximum loss:
premium plus cost of acquiring option (option expires worthless)	infinity minus strike price plus premium minus acquisition expenses

(continued)

Long (Bought) Put Option	Written (Sold) Put Option
Maximum profit: difference between strike price and underlying product becoming worthless, minus premium plus acquisition expenses	Maximum profit: premium minus cost of acquiring option (option expires worthless)
Maximum loss: premium plus cost of acquiring option (option expires worthless)	Maximum loss: difference between strike price and underlying product becoming worthless, plus acquisition expenses, minus premium

EXAMPLES

Mr. Stan Tahl buys a call on PIP Apr 60 for a premium of 3. The option costs $300, and the firm charges a $30 commission for a total cost of $330. The $330 represents all of the money Stan can lose. If the option premium goes to zero, Stan is out of pocket $330. His profit is determined by how high the value of the PIP stock can rise during the life of the option—$65, $650, $6,500, infinity? As PIP rises in value, so will the option premium and so will Stan's profit.

Mr. Pete Kole sold that option. The only money that Pete will see is the proceeds of the sale. If PIP should rise in value, it would cost Pete more to close out the position than he received on the sale; therefore, Pete would have a loss. If the option was exercised when PIP was selling at $90 per share, Pete would have to buy 100 shares of PIP for $9,000 plus expenses and deliver the stock for $6,000 (the exercise price) less expenses, for a $3,000+ loss. One mistake some people make in their thought process is to say, "What if Pete already owned the underlying stock and didn't have to buy it? He could use it to deliver against exercise." First of all, Pete would have to have bought 100 shares of PIP at some time to own it, which is a cost, but more important, he is delivering something worth $9,000 for only $6,000 (ignoring any expense).

Ms. Della Ware buys a put on ZOW Jul 40 for a premium of 5. The option costs Della $500 plus commission. If ZOW goes out of business and its stock becomes worthless, Della could theoretically buy the worthless stock and "put" out at the strike price of 40 for $4,000 less expenses. Her profit would be the difference between what she paid for the option and what she received when she exercised it and delivered the stock.

Ms. Toni Foote sold that option. The most money she will ever receive will be the proceeds from the sale of the option. That is her maximum profit. If the underlying company goes out of business and the stock becomes worthless, someone will exercise the option against Toni and she will have to pay $4,000 plus expenses for the now-worthless stock. Toni hopes that the price of the stock rises above the strike price, so that no one exercises the option against her position.

In reality, stocks do not rise in value to infinity, and few companies go bankrupt (and that process usually occurs over a long period of time). Therefore, a marketplace for options (known as listed options because they trade on exchanges) exists.

· LISTED VS. OVER-THE-COUNTER OPTIONS ·

Options trade on exchanges as well as over the counter. Options that trade on exchanges are called listed. Listed options have a fixed structure, whereas the terms of an over-the-counter option are negotiated between the buyer (holder) and seller (writer). Because the terms of a listed option are preset at the time of its listing, they are more liquid than those that are negotiated in the over-the-counter market.

In the case of an over-the-counter option, as all of the terms are negotiated between buyer and seller, they are customized and usually are one of a kind. They can include any strike price and any expiration date. Therefore, the contract between the buyer and seller remains in force throughout the life of the contract. Usually, the only place the buyer can sell the option is back to the original seller. At the time of the buy and the time of the sell-back, the prices are negotiated. Intrinsic value (i.e., the difference between the strike price and the underlying value) is a "hard" number. The time value of the premium is not, as it is arrived at through interpretations of the volatility and then negotiated. Listed options trade on option exchanges. They are issued by the Option Clearing Corporation (OCC) and guaranteed by it. After the trade has been consummated and is carried on the books of OCC, OCC guarantees performance. All exercises are made against OCC, and OCC assigns the exercises on a random basis to firms carrying written positions. In an over-the-counter option, the buyer and writer are locked together. Should the buyer (holder) exercise the option, it would be doing so against the writer. If the writer ceases to do business, the holder has no recourse except through legal channels.

The listing of options follows a regimented process. For example, say ZAP common stock, which is trading at $50 per share, is about to have listed options offered on it. First, the option exchange listing the option will want to establish strike prices that will be conducive to trading strategies. They will want to list one option *in the money*, one *at the money*, and one *out of the money*. With ZAP at $50 per share, that will translate to options being listed with strike price of $45, $50, and $55. This will give a call and a put "one option in, one option on, and one option out" of the money. If the volatility of ZAP warrants it, the exchange may even list an option between these three, such as a 47.5 and a 52.5, or further out, a 40 and a 60. As the underlying security price moves during the life of the option, the market-place on which the option is trading will apply to OCC to add additional option series as needed.

The expiration months are set as a quarterly cycle with the next two months. Let's assume that it is early December. An exchange will want to list options on a January quarterly cycle: January, April, July, and October. The longest-term option the exchange will list is nine months, and that will initially be the July option. It also wants to offer two near months, so it will initially offer January, February, April, and July. When the January option expires, the exchange will list a March option. That will offer the public February, March, April, and July. When the February option expires, the exchange will list the October option, giving those interested March, April, July, and October expiration month options to choose from.

Besides the standard options discussed above, OCC also lists long-term equity anticipation securities (LEAPS) options. These options have an expiration date up to three years from the date of issuance and expire the Saturday after the third Friday of the expiration month along with the standard option. When the option has eight months of life remaining, it takes on the symbol and all other characteristics of the standard option.

OCC also lists flexible exchange (FLEX) options, which can have a duration of up to ten years. Their expiration date must be a business day and cannot fall within two days before or after the expiration of a standard option, nor can it include the third Friday of the expiration month (or the day before that if the third Friday is a holiday). The FLEX option is a way that an option having some of the properties of an over-the-counter option can be recorded by a third party (Option Clearing Corporation). This would give the two parties to the trade the benefit of the clearing corporation, which acts as an independent third party and has a record of the transaction's terms should any questions arise at a later time. In addition, the clearing corporation guarantees performance should a counterparty to the trade fail. Over-the-counter options do not provide the third-party benefits or guarantees.

Listed options have symbol designations. For standard options, the first letters are the company's stock symbol, followed by the month and strike price. The months are designated $A–L$ for calls, with January being A, April being D, July being G, and December being L. For puts, the range is $M–X$, with M signifying January, P representing April, S for July, and X for December. The expiration months that fall in between would be represented by the corresponding letters.

The strike prices are based on 5-point intervals, with A representing a strike price of 5, D representing a strike price of 20, and T representing 100. The same letters are used for multiples of 100. Strike prices of 105, 205, et cetera, would also be A.

At the writing of this book, this process of identification, which dates back to April of 1973, when the concept of listed options was born, is currently being reviewed to address many of the inadequacies of the current system. The result will be a more flexible identification format.

The exercise of a listed equity option converts the option into the underlying security for settlement purposes. The exercise by a client of a broker-dealer is made by the broker-dealer against the Option Clearing

Corporation (OCC), which in turn assigns it to a broker-dealer the morning of the next business day. That broker-dealer in turn assigns it to a written position that is on that broker-dealer's books. The assignment instructs the receiving broker-dealer what category of account the assignment should be processed against (for example, "customer" or "proprietary"), and that instruction must be followed.

In the case of the exercise of a call equity option, once the client to be assigned is identified, the client must be prepared to deliver the required security. The exercise of the option is made on day one against OCC, which in turn assigns it the next morning. If the client has the security in his or her account at the broker-dealer, the broker-dealer will include the stock with other trades settling three days after the day of exercise. If the writer does not have the shares available, and as the writer does not know of the exercise until the following morning, the writer may have to acquire the stock that day. The rules give the writer a one-day grace period. The "uncovered" writer of the call must acquire the underlying stock on the day of assignment (the morning after exercise). If the position is acquired through trade, the settlement of the trade will occur three business days later, which is one day after the holder's exercise settles. But as the writer acted in good faith when acquiring the security, the rules allow the one-day delay in delivery.

· EXERCISE OF A CALL OPTION—TIME LINE ·

	Monday	Tuesday	Wednesday	Thursday	Friday
Position	Holder exercises	Writer receives exercise and buys underlying stock		Settlement day for holder's exercise	Settlement day for writer's trade
Holder	Exercises; this is the trade date for the exercise (TD)			TD+3; exercise trade is supposed to settle	

(continued)

	Monday	Tuesday	Wednesday	Thursday	Friday
Writer -		Receives assignment and buys stock for delivery; this is the TD for the purchase			TD+3; purchase trade settles and delivery is made

The called-in stock will be processed along with the broker-dealer's other equity trades through the equity clearing corporation, National Securities Clearing Corporation (NSCC).

Note: The rules of OCC are very clear. When an option position is opened on the books of OCC, it must state the category of the principal that owns the option. The opening firm designates "customer," "firm," or "specialist/market maker." This is how OCC controls the positions. An exercise of an option will state the firm and category initiating the exercise, and OCC will subtract the exercise quantity from that firm's category's position. It will then assign the exercise to a firm with a written category position on a random basis. The receiving firm must assign the exercise to a written position in that specific category. OCC then reduces the position in that category. The method the firm uses to assign exercises to clients is on file with the broker-dealer's regulator.

In the case of a put exercise, where the owner (holder) of the option has to make delivery of the underlying security, the time process is a little different. If the holder of the put option owns the underlying security, the security will be delivered in the normal equity trade cycle. If the put owner does not own the underlying security, the owner is expected to acquire the underlying security on the day of exercise so that it, too, will settle in the same cycle as a regular trade. The writer of the put, as he or she advised of the exercise against them the morning after exercise, has two days to get the money into the account to pay for the acquisition.

· Exercise of a Put and Call Option—Flow Chart ·

As over-the-counter options are not settled through Option Clearing Corporation, their exercise remains between the writer (seller) and holder (buyer). The holder notifies the writer of its intent to exercise. Both firms prepare trade-ticket entries, which are sent to National Securities Clearing Corporation (NSCC) for comparison. If the details of the two trade inputs agree, the exercise will settle. If not, both firms are notified of the discrepancy, which must be resolved so settlement can occur.

Exercise of a Put and Call Option, Including the Option-Clearing Corporation

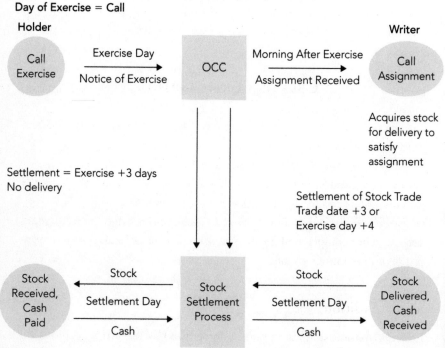

Day of Exercise = Call

Holder   Writer

Call Exercise — Exercise Day / Notice of Exercise → OCC — Morning After Exercise / Assignment Received → Call Assignment

Acquires stock for delivery to satisfy assignment

Settlement = Exercise +3 days
No delivery

Settlement of Stock Trade
Trade date +3 or
Exercise day +4

Stock Received, Cash Paid ← Stock / Settlement Day / Cash → Stock Settlement Process ← Stock / Settlement Day / Cash → Stock Delivered, Cash Received

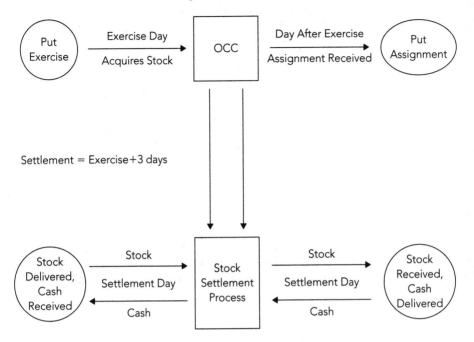

Day of Exercise = Put

· Uses of Equity Options ·

Options are a tool, and a tool in the hands of a novice could be an accident waiting to happen!!!

Options are a way of attempting to achieve a goal by putting at risk a minimum of capital. As with all such instruments, a mistake in some of the uses of options can be very costly.

Besides the standard buying and selling of options, there are strategies that are more complicated and are presented here for explanatory reasons and not as recommendations.

Simple Position

The most basic use of an option is simply the buying of the position. For example, say Justin Tyme is of the opinion that YEP common stock offers a good investment opportunity. The stock is trading at $25 and could rise to the $38−$40 range over the next six months. The $25-strike-price six-month call is trading at 6 points, or $600 per option, plus expenses. If he decides to buy the option, the most Justin can lose is the acquisition cost. If he is correct and the stock rises to $38, the $25-strike-price option will be worth a minimum of 13 points, less the 6 points plus it cost to buy the option and fees to unwind the position if closed out during its life, leaving Justin with at least a 5-point profit. If the option is held to expiration and is still selling at $25 or below, the unwinding fees will not be applicable, as the option will simply expire. Even if Justin is partly right, and the stock rises to $29, for example, at expiration, he can recoup part of his loss. If Justin does earn 5 points on the trade, it will be an 83 percent return on his investment. If he buys the underlying stock instead, he will have tied up $2,500 instead of $600, and if he sells it for $3,800, he will have earned $1,300, less expenses, for a return of less than 52 percent. He will also have put $2,500 at risk of loss, rather than $600. However, the option expires, and the stock doesn't. The stock could rise from $25 to $38 in the months after the option expires, which is worthless information to Justin.

Ms. Rose Flowers has been watching SLAP common stock fall in price. In reading research reports on SLAP and other stories, she can find no redeeming qualities in the company as long as the current management remains. The stock has already fallen in value from $90 per share to $85, and it looks as though $70 may not be the bottom. Rose does not own the stock. She wants to take advantage of a potential profit opportunity. She can sell the stock short, which will require a margin account that Rose may not have. If the stock is at $85, she will have put at risk a deposit of $4,250 per 100 shares for margin, the firm will have to arrange for the borrow of 100 shares to be used against the delivery of the short sale of 100 shares, and she faces the risk of the stock being bought should the supply of borrowing stock dry up due to some corporate activity. She can also buy a put! Let's assume a six-month window of opportunity. The most Rose can lose is the acquisition cost less the liquidation costs if she trades out of the position. Let's also assume there is a six-month, at-the-money option trading at 5 points. If she is correct in her estimates and the stock falls to $70, she will be able to buy the stock at 70 and exercise the put at 85, giving her a gross profit of 10 points (strike price of 85 minus market price of 70 = 15 points in the money, minus the cost of 5 points = 10 points), or simply sell out the option at 15 points intrinsic value (plus whatever time value may still be in the option's premium) for a gross profit of at least 10 points (15 points at sale − 5 points at purchase = 10 points profit). In all likelihood, Rose will do the latter, as it involves less expense.

However, if the stock takes a huge plunge after the option expires, Rose the option holder will not be happy, but Rose the short seller will.

Buy Write

Let's suppose Ms. Jenna Raite buys 100 shares of KOO stock at $60 a share because it pays a good dividend of $5.00 per share per year, or $1.25 every quarter of the year. (Important! She buys the stock for its dividend, not for capital appreciation.) After she buys it, she notices that there is a three-month, out-of-the-money KOO option with a strike price of 65 selling at $1.50. She decides to sell the out-of-the-money call and collect $150 the day after the sale. Jenna has collected more than one quarterly dividend payment within twenty-four hours. At the end of the three months, if KOO has never gone above $65 per share, she will employ the same strategy again, adjusting as necessary for changes in the strike prices of the option. If everything stays static, at the end of the year Jenna will have collected $500 in dividends and $600 in option premiums. But remember, the world is not static. KOO may have fallen in market value, thereby wiping out any benefit to the strategy, or KOO may have increased in value and the shares of stock been called away. The options have a strike price of $65, and Jenna purchased the stock at $60 per share, limiting her profit potential to the 5-point difference. Once KOO goes above $65, the stock could be called away. While the stock dividends and option premiums looked attractive at the time, they're not quite as attractive as if she had bought the stock at $60, never written an option position against it, and sold it at, let's say, $80. Go back to the beginning of this paragraph; Jenna bought the stock for its dividend, not for capital appreciation.

While a good feature of a buy write is the generation of income, the negative is that the underlying security may rise above the strike price of the call option. Once it does, the short option position negates the profit opportunity of the stock owner, as the stock cannot be valued higher than the strike price of the option because that is what it will be called in at. The other negative is that if the underlying stock falls in value and the owner wants to cut his or her loss by selling the stock, he or she is left with an uncovered short call option position, which could cause problems if the stock's price should turn and rise. An owner who closes out the option position in that case would incur additional expense.

Note: There is a major difference between a worthless option and an expired option. A worthless option could gain value if the market price of the underlying turns and runs toward the direction of the strike price. An expired option is dead. Covered writers—those that have the underlying security that the option was written against—sometimes learn this fact the hard way. In the case of a call writer, they write out-of-the-money calls against an equity position. The stock falls in value as the time value of the option dissipates. The options become basically worthless, so in order to pick up additional premium, they write more options on the same equity position that are closer to the current market price with a longer life remaining than the original options have left. The stock position covers the new and more expensive option, and as for the original, now deep out-of-the-money options, the writer must deposit margin on the uncovered deep out-of-the-money options, which have a minimal fee of $250 per option. If the initial options were long term when the position was opened, and the market price of the underlying continues to lose value, the writer may be able to do this again as the second round of written options becomes worthless. At this point, the covered writer has one set of covered options and two sets of uncovered options. Some event occurs that affects the underlying stock price favorably, and the price of the underlying stock starts to rise rapidly. The client is faced with the need to satisfy margin requirements on the uncovered options and worse; as the stock's price rises, the write will be getting assigned on its written uncovered call positions. One possibility for the option writer is, as these are listed options, to buy them in the open market and close the positions at the then-fair-market price of the option; but what is that cost to the entire position?

Spread

A spread consists of equal numbers of long and short calls or puts having the same underlying security and different series. In your typical spread, one position is the main option and the other acts as an insurance policy (if it's the long option) or a premium reducer (if it's the short option).

For example say Wanna Gogh thinks CIP, which is currently trading at $43 per share, is going to fall in value. Wanna writes an uncovered call (she doesn't own the stock) on CIP with a strike price of $45 and collects the premium. This option is out of the money by 2 points, so it won't be called away at the underlying stock's current price. She expects the stock to fall in value to $30 per share and the option to expire worthless. But what if she is wrong and the stock rises? Wanna would be facing unlimited risk, as there is no limit to how high the stock's price can rise. To limit her risk, she buys a call for the same period of time as the one she sold, but with a strike price of $50. If the stock rises above $45 per share, Wanna risks having the stock being called away, which would necessitate her buying the stock at the then current market price and delivering it against the exercise. If the stock rises above $50 and the stock is called away, Wanna can call in her long option at $50 and deliver it against the exercise at $45, thereby taking a 5-point loss between the two transactions. If the stock continues to rise, she has limited her maximum risk to 5 points, plus expenses, less the difference between the premium received on the option she sold and the premium paid on the option she purchased. This is a spread using the secondary option as an insurance policy.

An example of using the secondary option as a premium reducer is as follows. Polly Ester expects UMMM to rise from its current price of $31 per share to $35 per share over the next six months. Polly checks the price of the six-month call option with a $30 exercise price. It is trading for 5 points. If Polly is 100 percent correct, and the stock is trading at $35 per share when the option expires six months from now, the option will be worth exactly what she paid for it. Polly notices that the six-month call option with a strike price of $35 is trading at $2. Polly buys the $30-strike-price call and sells an equal number of the $35-strike-price calls, thereby reducing her cost to 3 points. If she is 100 percent correct, and UMMM is trading at $35 six months from now, the $30-strike-price option will be worth 5 points, and the $35-strike-price option will be worthless, netting Polly 2 points. That may not seem like a lot, but a 2-point profit (excluding fees) on a 3-point investment is a return of $66\frac{2}{3}$ percent in a six-month period. This is an example of the secondary option being used as a premium reducer. No matter how high the stock goes, at expiration the $30-strike-price option would be worth 5 points more than the $35-strike-price option.

Spreads are sometimes referred to as bull spreads or bear spreads. These terms indicate the direction the underlying security must go for the position to be profitable.

Note: Many novices believe that a bull spread is synonymous with a call spread and a bear spread is synonymous with a put spread. This is not true. . . . Read on.

The following are examples of bull spreads. (Note: Examples exclude fees.)

EXAMPLE

ZAW is trading at 50. Tom Atto takes on the following position:

> Buy one call ZAW Oct 50 for 5 points
> Sell one call ZAW Oct 55 at 2 points

The net cost to Tom Atto is 3 points. The buy at a cost of 5 points minus the sell at 2 points equals a 3-point cost. If ZAW is trading at 55 as the option is about to expire, and the position is unwound, the $50-strike-price call will be worth 5 points, and the $55-strike-price call will be worth 0. The sale of the $50-strike-price call will bring in 5 points, less the 3 points that the spread cost, for a profit of 2 points. If ZAW is trading for 50 or less when the options are about to expire, Tom would lose the 3 points paid. If the stock rose above 55, for every additional dollar per share Tom would earn on the $50-strike-price option, he would lose a dollar a point on the short option.

Value of the Options at Expiration

Price		Oct	50					Oct	55		Profit/loss
65				15						10	+2
60			10						5		+2
55			5						0		+2
50		0						0			−3
45	0					0					−3

EXAMPLE

Phil O'Dengrin's account has the following position:

Sell 1 put ZAW Oct 50 at 5 points
Buy 1 put ZAW Oct 45 for 2 points

The net received by client Phil O'Dengrin was 3 points. If the stock is trading at 50 or above when the option expires, both options will expire worthless, leaving the client with the 3-point profit from the premium received when the spread was put on. However, if the stock is trading at 45, the 50 put would cost 5 points to close out the position, and the 45 put would expire worthless. This would leave Phil with a 2-point loss. That 2-point loss would follow regardless of how low the price of ZAW became.

Value of the Options at Expiration

Price		Oct	50				Oct	45			Profit/loss
55	0					0					+3
50		0					0				+3
45			5					0			−2
40				10					5		−2
35					15					10	−2

Phil has a 3-point credit that, when subtracted from the 5-point loss, leaves him with a 2-point loss. As the stock falls below 45, the 5-point intrinsic value spread is constant.

Both of the above examples, one using calls and the other using puts, are bull spreads.

The following are examples of bear spreads. (Note: Examples exclude fees.)

EXAMPLE

Jack Rabbits believes Zaw is falling in value and takes on this position:

Sell 1 call ZAW Oct 50 at 5 points
Buy 1 call ZAW Oct 55 for 2 points

Jack Rabbits wants the stock to continue to fall in value, rendering both options worthless and allowing him to retain the 3-point difference from when the position was acquired. If, however, the stock rises to 55, the 50 call will be trading at 5, and the 55 call will be worthless. The 5 points Jack will pay to cover the $50-strike-price call, less the 3 points netted when the position was entered into, will leave Jack with a 2-point loss. As the stock continues to rise, the net 2-point difference will remain.

Value of the Options at Expiration

Price		Oct	50					Oct	55			Profit/ loss
65	15						10					−2
60		10						5				−2
55			5						0			−2
50				0						0		+3
45					0						0	+3

Ellie Fant is bearish on ZAW. Ellie decides to put on the following spread:

Buy 1 put ZAW Oct 50 for 5 points
Sell 1 put ZAW Oct 45 at 2 points

The net paid by Ellie Fant for the spread was 3 points. If the stock is trading at 45 when the options are about to expire, the 50 put would bring in 5 points when sold, and the 45 put would expire worthless. This would leave Ellie with a 2-point profit. If, however, the stock is trading at 50 or above when the option expires, both options will expire worthless, leaving Ellie with a loss of 3 points that was paid when spread was put on.

Value of the Options at Expiration

Price		Oct	50					Oct	45			Profit/ loss
55	0						0					−3
50		0						0				−3

(continued)

Value of the Options at Expiration

Price		Oct	50					Oct	45		Profit/ loss
45			5						0		+2
40				10						5	+2
35					15					10	+2

The two examples above are bear spreads, even though one contained calls and the other puts.

In the above examples, each spread had the same expiration month. These are known as price spreads, vertical spreads, or money spreads. The terms *price spread* and *money spread* originate from the fact that the series in the spreads have different strike prices. The term *vertical spread* originates from the display of option prices in most data providers. The options are listed by expiration month horizontally and strike price vertically.

Spreads can also have the same strike price but different expiration months, for example, "Buy 1 call LOL Apr 45" and "Sell 1 call LOL Jan 45." These are called time spreads, horizontal spreads, or calendar spreads. For example, say a company is bringing a new product to market in the next couple of months. It may be a success, or it may not be. The client, Carol Ling, wants to lock in the option price with the stock at the current price but doesn't want to pay all that time value. The option owned has a longer life than the one written. This spread will result in a reduced cost to Carol and give her a "second look" at the situation in January.

EXAMPLE

Sell 1 put ZUPP Aug 70 at 6 points
Buy 1 put ZUPP May 70 for 2 points

Let's assume that an out-of-the-money August put is trading for 6 points and has six months of life remaining. The May put with three months remaining is out of the money also and is trading for 2 points. Barry Toan does not see anything on the horizon that could affect Zupp favorably, so he takes on this position. Should ZUPP decrease in value below $70 per share, his sold put is covered by the bought put until it expires in May. In May, when the bought put expires, the August put would have three months of life remaining, which is the same time span the May put has now. If Toan's assessment is correct, and all other things being equal, the three-month sold put should be trading at 2 points. If Toan bought in the sold August put, he would be left with a 4-point profit.

There is also such a thing as a diagonal spread, where both the expirations and strike prices are different. For example, "Buy 1 put WOW Oct 60" and "Sell 1 put WOW Jul 55." This type of position may be the result of two independent events, the need for time with the ability for a look-see later on, and a cost/risk factor justifying the difference in strike prices.

A word of caution: At the beginning of the option chapter, there was the statement "Options are a tool, and a tool in the hands of a novice could be an accident waiting to happen." Before any of these strategies is employed, think it through. If you are not sure whether the right strategy is being applied, seek the advice of a person who truly understands the product and the goal.

In these transactions, and any transaction in any product, never forget to include expenses in your calculations.

Straddle

A popular strategy among professionals is called, appropriately, a straddle. This entails buying or selling equal numbers of puts and calls having the same underlying product and the same series designation.

For example, the account may own 10 calls on ZAP expiring in April with a strike price of 30 and 10 puts on ZAP expiring in April with a strike price of 30:

Long 10 calls ZAP Apr 30

Long 10 puts ZAP Apr 30

The owner of a call is hoping for an increase in the value of the underlying security, and the owner of a put is hoping for the value of the underlying security to decrease. The person with this position in his or her account is really straddling the proverbial fence. The owner of this position doesn't care which way the value of ZAP goes, as long as it moves enough to cover the cost of both options and then some. The owner is expecting some anticipated event to happen or fail to happen. If the anticipated event occurs, the stock's value will rise; if the event doesn't occur, the stock's value will fall. The owner is hoping that no matter what happens, there is enough movement in the stock's price to make the position profitable.

Let's assume the call is at three points and the puts are at two. The spread would cost the owner 5 points. The stock must move up or down enough so that the cost of the spread is covered. It can also move up and down enough during the life of the spread to cover the cost. Say a person holds the following position:

$$\text{Long 10 calls ZAP Apr 30} = 3$$
$$\text{Long 10 puts ZAP Apr 30} = 2$$

If the stock rises to $40 by expiration, the 30 call is worth $10 and the 30 put is worth $0 = 5-point profit.

If the stock falls in price to $20, the 30 put is worth $10 and the 30 call is worth 0 = 5-point profit.

Given time, the stock price changes, making one of the options profitable. That option gets closed out. Then the price turns to the point where the remaining option becomes profitable, and it is closed out.

Sellers of straddles want the opposite to happen. They are hoping the underlying security's value doesn't change much, so that the time value in the two options' positions' premiums will dissipate and the premium received from the sale will be their profit. They hope that if the underlying stock's value does change, it changes to an amount that will leave the writer with some profit.

EXAMPLE

Rumor has it that the ZAP Corporation may introduce a new product that will give it access to a market that it is trying to break into and needs badly. If it is successful in this new market, the benefits will flow to its existing products. Zap has risen from $18 a share to its current price of $30 on the rumor alone. It is speculated that if this new product is successful at launch, ZAP stock could be worth $45 per share or more. However, due to the amount of resources ZAP has thrown into this effort, if the new product in the new market is a failure, the firm will incur a huge loss.

Because of the uncertainty of the situation, six-month calls on ZAP common stock with a strike price of 30 are trading at $7 and six-month puts on ZAP with a strike price of 30 are trading at $5. Pete Cole is certain the options are undervalued. He perceives that if the product is a success, the value of the calls could triple in value, and if the product fails, the loss to the firm will be much greater than anticipated. Pete purchases the straddle. Tom Morrow thinks the hype about the pending product is skewing all the values. He also thinks that a product such as this will take at least a year to evolve into value. Tom writes the options; if his assumptions are correct during the next six months, the common stock of the ZAP Corporation should be trading around the price it is today or at a minimum will not move up or down to cover the 12 points he is receiving. If he is correct, the time value that is in the option's price today will decrease to his advantage over the next six months.

Let's look at the loss side. The most Pete can lose, regardless of what happens, is the cost of the two options, $700 per call contract and $500 per put contract, or $1,200 per straddle. Tom, on the other hand, has much more at risk. With the stock at $30 per share, if it rises above $42 per share (covering the $1,200 that he received when he sold the straddle) or falls below $18 per share (which also covers the $1,200 received) or experiences any combination of up and down movement covering the 12 points he received, Tom has a loss.

Let's suppose the new product is a dud and the impact on the company causes the ZAP stock to fall to $10 per share. With the stock at $10, the put side of the straddle mandates that Pete receive $30 for the stock he will deliver on exercise. Pete enters the market and purchases the stock at $10 per share and delivers it, netting a $20 gain per share, or $2,000 per contract. After subtracting the $1,200 Pete paid for the straddle, he has a net profit of $800. Tom receives the stock and pays the $30 per share. If he sells the stock at that point, he will incur a $2,000-per-contract loss. Subtracting the $1,200 Tom received when he sold the straddle from the $2,000 loss on the put for a loss of $800 per straddle. Let's say the new product is a huge success, greater than anyone expected. ZAP stock rises to $70 per share when the options are about to expire. On exercise, Tom would have to deliver stock worth $70 and receive only $30, for a loss of $4,000 (40 points × 100 shares) minus the $1,200 received, or a net loss of $2,800 per straddle. Pete would receive the stock, paying $30 per contract, and he could sell the stock in the market at $70 per share, for a gain of 40 points, or $4,000 per contract, less the $1,200 he paid for the straddle, leaving a $2,800 profit.

Combination

A variation of a straddle is combination. While it also includes the buying and selling of equal numbers of puts and calls, the series are different. Generally, one of the two legs of the position is further out of the money than the other, thereby reducing the cost of the position. For example: PIPP is trading at $38. Randi Miles is looking to buy a six-month straddle using $40-strike-price options. The $40-strike-price call is 2 points out of the money and trading for 2 points, and the $40-strike-price put is 2 points in the money and trading for 6 points. The cost of the position is 8 points. Randi notices that there is a $37.50-strike-price put trading at a price of 3 points. Rather than paying for the 2 points intrinsic value that is already in the $40-strike-price put's price, she opts to buy the $37.50 strike, which is out of the money by half a point, lowering the cost for the position to 5 points.

By buying the $37.50-strike-price put option instead of the $40-strike-price put, Randi has paid a minimum for the position that she wanted. She has two out-of-the-money options and is not paying a cost premium because one of them is in the money.

· Deep-in-the-Money Options ·

The cost of money, or the rate of return, plays an important role in the time value of the premium. To prove this, add the premium of a call option that is around the at-the-money position to the strike price to determine the approximate breakeven. Then take a call option with the same expiration month but a much lower strike price (much deeper in the money), add the premium to the strike price, and see how much closer the break-even point on the deep-in-the-money option is to the current market value than the at-the-money one is. The same holds true with put options, but the premium is subtracted from the strike price to reach the gross breakeven.

Stock ZXAP, last sale 50.29

Type	Expiration	Strike Price	Premium	Breakeven
call	6 months	50	5.90	55.90
call	6 months	30	20.60	50.60
put	6 months	50	5.40	44.60
put	6 months	70	20.40	49.60

Some people use options as a surrogate for the underlying stock. The deeper into the money an option is, the more expensive will be the premium. However, the deeper in the money the option is, the greater the percentage of the premium will be intrinsic value, and the less of the premium will be made up of time value.

EXAMPLE

With the Electra Corporation's common stock trading at $40 per share, a five-month call option with a strike price of 30 can be bought for 11.25 points (10 points intrinsic value + 1.25 time value). The breakeven on this purchase would be $41.25, or a payment of 1.25 points over the current market price of the stock. For that same expiration month, a call option with a strike price of 42.50 is trading at 3.30 (0 points intrinsic value and 3.30 points time value, for a breakeven of 45.80). With the stock trading at $40 per share, that is 5.80 points over the market price of the stock.

Let's suppose an investor thinks that the common stock could be trading at $50 five months from today and is interested in acquiring 1,000 shares. The investor could:

1. Buy the 1,000 shares at $40 per share in a cash account and pay $40,000 plus commission and fees;

2. Buy the 1,000 shares at $40 per share in a margin account, paying $20,000 plus commission and fees and borrowing the remaining $20,000 through the broker-dealer (the $20,000 borrow would involve an interest expense);

3. Buy 10 calls with a strike price of 30 at $11.25 per option, for a cost of $11,250 plus commissions and fees;

4. Buy 10 calls with a strike price of 42.50 at $3.30 each, for a cost of $3,300 plus commissions and fees.

Let's assume the investor is correct in the assessment, and the stock is trading at $50 per share when the option expires.

In scenario 1, the investor sells the stock at $50 per share. The investor makes $10,000, less two commissions and fees, on the $40,000 investment. The investor has received any cash dividends the company paid. The subject stock pays $1 per share per year, or $.25 per quarter. So at most the investor has received $.50 per share during the period the stock was owned, or a total of $500 (provided the stock ownership covered two dividend periods, e.g., the stock was bought in January and sold five months later in June, and the stock paid its dividend in February and again three months later in May). The investor lost the use of $40,000 plus costs during the period of stock ownership.

Scenario 2 has the investor selling at $50 per share the stock that was purchased on margin at $40 per share. The investor makes the same $10,000, less two commissions, fees, and interest charges (on the $20,000 loan) on his or her $20,000 investment. The investor has received a maximum of $500 cash dividends, as explained in scenario 1. The investor lost the use of $20,000 plus costs during the period of stock ownership and paid interest on the $20,000 loan.

In scenario 3, with the stock at $50 per share, the investor sells the $30-strike-price options at expiration for their full intrinsic value (in-the-money sum) for 20 points. The investor receives $20,000 on an investment of $11,250, for a profit of $8,750 less commission and fees. The investor does not receive any dividends and has lost the use of $11,250 plus costs during the period of option ownership.

Finally, in scenario 4, with the stock at $50 per share, the investor sells the $42.50-strike-price options at expiration for their full intrinsic value (in-the-money sum) for 7.50 points, or $7,500. The investor receives $7,500 on an investment of $3,300, for a profit of $4,200 less commission and fees. The investor does not receive any dividends and has lost the use of $3,300 plus costs during the period of the option ownership.

Let's do the same calculations as if the stock had risen to 45 instead of 50.

In scenario 1, the investor sells at 45 the stock that was purchased at 40. The investor pays $40,000 to earn $5,000 plus dividends minus expenses.

In scenario 2, the investor pays $20,000 to earn the same $5,000 plus dividends less expenses, which include interest on the $20,000 loan.

In scenario 3, the investor pays $11,250 for the $30-strike-price call and sells the options at their full value of 15 points, or $15,000, for a profit of $3,750 less expenses.

In scenario 4, the $42.50-strike-price options cost the investor $3,300. With the underlying stock at 45, the options would be worth 2½ points, or $2,500, for a loss of $800 plus expenses.

Note 1: The commission charged by broker-dealers is often based on the dollar amount of the trade. In those cases, the commission charged on the option trades would be less than that charged on the stock trade.

Note 2: The commission charged on the stock trades would be the same, as they both involve transacting 1,000 shares of stock at the same prices. The fact that one is a cash trade and one is a margin trade would differentiate the trades at the time they settle and not at the time they are originally made.

Note 3: Remember, the options expire in five months, but the ownership of the stock continues until the investor wants to sell it. If the option investor wanted to roll out of the expiring options into a new option position, the investor would face a new round of prices, commissions, and fees. If the investor decided not to roll the position forward, that would end the investor's involvement with this security. If the stock tripled in the following months, and the investor had maintained the positions, the investor would benefit from the rising price, and the option investor would not.

On a per-dollar-invested-and-at-risk basis, the deep-in-the-money option offered the better all-around return in each of the two sets of scenarios. This would not always be the case. Time and price affect the outcome. The example was presented here to show a popular strategy.

· Synthetics ·

Options can be used in combinations or with the underlying security to form synthetic positions. It is very important to understand these concepts, as this is the way option traders look at their positions. By mixing and matching these positions, option traders can develop a risk position far from what the position appears to be.

EXAMPLE

Long call + short put = synthetic long stock position

Buying a call and writing a put on the same underlying security and with the same series description will have the same effect as owning the stock. If the underlying stock increases in value, so does the value of the long call option, and the short put option loses value until it is worthless. The higher the stock rises in value, the higher the call's price rises in value, increasing the profit in the same way as owning the stock. If the underlying stock falls in value, the short put increases in value and the long call loses value until it reaches zero. As the underlying stock continues to fall, the loss in this position increases. This position has the same characteristics as the underlying stock.

EXAMPLE

Long put + a short call = synthetic short stock position

As the stock's price falls, the long put's value increases and the short call's value falls to zero. The lower the stock's price goes, the higher the put's value becomes, increasing the profit. If the stock becomes worthless, the put will be worth its strike price at expiration. If the price of the underlying security increases, the long put loses value, the short call gains value, and a loss emerges. As the stock price continues to rise, the short call gains value, increasing the loss in this position as the long put goes to zero. The effect is the same as shorting stock.

EXAMPLE

Long stock + long put = synthetic long call position

As the stock rises in value, the long stock gains value and the long put loses value until it becomes worthless. When it falls, the reverse happens. The long put gains value, and the stock loses value. The gain that is occurring in the put position as the stock loses value is offset by the loss being incurred on the long stock position. One neutralizes the other. This is the same pattern that a long call option would follow. A long call will increase in value as the underlying security increases in value but will eventually fall to zero as the underlying security loses value.

EXAMPLE

Short stock + long call = synthetic long put position

As the stock's price falls, the short stock position becomes profitable, as the call option's price falls to zero. If the stock should rise in value, the loss on the short sale would be offset by the rise in the value of the long call option. A long put becomes profitable as the underlying security value decreases. If the underlying stock increases in value, the long put becomes worthless.

EXAMPLE

Long stock + short call = synthetic short put position

A position including a long stock and a short call would react to changes in the value of the underlying security in the same fashion as a short put position. If the underlying stock rises in value, the profit from the long stock position is offset by the loss in the short call option position. If the price of the underlying security falls, the call's value falls to zero and the loss grows on the long stock position, replicating a stand-alone short put.

EXAMPLE

Short stock + short put = synthetic short call position

A short call becomes unprofitable if the underlying stock rises. A short stock–short put combination has the same result. As the price of the underlying security falls, the profit from the short sale is offset by the increase in the value of the short put. As the price of the underlying security rises, the loss of the short stock position grows as the short put goes to zero. A short call has the same properties. As the underlying stock gains value, the short call will also gain value, making it more expensive to close out, thereby developing into a loss. As the underlying stock loses value, so does the short call, making it less expensive to cover, thereby developing into a profit.

EXAMPLE

Long stock + long put + short call = dividend

This position is known as a conversion. The stock's price is sheltered by the two options so that it will neither be profitable nor lose money. If the value of the stock increases, it will be called away. If it falls, the owner of the stock will put it out. Assuming that the cost of the long option is offset by the proceeds received from the sale of the short option, the owner is left with a dividend-collecting, riskless position.

EXAMPLE

Short stock + long call + short put = interest or financing

Known as a reverse conversion, the short stock position can neither earn a profit nor incur a loss. If the stock value decreases, some will put the stock against the position. If the price rises, the owner of the stock will call it in. Assuming the cost of the long call is offset by the proceeds from the short put, the combination results in a riskless method of gaining cash flow or financing.

To effect the short sale, the stock must be borrowed for delivery purposes. The proceeds from the short sale are given as collateral to the security lender. The security lender pays interest to the security borrower for the money.

Firms that are financing margin customers' debit balances are permitted to use clients' securities in several ways to obtain the funds needed. This is one way to accomplish the need. The securities of a customer who has a margin account and has borrowed funds to leverage a purchase may be used in this manner.

· INDEX OPTIONS ·

Index options are different from equity options in many respects. First, these are cash-settling options, as there isn't any physical product to deliver on exercise. Cash is the vehicle that is used. The writer of the option will pay the owner of the option the difference between the closing value of the index and the exercise price of the option. Regardless of whether it is a put or call, the holder (owner) is paid. To better understand this, focus on when an option is in the money and when it is not. It is the in-the-money sum $\times$ $100 that is exchanged.

Example: The symbol for the particular index being traded is INDXE. The option in the example expires in October and has a strike price of $300. As this is a cash settling option, there isn't any physical product to be delivered, so options are exercised against the closing, or reported, value of the index each evening.

Index call option:

Ty D' Nott exercises a long call on INDXE OCT 300 when the reported final value of the day is 310. Ty would receive $1,000 on the exercise, which is derived from the in-the-money amount of 10 points ($310 - 300 = 10$) $\times$ $100 (the index multiplier that is used instead of the 100 shares of stock used in equity options), for a total of $1,000.

Index put option:

Deb Utant exercises an index put option on INDXE when the reported final value of the index is 290. Deb would receive $1,000 as a result of the difference between the exercise price and the final value of the index that day (300 − 290 = 10 × the index multiplier of $100 = $1,000).

While index options can, like any other option, be traded in and out of positions during the day, with the profit or loss based on the premium difference, exercise of an index option is different. For example, with equity options, Dan D'Lyon is the owner of a put option with an exercise price of $50 when the stock is trading at $42 per share. Dan processes the exercise through his firm and at the same time buys 100 shares of the stock at $42 to be used in delivery. Dan knows at that moment that he has locked in an 8-point profit. In the case of an index option, Dan couldn't do that, because the value of the index against which the exercise was made is determined by the closing value of the index that night. For example, say Dan owns a put on an index with a strike price of 500. During the day, the index falls to 420. Since Dan cannot buy the physical index to make delivery, Dan does not have a way to lock in that price at that moment. If he does exercise the put, the profit (or loss) would be based on what the index closed at that day.

In addition, there is a special formula that is used to compute the index value of certain index options on their expiration date. In these cases, the opening price of the securities in the index that underlies the option is used. Other indexes use a different methodology to arrive at the value. Option Clearing Corporation has produced an excellent booklet that can be obtained from the financial institution that is transacting your option business for you. The booklet is entitled *Characteristics and Risks of Standardized Options*. It is a must read.

Another difference between equity and index options is the time allocated to effect delivery on exercise of an option. Unlike equity options, where there is time built in to the exercise cycle for the deliverer to acquire the security to be delivered, the exercise of an index option is settled first thing in the morning of the next business day after exercise. The assigned account is charged the difference between the option's strike price and the closing value of the index that evening, and the recipient's account is credited that amount the next morning.

A picture of activity flows follows. On receipt of the exercise notice, the writer's account is charged the amount owed. This amount is netted with all

Exercise of an Index Option

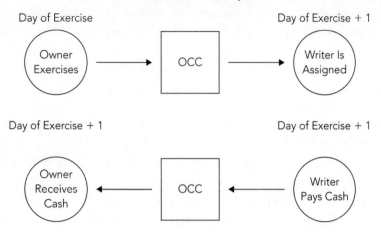

Day of Exercise

Owner Exercises → OCC → Writer Is Assigned — Day of Exercise + 1

Day of Exercise + 1

Owner Receives Cash ← OCC ← Writer Pays Cash — Day of Exercise + 1

other activity the broker-dealer has to settle with Option Clearing Corporation for that day's activity. The holder's firm also settles a net amount representing its daily activity with Option Clearing Corporation. That amount includes the sum owed to the holder whose account is credited the amount.

Due to the fact that there isn't a delivery of a physical product, which can be used to lock in a profit or loss, the maximum gain or loss found in a spread is lacking. For example, in the case of stock options, consider the following position:

$$\begin{array}{l} \text{ZAP is selling at 49} \\ \left.\begin{array}{l} \text{S 1 call ZAP Apr 50} = 5 \\ \text{L 1 call ZAP Apr 55} = 2 \end{array}\right\} = 3 \text{ Credit} \end{array}$$

This is a bear spread position, and as the lower-priced call has the most value (because it will go into the money first), the owner of this position wants ZAP to fall in value so that he or she can keep the credit that remains when the higher-strike-price sale is netted with the lower-strike-price purchase. If the client is wrong and the stock rises in value above $50 per share, but not above $55 per share, someone who calls the ZAP stock away from the client at $50 per share will force the client to obtain the stock, which has a higher value than the option's strike price, and make the delivery for $50 per share. If the stock has risen above $55, the client will satisfy the call against him at $50 per share by calling in the $55 stock from the option owner. The loss will be limited to the 5-point spread between the two options (plus expenses). In the case of a cash-settling option, the price against which the exercise is made is set at night. Therefore, assume the index is at 300 and the following position is acquired:

> Sell 1 call INDA April 300
> Buy 1 call INDA April 310

At a later date, the index closes at 350 and someone exercises the 300 call option against the client, the client owes 50 points, or $5,000 (50 points × $100 = $5,000). The next day, if the client exercises the owned (long) option and the index closes at 380, the client would receive 70 points (70 × $100 = $7,000) netting a $2,000 profit. Even though the position was set up as a bear spread, in reality it behaved as a bull spread.

Comparing the behavior of the two spreads once the ZAP stock rises above $55, it behooves the client to exercise the long option to limit or cap the loss. However, in the cash-settling option, exercise of the long option to cover the "loss" on the short option may very well turn out to be profitable.

As index options are used in many combinations with index futures, many index options expire on the same day as the index futures become deliverable, while others expire in the same cycle as the equity options. Perhaps one of the most infamous strategies, which caused market volatility, was the "triple witching hour." This will be discussed more in the chapter on futures.

· CURRENCY OPTIONS ·

Individuals who are involved with foreign exchange are most likely to get involved with currency options and currency futures. Currency options will be discussed here, currency futures in the chapter on futures.

Like other types of options, currency options are traded over the counter as well as on exchanges. The currency option exchange in the United States is the Philadelphia Stock Exchange (PHLX). At the writing of this book, the PHLX was being acquired by NASDAQ.

The put and call options that trade on the PHLX are:

Amount	Currency per Option
10,000	Australian dollars
10,000	British pounds

10,000	Canadian dollars
10,000	euros
1,000,000	Japanese yen
10,000	Swiss francs

Unlike equity options, these options are European style, which means that they can only be exercised at the end of their lives. The options expire on the Saturday after the third Friday of the month. The last day for trading options is the third Friday of the month. Settlement of transactions is in U.S. dollars.

Like all exchange-traded options, trades are settled through Option Clearing Corporation (OCC). Once the buying member and the selling member agree to the terms of the trade, OCC steps in between the two parties and becomes the contra party to the trade. Because OCC guarantees performance, the buying member and selling member do not have to worry about the other party to the trade not being able to perform the terms of the trade.

To differentiate between the two currencies under discussion, let the option used in settlement be U.S. dollars and the currency underlying the option be the commodity. For example, it costs $1.9959 to buy one British pound sterling (BPS). It would cost £0.5012 to buy one U.S. dollar. In British pound sterling options, if the dollar fell against the British pound, outstanding calls would rise in value and puts would lose value. The calls would increase in value because you would need more dollars to buy the pound.

This is no different from an equity option. When a stock (the commodity) rises in price, more dollars (the currency) are needed to buy it. It could be said that the dollar lost purchasing power against the stock; the same is true with currency and currency derivatives. When the dollar fell in value against the pound, the value of the pound (the commodity) rose against the dollar (the currency).

Settlement of exercises requires the delivery of the foreign currency vs. dollars. If the option owner does not want to get involved with the actual foreign currency, he or she has to trade out of the position. Currency option trades settle in U.S. dollars on the next business day. Option exercises settle in dollars vs. the underlying foreign currency two days after exercise. Therefore, there is an exchange of dollars for the foreign currency on the exercise of the option.

There is a large market for over-the-counter currency options. Again we are faced with the same put or call option. However, that is where the similarity ends. The listed currency options trade on a limited number of currencies (the major currencies), whereas the over-the-counter option can be on any currency. The listed option has a fixed quantity, strike price, and expiration date. The over-the-counter option can have any quantity, strike price, and expiration date.

Over-the-counter options involve a much higher risk than listed options, as Option Clearing Corporation does not guarantee performance. In listed options, OCC becomes the counterparty to the trade after the buyer and seller have agreed to the terms. As the terms of a listed option are regimented, secondary trading (going in and out of a position before expiration) in listed options far exceeds that of the over-the-counter market.

The product being addressed here should not be confused with future currency options. This one has as its underlying security the physical currency. Trading of the option being discussed in this section settles in dollars. Exercise of the option involves the delivery of the foreign currency. The future currency option has as its underlying security the future product itself. The future product is on the currency. Trading in and out also settles in dollars. Exercise of the future option involves delivery of the future that is on the currency not the currency itself. The exception is at the end of the future's life, when exercise of the option flows through the future to the currency.

· INTEREST-RATE OPTIONS ·

Interest-rate options that are listed are European form, as they are only exercisable at the end of their life. The options are based on specific U.S. Treasury instruments. As with the other option products, the buyer of a call is expecting underlying yields on the particular instrument to rise above the strike price, whereas buyers of puts are expecting yields to fall below the strike price. The reverse holds true also. The seller of an interest-rate call is expecting interest rates to fall below the exercise price, and the seller of an interest rate put is expecting interest rates to rise above the exercise price. One must remember that as interest rates rise, bond prices fall and yields rise. The reverse, that as interest rates fall, bond prices rise and yields fall, is also true. (This is discussed in more detail in the bond chapter of this book). Therefore, in trading these products, one must be careful and differentiate between the expected bond-price activity and the expected interest-rate activity.

Presently, interest-rate options trade on the Chicago Board Options Exchange. The underlying instruments are the newest-issued thirteen-week Treasury bill, the five-year note, the ten-year note, and the thirty-year bond. They are offered in the March cycle, with up to three nearest months and the next three quarterly months being offered at one time.

Their exercise price reflects the yield to maturity. A strike price of $67.50 equates to a yield of 6.750 percent. The settlement of an exercise is the currency difference between the strike price of the option and the spot yield on the last trading day, as determined by the Federal Reserve Bank of New York at 2:30 PM.

The thirteen-week Treasury bill option uses a multiplier of $100. The minimum tick, or price movement, is $.05 ($5.00) for options trading below $3.00 and $.10 ($10) for options trading at $3.00 and above. They are issued in 2½-point intervals.

The exercise of these options results in cash payments similar to those discussed with regard to index options. The settlement price is determined by the "spot price" at the end of the trading period. *Spot price* refers to the cash price or actual annualized discounted rate for the T-bills at expiration or the yield to maturity of the instruments at the end of the last trading day.

· DEBT OPTIONS ·

Debt options are similar in behavior to interest-rate options. However, the settlement of exercise calls for either cash or physical settlement. Known as priced-based options, they follow the typical in-the-money, out-of-the-money regimen of equity and index options. When the exercise of these options calls for physical delivery, a slate of acceptable instruments, called a basket, may be selected to ensure availability for delivery. This basket causes a "cheapest-to-deliver" (CTD) concept to be employed for pricing and other requirements.

Very important: There is a major difference between interest-rate options and debt options. Interest-rate options work off yields, and debt options work off price. As bond prices rise (good for long call and short put positions in debt-product options), yields fall (good for long put and short call positions in interest-rate options). As bond prices fall (good for long put and short call positions in debt options), yields rise (good for long call and short positions in interest-rate options). In other words, the effect of price movement is the opposite in debt options from what it is in interest-rate options.

· BINARY OPTIONS ·

As the name implies, binary options have one of two outcomes during their life. They are either exercised for a predetermined amount or expire. With a predetermined exercise amount, the writer has limited their exposure and is therefore willing to write the option for a lower premium.

Example: Mel Back writes an uncovered, out-of-the-money call on the shares of ZAPP APR 40s and collects a premium. ZAPP is currently trading at $37 per share. Included in the premium's computation is the price volatility, both past and present, of ZAPP. However, not all contingencies can be accounted for and Mel has opened himself to unlimited loss because there isn't any ceiling as to how high ZAPP can rise in value. If something spectacular happened to ZAPP after the close of business one day and it opened for trading the next day at $100 and continued to rise from there, even if Mel bought ZAPP at the opening of the market and paid $100 per share, he would be facing a 60-point loss, or $6,000, per contract. Instead, suppose Mel enters into a binary option contract that states if ZAPP rises in value and closes at $45 per share or above any given day, the option will be automatically exercised and Mel pays 10 points, or $1,000, per contract. To the buyer, Val Polichetta, he is willing to forgo the unrealistic "big profit" because if the stock closes at $45 or above, he is assured of the $1,000 payment. That amount he wouldn't otherwise realize until the stock reached $50 per share.

Binary options are also used with structure products such as credit default swaps. In this case, some event such as missing an interim payment would trigger the binary option and the option writer would have to satisfy the terms of the option contract.

· Capped Options ·

Usually issued in the European form, these options will be automatically exercised during their life if the capped price is reached or passed at the close of a trading day. Call options will have the cap price higher than the strike price, whereas put options will have the capped price below the strike price.

For example: The IND Index is valued currently at 380, Merl Lowe buys a six-month over-the-counter put with a 380 strike price. During the months, the index closes several times below 375. At expiration, the index closes at 382. As this was an over-the-counter market transaction, there wasn't any liquid market for Merl to trade out of or close the position. Merl was unable to take advantage of the in-the-money closing prices. However, had Merl bought the 380 strike price put option with a cap price of 375, the first time the index closed at 375 or below, Merl would have had an automatic early exercise.

· Conclusion ·

The main option products have been reviewed in this section. Many of the products also trade in major markets around the world. As options are a derivative, their structure and basic characteristics remain the same regardless of where they are traded.

Those that are listed on exchanges and trade with their preset structure usually also trade over the counter in their negotiated format.

They may be European or American form.

They are either puts or calls.

Exercise results in either physical or cash settlement (depending on the product).

Options expire.

They are either *in the money, at the money,* or *out of the money.*

Their premium is made up of intrinsic value and time value, either or both of which may be at zero.

9

Exchange-Traded Funds

· THE ETF PRODUCT ·

One of the newer products being offered is the exchange-traded fund (ETF). This instrument tracks an index much as a mutual fund does, but with one major difference. When we compare ETFs to mutual funds, we are referring to open-end mutual funds that are priced after the market closes, and all trades in that fund that day settle at that one price. ETFs trade during the day, and their price is revealed in a real-time environment in the same manner as common stocks. An ETF trade is treated the same way as shares of common stock, with the same trade-processing "trade date +3" settlement routine.

An ETF is backed by a basket of stocks, other securities, or other assets that make up an index, such as a commodity like gold bars. The index is of the passive type and not the aggressive type. The component parts of a passive index are adjusted periodically to stay true to the index's core, whereas the component parts of an aggressive index are traded regularly, making it impossible to maintain and control the value represented by the index. The component securities in the index can be broad based, covering an industry in general, or they may be more focused, for example, by sector, geographical area, type of asset, country, commodity, sector in a country, and so on.

Exchange-traded funds offer investors many of the strategies afforded them in their trading of stocks. Unlike shares of mutual funds that focus on indexes, investors can sell short ETFs and, due to the moment-by-moment pricing, they can go in and out of positions on the same day at the then-present market price, thereby incurring a profit or loss. They can also enter step orders, which are a series of limit orders to be filled if and when the index reaches specified price limits during the day. Another advantage to ETFs is that owners cannot be forced to accept taxable events because other shareholders are selling their ETF shares. When mutual fund shareholders sell their shares back to the fund, the mutual fund may be forced to liquidate positions so that it can raise the cash necessary to pay the fund share sellers. In other words, mutual fund shareholders incur capital gains tax liabilities through the normal workings of the mutual fund's advisers, whereas the ETF shareholder's capital gains tax liability is based solely on his or her own buying and selling of ETF shares.

· ETFs vs. Mutual Funds ·

Open-end mutual funds are priced at their net asset value. The net asset value is the value of the fund's portfolio, plus money awaiting investment, less expenses, divided by the shares outstanding. As an open-end fund stands ready to buy or sell its shares against the public, there isn't a secondary market. Should a large number of fund shares be sold back to the fund, the fund would have to sell off investments to raise the cash necessary to pay the fund share sellers. The sale of those investments creates a taxable event for all of the mutual fund shareholders. These taxable events may not be in the best interest of the remaining mutual share owners. The price of an ETF is also determined by the net asset value of its contents. The buying and selling of the ETF's shares is accomplished in the marketplace between public participants. The transaction does not have any effect on the other ETF holders. If there is a large enough price difference between the market price of an ETF and the true value of the ETF, arbitrageurs will take positions that will cause the market price to realign with the portfolio value. Remember, an ETF, given enough size, can be brought back to its originator and dissolved into its component parts, and the parts then can be owned or sold. In the case of dividends and other cash distributions, both the mutual fund shareholders and the ETF shareholders pay income taxes. The exception is some municipal bond funds.

However, as the ETFs trade on an exchange or through electronic commerce networks (ECNs), buying and selling shares requires the use of a broker, which in turn would cause the investor to incur a brokerage fee in the form of a commission. The commission fee would be charged when the investor entered into the position and again when the position was closed out. In the case of mutual funds, the fee, known as a load or sales charge, is a one-time charge, if the fund charges at all. Those mutual funds that do not charge a fee are known as no-load funds, but generally speaking, no-load funds charge higher operational fees. The difference between the total cost of owning a mutual fund and the total cost of owning an ETF differs from fund to fund and from broker-dealer to broker-dealer and is affected by the amount involved in the transaction.

· ETF Creation Units ·

The first ETF was Standard & Poor's depositary receipts (SPDRs), known as spiders or spyders. Its trading symbol is SPDR. The original SPDR was on the S&P 500 Index. ETFs are created when a large bank or institution acquires blocks of securities that replicate the composition of a particular index and, along with the deposit of cash needed to satisfy pending dividend and other payment requirements, form "creation units." The units are placed with a trustee, which allows for the issuance of ETF shares. The reverse is also workable. An investor who amasses enough ETF shares can surrender them to the trustee and receive the component securities and appropriate cash or other underlying collateral.

While both the mutual fund and the ETF that are based on indexes offer the investor diversification through the index portfolio, ETFs are required to report their holdings each evening. The same is not true with mutual funds, which report their holdings only periodically.

An ETF based on the Standard & Poor's 500 Index has its securities maintained in a trust managed by State Street Global Advisors (SSgA).

The trust is a unit investment trust (UIT). The ETF is priced at one-tenth of the index value. The index pays cash dividends quarterly on the securities held in the trust, less any expenses. SPDR has grown into a family of ETFs that includes international and domestic, long to short term, stock and debt, income to growth, and much more.

A similar product is iShares. They are offered by Barclays Global Investors. They also trade in an exchange environment or through ECNs. They offer a wide range of ETFs also, encompassing both the domestic and international markets, with a wide range of products.

Vanguard Index Participation Equity Receipts (VIPERs) are similar to the above and are issued by Vanguard.

Power shares ETFs are offered by Invesco, which has many different ETFs available. Most are custom made. Northern Trust offers NETs, which are also ETFs and are on the major international indexes such as NETs, FTSE, 100 Index (United Kingdom), the NETs Dax Ind Fund (Germany). As is evident, there are many issuers of ETFs. The investor should read the attributes et cetera of each ETF before investing.

10

Futures

First and foremost, futures and forwards affect our daily lives more than any other product that we trade, with the possible exception of foreign exchange and interest rates. Second, for a future or forward product to exist there must be risk, either real or perceived. If there isn't any risk, there isn't a need to have a future or forward product, and trading in these products would be discontinued because of a lack of need.

A future or forward determines the price at which a delivery will occur at a later date. Futures trade on exchanges; forwards trade over the counter. The contract specifications of a future product are set by the exchange on which it trades. This standardization of terms allows for liquidity, and through the liquidity a ready market to trade in and out of positions. All of the terms of a forward contract are negotiated, and due to this customization of terms, therefore the ability to trade in and out of a position is limited to nil. The exception to this is foreign exchange (currency trading), as the liquidity is based on currency itself.

· EXAMPLE OF A FUTURE PRODUCT ·

Let's assume a commodity called widgets. A widget sells for $1, and there are 1,000 widgets to a bushel (bu). It takes six months to bring a widget to market. One of the futures exchanges lists a widget contract containing 100 bushels. Therefore, the value of the widget contract currently is $100,000 ($1 × 1,000 × 100). However, widgets have been known to fluctuate between $.90 and $1.10 over short periods of time. The price movement is based on widget production, as well as the pricing of competitive or substitutable products.

At the current time, the six-month future contract is trading at $1.03. A widget producer and a widget processor must determine a course of action that will directly affect their individual businesses' profitability. If the producer sells the contracts, the producer is assured of the $1.03 price, regardless of where widgets are trading at the time of delivery. If the processor buys the contract at $1.03, that is the price the processor will pay, regardless of what price widgets are trading at when delivery occurs. The mechanics behind this will be explained later in this section. Also, keep in mind that there is a marketplace for widget contracts that permit participants to enter into and close out positions during the period that particular contract is being traded.

· STRUCTURE OF A FUTURE PRODUCT ·

A future contract is composed of the following parts, which are set by the exchange on which it trades:

1. Underlying product
2. Quantity required
3. Quality level

4. Delivery month
5. Predetermined delivery location
6. Predetermined payment terms and conditions

· STRUCTURE OF A FORWARD PRODUCT ·

A forward contract is composed of the following parts:

1. Underlying product
2. Negotiated quantity
3. Negotiated quality
4. Agreed-to delivery dates
5. Agreed-to location for delivery
6. Agreed-to payment vehicle
7. Agreed-to payment location

· BASE CASE ·

Let's take two interests: a farmer and a miller.

The farmer faces a large risk every spring. The farmer is going to plant a crop of some kind of grain, tend to it, and take it to harvest many months later. The farmer is at market risk during the entire growing season. If the cost of growing the crop exceeds the price received at harvest time, the farmer will incur a loss. If the farmer is accurate in his expense and sale price assumptions, there will be a profit at the end of the cycle.

The miller faces a similar problem. The miller must buy the harvested product at a price that will permit a profit to be obtained when the finished product is sold in the market. The public will tolerate a certain price level before it seeks an alternative product or cuts down its consumption of that product. Take wheat that is used in making bread, for example: As the price of wheat increases, the cost of bread made of wheat increases also. At some point, the public will start to switch to alternatives for starch, such as rice bread or potato bread.

To hedge the market risk, both the farmer and the miller would enter into the future market. The farmer, looking over the acreage to be planted, checks the future prices of the commodities that he may plant. Special attention is paid to the future contract that becomes deliverable when the products about to be planted will be harvested. The farmer has an idea of the expenses involved in tending the crop and, with a cost estimate in mind, determines which product has the best chance of netting the largest profit. Once the product is decided upon, the next step is even more difficult. Future contracts specify the amount per contract, along with other criteria that the delivery must satisfy. And unlike option products, which expire if not exercised, delivery must be made and accepted on open contracts at the specified delivery time. The farmer must determine what percentage of the expected crop is to be hedged by the future contracts. For example:

Contract	Size
wheat	5,000 bu
oats	5,000 bu
corn	5,000 bu
soybeans	5,000 bu

The agricultural contract that is listed for trading is for a generic product. When actual delivery is made, the future price is adjusted to accommodate the quality or type of the product being delivered. Quality or type specifications for each generic product are as follows:

- Wheat delivery grades: No. 2 Soft Red Winter, No. 2 Hard Red Winter, No. 2 Dark Northern Spring, and No. 2 Northern Spring at par; No. 1 Soft Red Winter, No. 1 Hard Red Winter, No. 1 Dark Northern Spring, and No. 1 Northern Spring at 3 cents per bushel over contract price.
- Oats delivery grades: No. 2 Heavy and No. 1 at par; No. 1 Extra Heavy at 7 cents per bushel over contract price; No. 2 Extra Heavy at 4 cents per bushel over contract price; No. 1 Heavy at 3 cents per bushel over contract price; No. 2 (thirty-six-pound total minimum test weight) at 3 cents per bushel under contract price; No. 2 (thirty-four-pound total minimum test weight) at 6 cents per bushel under contract price.

- Corn delivery grades: No. 2 Yellow at par; No. 1 Yellow at 1½ cents per bushel over contract price; No. 3 Yellow at 1½ cents per bushel under contract price.
- Soybeans delivery grades: No. 2 Yellow at par; No. 1 Yellow at 6 cents per bushel over contract price; No. 3 Yellow at 6 cents per bushel under contract price.

(The above can be viewed on the Chicago Board of Trade Web page, www.cbot.com.)

Focusing on the soybean contract, say the standard, or generic, product being traded is No. 2 Yellow. A delivery of that grade of soybean will receive the price at which the future was contracted. A delivery of No. 1 Yellow, which has 13 percent or less moisture, is supposed to get $.06 more per bushel, or $300 more per contract (5,000 bushels × $.06 = $300). Delivery of No. 3 Yellow, which contains more moisture, will get $.06 less, or $300 less per contract, provided that all specifications meet or exceed No. 2 Yellow (except for foreign materials, which cannot exceed 3 percent). The moisture in No. 2 and No. 3 Yellow cannot exceed 14 percent. This is an example of the way many commodity future products trade. There is the generic product traded, and at delivery, adjustments are made in its price due to quality of the physical product delivered.

The farmer must decide how large a crop is expected to be grown and what percentage of it is to be hedged with future contracts. If there is a poor growing season and the farmer's harvest fails to fill the contracts sold, the farmer must go into the market and purchase the shortfall for delivery or try to buy back the unfilled contracts. As these contracts trade on an exchange and are standardized, the farmer can purchase the contracts from any seller. Either way, the farmer will be facing a loss. If there is an excellent growing season, then the farmer may have excess crops that could be sold in the open market. However, if the supply of the commodity outstrips the demand, the price in the open market will fall and possibly negate the supposed profit on that part of the crop that was not hedged.

Using the widgets from the previous example:

1. If the expected crop of widgets is what was actually grown, and the farmer has hedged 80 percent of the crop with the contracted price of $1.03, and, with all costs included, the expense to bring

the widgets to market is $.98, the farmer has locked in a $.05-per-widget profit. If widgets are trading at $1.05 at the time of delivery, the farmer has missed the opportunity to earn $.02 per widget on 80 percent of the widgets sold under contract but can earn the additional profit on the remaining 20 percent of the crop not sold under contract.

2. If instead of the widgets trading at $1.05 per widget, they are trading at $.95 at the time of delivery, the farmer will still receive the $1.03 required under contract on 80 percent of the widget crop but will lose $.03 per widget on the remaining 20 percent of the crop not sold under contract.

3. If, due to a very poor growing season, the farm is only able to produce 70 percent of the expected crop, the farmer will receive $1.03 for the crop grown at the cost of $.98. For the 10 percent shortfall, the farmer will have to acquire widgets at whatever price they are trading at in the open market and deliver them. Due to the shortage, the price of the widgets would most likely be above $1.03, which would mean the farmer would incur a loss on the 10 percent that was not filled by the farmer's own crop.

The miller faces a similar situation. The miller's representative must acquire wheat at the best price possible. To lock in a price that could be used in determining the miller's profit, the representative would buy future contracts. This removes market risk on the wheat covered by those contracts. At the time of delivery, if wheat is trading at a price higher than the contracted price, the miller's representative made a good decision; if the price is lower than the contracted price, the miller missed an opportunity to earn a larger profit. BUT remember, neither the farmer nor the miller is in the market to take that kind of trading risk. That is what traders do. The farmer and miller are in the market to maintain a business franchise.

· FUTURE PRODUCTS ·

As stated earlier, the future and forward market affects our personal lives more directly and faster than any other product traded. The future products traded have as their underlying:

1. Grains: corn, oats, rice, soybeans and wheat
2. Livestock: cattle, hogs, broilers (chickens), and frozen pork bellies
3. Dairy: butter, cheese, milk, and whey
4. Sugar, coffee, orange juice, and cocoa
5. Greasy wool, fine wool, and cotton
6. Fuels: ethanol, brent crude, crude oil, heating oil, reformulated gasoline blendstock for oxygen blending (RBOB), natural gas, Phelix (Physical Electricity Index, which is German/Austrian), electricity, and coal
7. Foreign exchange: Australian dollars, Canadian dollars, euros, Japanese yen, Swiss francs, U.S. dollars, and cross-currency versions
8. Forest products: random-length lumber and wood pulp
9. Metals: gold, silver, copper, aluminum, aluminum alloy, nickel, tin, zinc, lead, steel, uranium, platinum, and palladium
10. Indexes: Goldman Sachs Commodity Index, Goldman Sachs Commodity Index Excess Return, Standard & Poor's 500 Index, NASDAQ 100, Russell 2000, Nikkei 225, and variations of these
11. Interest rate: three-month euro, one-month LIBOR, ten-year SWAP rate, five-year SWAP rate, thirteen-week Treasury bill, and others (Note: SWAP rate is the difference between a forward exchange rate and a currency's spot rate.)
12. Weather: various heating or cooling degree days
13. Special indexes called *TRAKRs* (Total Return Asset Contracts)
14. Real estate contracts, based on the S&P/GPA Commercial Real Estate Index or the S&P/Case-Shiller Metro Area Home Price Index
15. Plastics: polypropylene and polyethylene

The underlying for forward products are:

1. Foreign exchange
2. Interest rates
3. Any commodity of different quantity, quality, and/or delivery specifications from the standardized future product (which can be negotiated between two or more participants)

Many of these products trade in the international markets, while others (especially electrical energy futures) trade only in local markets.

Not all contracts are truly global. The origin, type, or characteristics of a commodity may change from area to area, the location at which delivery is supposed to be made may affect the pricing due to transport complications, and these in turn may render the underlying commodity in one contract not good delivery for the "same" contract traded on another exchange.

Upon delivery, most products must be certified or inspected by some authority before they can be accepted as what was contracted and paid for.

Soybean Products

Some products have a direct relationship to other products. For example, the futures market trades soybeans, soybean meal, and soybean oil. Sixty tons of soybeans produce forty-seven tons of soybean meal and eleven tons of soybean oil. The remaining two tons are lost in the crushing.

Besides being used to make the other two products, soybeans are also used in Asia and other parts of the world as food in their own right. In Japan they are known as *edamame*, and they are growing in popularity in the United States. A fermented form of them is the key ingredient in soy sauce.

Soybean meal, aka soybean flour or soy flour, is used in the preparation of soy cakes, tofu, and rice balls, as well as for animal feed and fertilizer.

Soybean oil is used in cooking oil, margarine, shortening, soaps, and bath oils. Soy oil supplements are believed to cut the risk of heart-related death. Soybean oil competes in the marketplace with other products, such as corn oil, butter, and lard. Other products that compete with soybean oil are sunflower, coconut, palm, and rapeseed oils. And to add to the mix, different oils are preferred in different countries.

Soybean oil, or an extract thereof, could be the fuel of the future. It is one of the possible fuels that replenish themselves, along with corn and other grains. Henry Ford, founder of Ford Motor Company, had a workable automobile (circa 1940) whose body was made out of soybean plastic. He actually had a suit of clothes made from the product, which attests to its versatility.

So here we have a product that is directly interrelated with two other products, and each of the three has its own market. A sudden demand in one would have an effect on the other two. Suppose it was discovered that taking a tablespoon of soybean oil three times a day would prevent and/or cure a fatal disease plaguing the world. What would happen to the price of soybean oil? And what effect would it have, if any, on the other two products: soybeans and soybean meal? It is most likely that the price of soybean oil would rise. And as the needed supply would put pressure on the growth of soybeans, their price would increase also. As the growth of soybeans increased to meet the demand, the supply of soybean meal would increase also. Unless there was an increase in the demand for meal, its price would fall. In theory, there are three actions that could be taken. One would be buy the soybean oil future contracts. The second would be to buy the soybean future contracts and wait for the price of the underlying product to rise. The third would be to sell the soybean meal future contracts and wait for the price of the underlying product to fall.

If the strategies play out, the soybean and soybean oil contracts would be worth much more at delivery than the price the contracts originally called for and could thus be sold at a profit. The soybean meal, at delivery, should be at a lower price than contracts require, and the contracts could be bought in at the lower price, locking in the profit.

As the price relationship between the three gets out of line, participants could trade options on a synthetic product called soybean crush. The discrepancy between the price of soybeans and the price of soybean meal and soybean oil widens and narrows in the course of the individual products' trading. If one thinks the spread will widen, one would buy crush call or sell crush puts. If one thinks the spread will narrow, one would buy crush puts or sell crush calls.

Like all the examples in this book, these are for explanatory purposes only and are not recommendations. As with all strategies, timing and market conditions are of critical importance.

Multiclass Coffee Product

All coffee is not the same. Though there are many types of coffee, the two main types are arabica and robusta. Arabica is the more popular of the two and dominates the market. A future contract for coffee trades on the Intercontinental Exchange (ICE). This contract is for arabica coffee grown in several Central and South American countries, as well as Asia and Africa.

The delivery months are March, May, July, September, and December. Delivery points are exchange-licensed warehouses in the Port of New York District (at par), the Port of New Orleans, the Port of Houston, the Port of Bremen/Hamburg, the Port of Antwerp, the Port of Miami, and the Port of Barcelona* (at a discount of 1.25 cents per pound). (Source: ICE Futures Web page, www.nybot.com)

The coffee being delivered must be certified by the grade of the bean and by cup tasting for flavor. The exchange sets the base by which all coffees are judged. Those that are superior will settle at a premium; those that do not stack up against the base will trade at a discount. The certificates are sent by the exchange from those delivering to those receiving. This opens another trading opportunity, as receivers adjust the grade that they are receiving against the grade they need. The proprietor of an upscale restaurant would want a higher-grade coffee than the local morning coffee shop and therefore would trade up for a higher grade. The period of trading generally lasts from the seventh business day prior to the first trading day of the delivery month to the seventh business day before the last trading day of the delivery month.

· WORKINGS OF A FUTURE PRODUCT ·

Let's refer back to our widget product. Say the exchange that lists the widget for trading has determined that at approximately $1 per widget, a contract of 100,000 widgets will be the right size to stimulate interest and trading in the product. Looking back over the price of widgets for the last three or four years, the economists at the exchange have discovered that the price of widgets has fluctuated by 3 cents or less per day 95 percent of the time. Another way of saying this is that the value at risk (VaR) is that the movement of widgets' price by 3 cents or less will occur in the ninety-fifth percentile of the observed sample data time period. This gives them the comfort level to recommend that the standard margin be $5,000 per contract and the maintenance margin be set at $2,000 per contract, thereby accommodating the 3-cent boundary while leaving a cushion incase the widget's price exceeds that amount on a rare occasion. Each evening, the

---

* Effective with the March 2008 contract.

exchange sets a closing price on every contract that is offered for trading. Those contracts that do not trade on a given day have their closing price determined (extrapolated) from the next-nearest future on that product that did trade. Against these closing prices all positions are adjusted. This is known as mark to the market.

(Notice the amount of leverage being offered. At $5,000 per contract, the widget-future practitioner is controlling $100,000 worth of widgets. This degree of leverage is common in future trading.)

The firms that do business with the public in future contracts must be Futures Commission Merchants registered with the Commodity Futures Trading Commission (CFTC), a federal regulator.

On day one of trading the new widget contract, a client of Stone Forrest and River (SFR), Lauren Auder, buys 10 six-month contracts at $1 and deposits the required $50,000 (10 contracts at $5,000 per contract equals $50,000).

At the same time, a client of Giant Reckor and Crane (GRC), Justin Tyme, sells 10 contracts of the same future contract and deposits the required $50,000.

SFR	GRC
Lauren Auder Account	*Justin Tyme Account*
long 10 widget 6mo. @ $1.00	short 10 widget 6mo. @ $1.00
standard margin $50,000	standard margin $50,000

Lauren's contract states that she is going to buy 10 contracts of widgets, for a total cost of $1,000,000. She has deposited $50,000, leaving a balance of $950,000, which is to be paid when the widgets are received

Justin's contract states that he must deliver 1,000,000 widgets, and he will be paid $1,000,000 plus his deposit of $50,000, for a total of $1,050,000.

On day two, widgets are marked at $1.01.

As Lauren has a profitable position, her account will be credited the one point, or $10,000, whereas Justin has a loss of $10,000, and his account will be charged. These entries to their respective accounts are called a variation margin. This money adjustment is necessary, as it will enable the firms to honor Lauren's and Justin's contracts at $1,000,000.

If delivery was to occur at today's price, SFR would pay the $1,010,000 required by the market using Lauren's $1,000,000 (the $50,000 that she deposited, plus the $950,000 that she still owes and will pay upon receipt of the widgets), plus the $10,000 variation margin, for a total of $1,010,000.

Justin, on the other hand, has a paper loss of $10,000. His account will be charged $10,000, leaving only a $40,000 credit balance. If delivery of the widgets was to occur, Justin would receive the current market price of $1.01, or a total of $1,010,000. The $40,000 that remains in his account would be returned to him and, when added to the $1,010,000 received for the widgets, would total $1,050,000, which is what his contract calls for.

SFR Lauren Auder Account	GRC Justin Time Account
long 10 widget 6mo. @ $1.01	short 10 widget 6mo. @ $1.01
standard margin $50,000	standard margin $50,000
variation margin +10,000	variation margin −10,000
$60,000	$40,000

On day three, widgets are at .99, having fallen 2 points in value from the previous day.

Justin now has a profitable position; his account will be credited the 2 points, or $20,000, to account for the 2-point move from the previous day's closing. Lauren now has a loss of a point against her contract, and her account must be adjusted with a charge of $20,000 to account for the 2-point move. These entries to their respective positions will be reflected in their variation margins. The variation margin will enable the firm to honor Lauren's contracts at $1,000,000, and, if delivery was to occur at today's price, pay the $990,000 required by the market by taking Lauren's $990,000 ($40,000 remaining in her account from her deposit of $50,000 plus the $950,000 that is still owed and will be paid on receipt of the widgets, for a total of $990,000).

Justin, on the other hand, has a paper profit of $10,000. His account will be credited $20,000, leaving a $60,000 credit balance. If delivery of the widgets was to occur, Justin would receive the $.99 price, or $990,000. When this is added to the $60,000 that remains in his account, Justin would receive a total of $1,050,000 that his contract calls for.

SFR	GRC
Lauren Auder Account	*Justin Tyme Account*

long 10 widget 6mo. @ $.99	short 10 widget 6mo. @ $.99
standard margin $50,000	standard margin $50,000
variation margin −10,000	variation margin +10,000
$40,000	$60,000

On day four, widgets continue to fall in price to .97.

Lauren's account is charged $20,000, and Justin's account is credited $20,000.

SFR	GRC
Lauren Auder Account	*Justin Tyme Account*

long 10 widget 6mo. @ $.97	short 10 widget 6mo. @ $.97
standard margin $50,000	standard margin $50,000
variation margin −30,000	variation margin +30,000
$20,000	$80,000

When listing the future on widgets originally, the exchange decided to set the standard margin at $5,000 per contract and the maintenance margin at $2,000 per contract. As Lauren's account is now at $20,000 per contract ($2,000 × 10 contracts), Lauren will get a margin call for $30,000 that will bring her account back up to standard margin. With the deposit of the $30,000, Lauren's and Justin's accounts would be as follows:

SFR	GRC
Lauren Auder Account	*Justin Tyme Account*

long 10 widget 6mo. @ $.97	short 10 widget 6mo. @ $.97
standard margin $80,000	standard margin $50,000
variation margin −30,000	variation margin +30,000
$50,000	$80,000

If delivery was to occur at $.97, the following steps would occur: Lauren has now given SFR a total of $80,000 ($50,000 + $30,000). Under the terms of her contract, she still owes $920,000. Upon delivery of the widgets, SFR would collect the $920,000 from Lauren, take the $50,000 remaining in her account, and acquire the widgets for $970,000 ($920,000 + $50,000 = $970,000). The contract still cost Lauren $1,000,000 ($80,000 + $920,000 = $1,000,000). Justin would deliver the widgets and get paid $970,000. When this was added to the $80,000 remaining in his account, the total would be $1,050,000, the exact sum Justin is owed.

Let's assume that over the next few weeks, widgets work their way up in price to $1.03. The change in widget pricing over that time would reflect the 6-point change between $.97 and $1.03. Lauren's account will be credited a net adjustment of $60,000, and Justin's account will be charged that sum.

| *SFR* | | *GRC* | |
Lauren Auder Account		*Justin Tyme Account*	
long 10 widget 6mo. @ $.1.03		short 10 widget 6mo. @ $1.03	
standard margin	$80,000	standard margin	$50,000
variation margin	+30,000	variation margin	−30,000
	$110,000		$20,000

Now it is Justin's account that is on call for money. Justin would have to bring the account back up to standard margin. If Justin meets the call of $30,000, the two accounts will look like this:

| *SFR* | | *GRC* | |
Lauren Auder Account		*Justin Tyme Account*	
long 10 widget 6mo. @ $1.03		short 10 widget 6mo. @ $1.03	
standard margin	$80,000	standard margin	$80,000
variation margin	+30,000	variation margin	−30,000
	$110,000		$50,000

We will discuss Lauren's account shortly. Justin's contract states that he will receive $1,000,000 for his 10 widget contracts and his money back. His "money" was $50,000, but after the deposit of $30,000, that figure rose to $80,000. Therefore, Justin is to receive a total of $1,080,000. Justin delivers the widgets and receives a payment of $1,030,000. GRC returns the $50,000 remaining in Justin's account, for a total payment to Justin of $1,080,000.

Lauren can take several actions. She can do nothing and deposit the $890,000 due on delivery of the widgets ($890,000 + $110,000 = $1,000,000), plus the $30,000 in variation margin, for a total of $1,030,000. She can withdraw $30,000, which would put standard margin back to its original position of $50,000 ($80,000 − $30,000 = $50,000) and $30,000 in variation margin, to accept the delivery of the widgets upon her deposit of $950,000, for a total $1,030,000. Or she can withdraw a total of $60,000 (standard margin of $80,000 − $50,000 = $30,000, plus variation margin of $30,000 − $30,000 = 0), which would change Lauren's contract price from $1 to $1.03 per widget. With only $50,000 in her account, representing the standard margin requirement, Lauren would have to deposit $980,000 ($980,000 + $50,000 = $1,030,000) to satisfy her commitment. The difference between the actions Lauren can take is the variation margin. The last one would necessitate Lauren depositing $980,000, as opposed to the original contract requirement of $950,000, which, when added to the $50,000 remaining in her account, would total $1,030,000.

It's important to understand that the variation margin is needed by the firm to honor the contract. If the client removes the variation margin, it changes the terms of the agreement. For example say two people are going to be partners on an automobile that costs $30,000. They agree to pay $15,000 each. As they leave the dealership, partner 1 asks partner 2 to lend him $5,000 and says they will settle up when the automobile is delivered by the dealership. When partner 1 borrows the $5,000, the terms of the original agreement change. Partner 1 now owes $20,000, and partner 2 owes $10,000 when the automobile is delivered. Likewise, when Lauren removes the $30,000 from variation margin, the contract changes from $1 per widget to $1.03. Laruen must deposit $980,000 (which includes the $30,000 that she removed), rather than the $950,000 originally required, because she removed the firm's ability to honor the original contract.

This is where users of future products get into trouble. Variation margin is what permits the firm to honor the contract. When the variation margin is removed or used for another purpose, the terms of the original contract change.

EXAMPLE

A client buys one widget contract at $1.00 and deposits the required $5,000.

Widgets increase in price to $1.05. The client then has a paper profit of $1,000 per point, or $5,000. The client also has $5,000 in variation margin.

The client takes the variation margin and buys a second contract at $1.05. As the variation margin that was generated from the $1.00 contract has been used and is no longer available to support the $1.00 contract, the client has two contracts at $1.05 and is now earning a paper profit of $2,000 per point.

Widgets increase in price to $1.10. As there are two contracts in the account at $1.05, the market on the positions gives $10,000 (2 × $5,000) to the variation margin.

The client takes the $10,000 variation margin and buys two more contracts at $1.10. The client now has 4 contracts at $1.10 and will have a paper profit of $4,000 per point if widgets continue to rise.

Widgets rise to $1.15. At that price, the variation margin reflects a balance of $20,000 (4 × $5,000).

The client takes the variation margin and buys 4 more contracts, giving him a position of 8 contracts at $1.15 and the opportunity to earn $8,000 per point.

Widgets rise to $1.20. The client's variation margin is now $40,000 (8 × $5,000), and of course the client uses it to purchase 8 more contracts, for a total of 16 contracts at $1.20. The client will earn $16,000 per point if widgets continue to rise. At $16,000 a point, the client will have a paper profit of $80,000 (16 × $5,000) when widgets reach $1.25. But they don't. Instead they fall in value 3 points in one day. The client receives a maintenance call for $3,000 per contract on 16 contracts, or $48,000. The client owes $48,000 on a $5,000 initial investment. If widgets continue to fall the next day, the client will receive yet another call. The client liquidates the position and honors the $48,000 call.

Had he stayed with his initial single contract at $1 per widget, he would have had a 17-point profit ($17,000) when he sold the widget contract after the 3-point drop.

Caution: At the beginning of this section, it was noted that the exchange on which a future trades does an analysis of risk before setting margin requirements. It would be impractical and expensive to set the margin rates to cover all contingencies. A rate is set that covers a high percentage of occurrences, such as those events that would appear within a graph capturing 95 percent of the occurrences. What happens when an event occurs that is outside the accepted sample? In the case of widgets, what would happen if the price of widgets rose or fell more than 3 cents in a given day? The future exchange on which they trade would stop trading the product, giving the firms time to call in additional collateral from those clients on the wrong side of the market. The next day, the trading range would be widened, and if the change of price exceeded this range, trading would cease and the call for additional collateral would again go out. By this time, the firms should have called for (and, they hope, received) sufficient collateral for the exchange to begin trading. In the meantime, those who were on the wrong side of the market would be locked in and see their loss growing every day. Those on the right side of the market would be seeing their profit grow every day.

· Who Are the Exchange Market Participants? ·

While the market has many participants with different agendas, it is these different agendas that develop the liquidity these markets are known for. The ability of a participant to get in and out of positions makes these markets attractive to a diverse group of participants from all over the world and invites the employment of all types of strategies. While not 100 percent accurate, let's divide the participants into three primary groups:

1. hedgers
2. speculators
3. traders

Hedgers

There are several types of hedgers. The "futures against physical" hedger is one of the more common. This hedger's strategy is used by both producers (those that bring the product to market) and consumers (those that take the product from the market). Farmers who grow wheat, for example, may sell all or part of their expected crop through the use of futures, even before the wheat's seed has been placed in the ground. By doing so, the farmer has locked in the price that will be received when the wheat is brought to market. If the price of wheat is higher when delivery occurs, the higher price received for the wheat is offset by the loss incurred on the future position. If it's lower, the weak price received for the wheat is offset by the profit on the future position. As the wheat future contract trades in a liquid market, if the farmer sees that the future position is hindering a profit potential, the future position could be closed out, leaving the farmer with a nonhedged position. Farmers are not usually market risk takers, so the hedge would only be removed if the difference between the future contract price and the projected price of the physical wheat was dramatic enough to warrant taking the risk.

On the other side of the market is the miller, who must buy wheat at a price at which he can earn a profit and stay competitive with other grains that can be substituted for wheat. The miller will buy the wheat future as a hedge against what the price is going to be at the time of delivery. If the deliverable price of the wheat is below the future's price, the miller missed the opportunity to earn a larger profit, as long as all other factors stayed the same. The lower price being paid for the wheat is offset by the loss on the future contract position. If the price is higher than the future's price, the miller can stay competitive due to the profit on the long future position. As with the farmer, if the physical price begins to stray away from the future's contract price to where the difference is detrimental to the miller, the miller will close the position out.

Let's take a look at the relationship of the price of wheat to an established future contract position.

Wheat

Farmer	Price per Bushel	Miller
−$.100	$1.050	+$.100
−075	1.025	+.075
−.050	1.000	+.050

(continued)

	Farmer	Price per Bushel	Miller
	−.025	.975	+.025
Future's contract price		.950	
	+.025	.925	−.025
	+.050	.900	−.050
	+.075	.875	−.075
	+.100	.850	−.100

With the deliverable wheat at $1.050, for every bushel that is delivered, $1.05 will be paid. As the future contract is for five thousand bushels, that equates to $5,250. However, the farmer's account will have been charged $500 against the future's price of $.950 ($.10 per bu, × 5,000 bu = $500), netting the farmer $4,750. The contract called for $4,750 (5,000 bu × $.950). The miller, who had to pay $1.050 per bushel, or $5,250, would have his futures account credited $500, the profit on the future contract, for a net cost of $4,750, which is what the terms of the contract require. Had wheat fallen in price to $.850, the charge and the credit of $.10 per bushel would have been on the opposite sides. The farmer would have received $4,250 ($.85 per bushel × 5,000 bu) and $500 from the future contract position, for a total of $4,750. The miller would have paid $4,250 for the five thousand bushels of wheat and been charged $500 for the loss of the future position, for a total cost of $4,750.

To recap: The farmer sold the wheat contract at $.95 per bushel. At delivery, the settlement price for wheat is $.85 per bushel for a trading profit of $.10 per bushel ($500 for 5,000 bushels). The miller bought the wheat contract at $.95 per bushel. At delivery, the settlement price for wheat is $.85 per bushel, for a trading loss of $.10 per bushel ($500 for 5,000 bushels).

Both the farmer and the miller could have closed out the hedge, independent of each other, any time they wanted. At the point of closeout, their respective futures accounts would carry the then-current profit or loss.

A hedge may be a buying hedge or a selling hedge. A buying hedge is one in which the future is purchased against a deliverable due at a later date. The underlying product can be short, as in an index future, or presently nondeliverable, such as an agricultural product that is not ready to be harvested. The price for the product to be delivered at a later date is locked

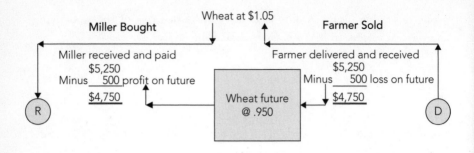

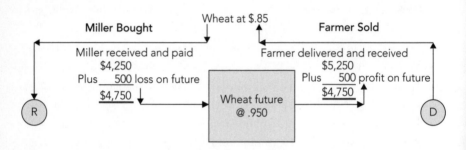

in. A selling hedge is where the underlying product is owned currently and the future sets the price that the underlying product will bring in at a later date. This type of strategy is used by a manufacturing operation when the product exists but delivery will occur at a later date or by a storage warehouse when the product has been accumulated for delivery at a later date.

Hedging is not a cure-all, as it has its own inherent risks. Take the buying or "long" hedge. A future is purchased against a short product position. The purpose of the hedge is to protect the position against rising prices. As the price of the future delivery product increases, it will cost more to cover (buy in) the short position. However, as the product increases in value, so does the future, thereby offsetting the loss generated when the short is covered. But what if the price of the product falls? While the short product position is beneficial for the ability to cover the short for less than the original sale price, the long future position is also losing value. As the prices of the two move up or down, the spread (or basis) between the two changes also. Therefore, it is imperative that the hedger knows the basis at which the hedge was put on. This gives the hedger an additional opportunity. The long or buying hedge is only valuable if the price risk of the underlying product is greater than the basis spread of the hedge.

Speculators

The speculator is one who sees a possible opportunity and takes advantage of it. Sometimes the opportunity is hidden in some catastrophe or disaster, other times it is a shift in consumer demand, and still other times it is caused by changes in the market mix.

Unlike equity and other security products, it is as easy to sell a future contract as it is to buy one. Nothing special has to be arranged. There isn't any borrowing or chance of being bought in because the supply of the borrowed security has dried up, or any of the other potential problems that the security short seller faces. The buying or selling of future contracts is so common that the closing out of a position is simply referred to as a liquidation. As many future contracts are sold against products that do not exist at the time of sale, the terms *long sale* and *short sale* are not used. The seller of contracts is simply said to be in a short position. If the position remains at the delivery time, the short position is satisfied either by the short contract position being bought in or by the delivery of the contracted amount. This is an important difference between being short an option contract and being short a future contract. Like a future contract, an option contract can be sold as easily as it can be bought. The difference is that when an option contract is in a short position at expiration, the seller does not have to do anything if a long option has not been exercised against the short position; the short option position will simply expire. This will occur with out-of-the-money options. The short future position holder must take some action to close out or satisfy the obligation.

Hurricanes, tornadoes, earthquakes, and other natural disasters stimulate the demand for raw materials to rebuild. Most of those materials are underlying products on which futures trade. Some of these disasters may even affect the food supply, requiring governments to enter the spot market and acquire huge amounts of food to ward off starvation, dehydration, and disease. This sudden demand for available supplies will cause a temporary shortage, which will in turn cause the price of the commodity to rise and the futures that trade on it to increase also. Savvy speculators, who have trained themselves (or have been trained) to study every event that occurs anywhere in the world and predict how that event may affect a product and its overlying future, will speculate and take a position on the outcome of the event. This is often referred to as reading the market.

The speculator must have a feel for the market insofar as what is considered fair pricing. An occurrence could cause the market to overreact, thereby skewing the price of the future. The savvy speculator would take a contra position and wait for the market price to correct. Such was the case with the "market correction" of 1988. Market participants jumped on index futures and option contracts, and their volatility exploded, which in turn exaggerated their prices. Many savvy speculators waited until they thought the volatility would subside and took opposite positions. As the market recovered and prices returned to a fair level, these speculators profited.

Traders

These individuals add liquidity to the market through their trading activity. The more successful ones have a "feeling" for what the market is doing or is about to do and act on it. Such slogans as "The trend is my friend" and "No pain no gain" are their mantra. Their tools are the other products that augment future contracts, such as options on the underlying, options on futures on the underlying, related products, and competitive products.

As to the use of options, traders understand the working of the different option series premiums in relation to each other. As discussed in the option section, option premiums, based on the movement of the underlying product, are not in lockstep or dollar for dollar. There is a whole slew of Greek letters that are used to describe the tracking of these movements. For example the term *delta* is used to describe the movement of an option premium as compared with the movement of the underlying product. An option with a delta of 75 will move $.75 to the underlying issue's $1.00 move. An option with a delta of 50 will move $.50 to the underlying product's $1.00 move. In the latter example, a trader who is long a future contract could sell two calls on that future and be "delta neutral." A $1.00 gain in the future product is offset by a $1.00 loss in the option position (2 × $.50 = $1.00). As long as the options retain the delta, the trader cannot earn or lose money, as the net position is flat. A trader can be long 50 future contracts and, through the strategic placement of options in position, maintain an overall position that acts as if the trader were short 50 contracts. The trader might do this because some client somewhere wanted to sell that particular future and so the trader bought it (liquidity). This is a very narrow picture of what traders are actually doing, as they juggle their positions during the day.

Of course, time and price will change the options' delta over time. Therefore, the trader must constantly monitor and adjust the positions. Trading in and out of or adding to or subtracting from positions adds liquidity to the marketplace.

Traders will also look at two products that may or may not be similar but over time have had a pricing pattern. Let's assume that product A trades at a premium of 5 points over product B. If that premium should temporarily widen for no apparent reason, traders will take a long position in the less expensive side and a short position in the higher-priced side and wait for the spread to return to normal. If the spread narrows, the reverse position is taken; the lesser value is sold, and the higher value is bought and held until the norm returns. An example of this is the relationship between the two-year and five-year U.S. Treasury note futures. A similar situation exists between soybean product futures. Traders enter into and liquidate these positions several times a day. A side effect of this type of trading is the liquidity it brings.

· RESEARCH ·

As with securities, the world of futures includes both fundamental and technical research. Fundamental research is based on hard facts, such as supply and demand and other related forces that act on the product. Technical research is based on the price movement and behavior of the underlying product and the future product itself in the marketplace.

Fundamental

While supply and demand are the primary forces considered in the analysis, fundamental research goes way beyond them. First of all, like equity research, fundamental research is not a precise analytical tool. There are many known variables and unknown events that will affect price. In looking backward, the research analyst can accurately justify the current market condition in a particular future product. That is because all factors that go into the research mix are now known. There aren't any assumptions or surprises. If there were any, they have now been accounted for. It is when the analyst moves from now to the near term to the far term that accuracy wanes and in its place come assumptions, averaged statistics, and, when necessary, a complete change in the assessments used in the recommendations.

It is a common belief that the neutralizer between supply and demand is price. It is also a common belief that price affects supply and demand. The lower the price, the less profitable is the production of the product. Producers will seek out alternative products that will generate a better profit. At the same time, as prices drop, demand increases. Likewise, as prices rise, more production becomes viable as less efficient producers enter the market. Also, demand will fall as consumers seek out alternatives. The degree to which these situations evolve depends on the public's need for the product. The term that is used to measure demand is *elasticity*. How much can the price of a product change before it affects the demand?

Fundamental research as applied to products that are used directly or indirectly in manufacturing or the commercial market most closely follows the methodology of security research. The concern focuses on what the demand for the product will be, as the flow from raw material to finished product must adjust to what the assumed demand will be at each step along the way. An accurate assessment of the demand is necessary to maximize profit. Each step along the way necessitates its own assessment of what and how much is needed to get to the next step. From this the amount of "cushion" that should be on hand at all times is determined. The "cushion" could be referred to as inventory, or stock, or warehoused. Different products use different terms. The amount of inventory that it is necessary to have on hand is determined by the level of demand, the cost of carry, and the speed at which the inventory can be replaced. As many of these products are combined in the manufacturing process, any delay caused by shortages or other problems in one component could upset the availability of the finished product. Taking this process backward, from sale (demand and the elasticity thereof) to the raw material to the future on the raw material, the analyst must factor in all of the elements that may or do play a role in pricing the future contracts.

Livestock

Analysts who review livestock futures begin their assessment from the supply side. While demand is still important, the number of animals available for slaughter is the more dominant factor. Maintaining live animals by keeping them off the market and waiting for higher prices, a practice followed in other products, is almost cost prohibited and also exposes the livestock to disease.

The breeding period for these animals is critical to the price of the product in the supermarket, as a sudden increase in what was a stable demand will take many months to adjust for. Hogs, for example, take almost one year to develop from the breeding time to the slaughter period. Cattle take about two and a half years from breeding to slaughter. In addition, veal competes with beef in the marketplace. As the profit potential from beef falls below that which can be obtained from veal, ranchers will alter the directions their herds will take on the way to market.

Precious Metals

The metal market consists primarily of base metals (aluminum, copper, lead, tin, and zinc) and precious metals (gold, palladium, platinum, and silver). For the most part, they are price-driven commodities. The higher the price, the more of the metal it becomes economically viable to mine. Gold, for example, has a very elastic demand due to its use in jewelry. Changes in the price of gold have little effect on its consumption. In addition, as the price of gold rises, sources other than mining begin to enter the gold supply. An individual's special, precious, never-to-be-parted-with gold chain and pendant take on a different dimension when gold goes from $300 to $900 per troy ounce. While the gold supply that is mined can be measured and forecasted, the influence of the secondary gold supply, which is made up of unwanted jewelry and manufacturing scrap, can only be estimated. This adds to the difficulty that an analyst has in forecasting gold prices.

Silver is used in jewelry and silverware, where appearance is important. It is also used in dentistry, photography, printed circuitry, electrical contacts, mirrors, batteries, et cetera. The level of consumption is dependent on these industries. When combined with copper at a ratio of 92.5 percent silver to 7.5 percent copper, it becomes sterling silver. Silver when mined is never found by itself. It usually is found in rock containing copper and lead.

The amount that can be mined depends primarily on the price of silver in the market.

Platinum is one of six elements (platinum, osmium, iridium, ruthenium, rhodium, and palladium) that all have the same characteristics. The metals are used as catalysts, and some are used in jewelry, in dental ingredients, as a coating for razor blades, et cetera. In 1975 the uses of these elements changed drastically as the automobile became the number one user. Platinum, rhodium, and palladium are used in the manufacturing of automobiles' catalytic converters. The converter is added to the exhaust system of a vehicle to reduce emissions. This is a good example of how a nontraditional user of a commodity can become a major player overnight.

Base Metals

Base metals are common metals. They include aluminum, copper, lead, tin, and zinc. One trait of base metals is that they oxidize and corrode easily. They are also nonferrous. Their main use is industrial. Aluminum is used in many types of cans, food wrappers, and packaging. It is also used for automobile body parts and in construction. Copper is a mandatory ingredient in computers, electric circuitry, and currency. Lead is used in construction, bullets and shot, solder, and pewter. Tin is used to coat other metals in order to slow down or eliminate the corrosive process. Tin cans and tin foil are coated with tin but are made from steel and aluminum respectively. Finally, zinc is used on steel to prevent rusting. It is also used as a supplement in food. Animals and plants could not multiply without zinc in their systems. It is also used as a water purifier, and the U.S. penny is 98 percent zinc and 2 percent copper coating. Iron, which is a ferrous metal, is one of the oldest elements known and is used in construction.

Research analysts focusing on base metal futures usually specialize in one or two because of all the factors affecting their uses. Base metals' prices are fed by demand and therefore are dependent on the economy.

Fuels

There are several types of fuels on which futures trade. The New York Mercantile Exchange (NYMEX) trades futures on crude oil (light, sweet oil), brent crude oil (a blend of oil from the North Sea), heating oil (made from crude oil), RBOB oil (reformulated gasoline blendstock for oxygen blending), blending (gasoline production), and natural gas (a plentiful non-oil-based fuel used in heating houses). Oil future products trade on exchanges worldwide, such as the InterContinental Exchange (ICE) and the Shanghai Futures Exchange (SHFE).

It is from crude oil that heating oil, gasoline, aviation fuel, and many other products, such as plastics, are derived. The refiner has to determine what crude oil will be converted into. As more countries become industrialized, the demand for fuel increases, causing the demand for crude oil to rise, causing the price of crude to increase. OPEC controls the supply of crude. The earth also controls the supply. The analyst must study the demands for the particular source of fuel. Many of the biofuels that are pointed to as an escape from fossil fuel if successfully employed, will cause the cost of food and feed to increase. The analyst must assess all of these factors.

The analysis of noncommodity futures, such as interest rates, debt instruments, stock indexes, and the like, follows the analysis of the underlying product.

Technical

As stated earlier, technical analysis is based on price movement. Therefore, the analyst believes the market accounts for and discounts all factors that affect the product's current price. To keep a record of the price and its movements, the technical analyst uses charts. (Caution: There are many, many chartists, but few true analysts.) As the analyst tracks market-price activity, the type of charts used are the same as for other products (see: equities).

· INTEREST-RATE FUTURES ·

Interest-rate futures are based on specific debt instruments. The majority of interest-rate futures are based on the sovereign debt of the country. These instruments are traded all over the world. There are futures on the U.S. Treasury thirty-year bond and ten-year, five-year, and two-year notes that are offered domestically. Interest rate futures are a global product. For example, from the European Community comes the Euro Bobl (Bundesobligationen), from Japan come JGBs (Japanese government bonds), from the United Kingdom come Gilt futures. Because of the limited number of a particular bond outstanding, the acceptable delivery against a particular future is a range of bonds or notes. For example, the accepted delivery against the thirty-year U.S. government bond future is either (1) a U.S. Treasury bond with a noncall feature that becomes a call feature fifteen years from the first day of the delivery month or (2) a U.S. Treasury bond that is noncallable, with a fifteen-year or longer maturity from the first day of the delivery month. The price of the delivered bond must be converted so that the bond price will have a yield to maturity of 6 percent.

Against the five-year note future, the delivered note would have to have an original maturity of not more than five years and three months and a remaining period of at least four years and two months before maturity. The price must be converted so that the price will have a yield to maturity of 6 percent (Source: Chicago Board of Trade).

The conversion exercise is necessary to level the playing field at the time of delivery. Bonds may not be trading at a price that gives a yield equal to, say, 6 percent, which is what is called for in the contract. To determine the amount that will yield 6 percent, a factor is employed.

The factor formula for 6 percent is

$$CF = \left[C/2 \; \frac{\frac{1}{1-(1.03)^n}}{0.03} + \frac{1,000}{1.03^n} \right] / 1,000$$

CF = conversion factor

C = coupon rate of the bond

0.03 = half the yield of 6 percent, as the instrument pays interest semiannually

n = number of times the event happens

The factor is an attempt to standardize deliverable bonds with different coupon rates. Due to changes in market conditions and differences in the price of the bonds in the cash market, one bond will stand out as the "cheapest to deliver" among the basket of acceptable bonds that are good for delivery. As it is easy to identify the cheapest to deliver, the future product will be priced off this bond. Should market conditions change to the point where a different bond becomes the cheapest to deliver, the market will price the future off that bond. As a rule of thumb, the cheapest to deliver against a 6 percent obligation would be the bond with the highest or lowest coupon and with the shortest maturity.

Note: In the case of any derivative product, where "good delivery" is not set to one instrument but a choice of acceptable instruments, there will be a "cheapest to deliver."

· INDEX FUTURES ·

Index futures are a cash-settling product. On delivery, the recipient receives cash, not the component part of the index. The value paid is the difference between the closing value of the index and the contract at the time of trade. As explained in the "Workings of a Future Contract" section earlier in this chapter, the contract positions are marked to the market daily, with adjustments being made against the account's variation margin. Therefore, barring any other activity, the difference between the original index value of the contract and the closing value of the contract should have been accounted for through the variation margin, as the value of the future contract and the value of the index at delivery are the same.

The future indexes that are traded are too numerous to name. Stock index futures are traded globally. These include indexes on the stocks traded on local exchanges. The TOPIX index (Tokyo Stock Price Index) has a future on it and trades on the Tokyo Stock Exchange. The Dow future index is traded on the Chicago Board of Trade. The Commodity Research Bureau (CRB) Index future is traded on the New York Board of Trade (NYBOT), now part of the InterContinental Exchange. It trades with delivery months January, February, April, June, August, and November, with cash delivery occurring the second Friday of the month. A strategy that caused much concern a few years ago involved indexes, index futures options on future indexes, and option-on indexes. The strategy was known as program trading. The main index products involved were the index and the index futures. Say a future index, deliverable three months from now is trading at a premium of 7 percent over the current index value. An institution acquires a basket of stock in such proportions that it replicates the current index value, and it sells the future contract. Assume the cost of carry for the securities is 6 percent, less 2 percent for dividends received, or 4 percent. As the current index's value changes, so does the basket of stock. Three months from now, the future comes in for delivery; it has a value that equals the then-current index value. The institution locked in the 3 percent difference. To be sure of the profit, the institution must dump the basket of stock immediately. This causes the market prices to drop violently, which is reflected in the index value. Other investors position options on indexes and options on futures on indexes to take advantage of the price swings. This adds to the volatility. The entire trading action was known as the triple witching hour. It was when the three derivative products ended their trading period, the futures became deliverable, and the two option products expired or were exercised.

· CURRENCY FUTURES ·

Currency futures came into being due to the potential risk of intercurrency fluctuations. As stated in the currency chapter of this book, to understand currency futures you must think of one currency as a commodity and the other currency as cash or the money that will be used to pay for the commodity. Generally, we think of currency in terms of our home currency, U.S. dollars. We trade futures on British pounds sterling or Japanese yen and settle delivery of positions in U.S. dollars. Yet Australian business conducts commerce with Japanese business, and many other countries trade with each other; all have needs for the benefits offered by currency futures.

The following currencies are traded on the Chicago Mercantile Exchange, with the standard contracts noted:

British Pound Sterling (GBP)

Trading symbol BP; quantity 62,500 GBP, deliverable quaterly in the March cycle for one and a half years, with the last trading day being the second business day before the third Wednesday of the delivery month. Continuous linked settlement (CLS) may be used for settlement.

The March cycle is March, June, September, December (next year), March, and June.

Canadian Dollar (CD)

Trading symbol CD; quantity 100,000 CD, deliverable in six quarterly deliverable months (one and a half years), starting with the March quarter.

The contract is physically settled, with the last trading day being the business day before the third Wednesday of the delivery month.

Japanese Yen (JPY)

Trading symbol JY; quantity 12,500,000 JPY, deliverable in six quarterly deliverable months (one and a half years), starting with the March quarter. The contract is physically settled, with the last trading day being the second business day before the third Wednesday of the delivery month.

Swiss Franc (CHF)

Trading symbol SF; quantity 125,000 CHF, deliverable in six quarterly deliverable months (one and a half years), starting with the March quarter. The contract is physically settled, with the last trading day being the second business day before the third Wednesday of the delivery month.

All of the above settle in U.S. dollars. The owner of the future pays dollars and receives the foreign currency. Settlement occurs at a bank in the foreign country, as long as neither it nor the U.S. bank (located in New York or Chicago) is on holiday.

Dollar-denominated futures also trade on the Brazilian rea, Czech koruna, Hungarian forint, Israeli shekel, Korean won, Mexican peso, New Zealand dollar, Norwegian krone, Polish zloty, South African rand, and Swedish krona.

Cross-Currency

Also traded are:
- Australian dollar (AD)/Canadian dollar (CD); AD/Japanese yen (JY); AD/New Zealand Dollar (NE)
- British pound (BP)/Japanese yen (JY); British pound (BP); BP/Swiss franc (SF)
- Canadian dollar (CD)/Japanese yen (JY)
- Chinese renminbi (RMB)/euro (EC); Chinese renminbi (RMB) / Japanese yen (JY); Chinese renminbi (RMB)/U.S. dollar
- Euro (EC)/Australian dollar (AD); EC/British pound (BP); EC/Japanese yen (JY); EC/Norwegian krona (NOK); EC/Swedish krona (SEK); EC/USD; EC/Czech koruna (CZK); EC/Polish zloty (PLN)

Currency futures trade globally. Besides the Chicago Mercantile Exchange, the various products trade on the London International Financial Futures and Option Exchange (LIFFE) (now part of NYSE Euronext), the New York Board of Trade (part of the InterContinental Exchange), the Brazil Mercantile & Futures Exchange (Bolsa de Mercadorias & Futuros, or BM&F), the Tokyo Financial Futures Exchange (TFX), and others.

Currency futures are priced in the same manner as other futures. The British pound sterling future traded in America is priced in U.S. dollars. As the dollar gets stronger against the British pound sterling, a buyer needs fewer dollars to buy it, so one would say that the British pound future fell in price. Again, the British pound sterling is the commodity; the dollar is the currency. In cross-currency futures, the first currency listed is the commodity, and the second currency listed is the settlement cash (e.g., in the EC/BP future, the euro is the commodity, and the British pound sterling is the currency that will be used in settlement).

The main advantages of the currency future market over the forward currency market are:

1. Prices are determined in an actively traded, competitive market.
2. The market is composed of participants with a wide spectrum of different interests.
3. As the products trade globally, the observation of values from different parts of the world justifies the prices in the market.

These three together give a sense of fairness and reliability to the price-discovery process.

One disadvantage that the future product has against the forward market is its rigidity. The quantity of currency per contract is set and is not flexible. For example, for the British pound sterling, it is set at 62,500. Industrial use of foreign exchange is hardly ever that exact. The second negative is that the delivery dates of the futures may not mesh with the need dates of the users.

Due to the size requirement of many of the commodities that trade in the futures market, mini contracts have been introduced. These include the mini gold contract, which is 33.2 troy ounces instead of 100; mini silver contract, which is 1,000 ounces instead of 5,000, mini wheat contract, which is 1,000 bushels instead of 5,000, and so on. The mini future contracts that are traded cater to smaller users. Previously, those who needed smaller amounts than specified in the future contracts had to turn to the forward market, with its liquidity limitations.

· TRAKRs ·

TRAKRs (Total Return Asset Contracts) are nontraditional future contracts. The product was developed by the Chicago Mercantile Exchange and Merrill Lynch. It was designed to give participants a way to invest in a broad-based index of stocks, bonds, currencies, and other financial instruments. A TRAKR may allow an investor to buy the S&P 500 Index and, under certain conditions, write out-of-the-money covered calls on some of those securities with one transaction. A TRAKR may track a commodity index that contains futures on commodities consumed on a global basis. As this concept catches on with institutional and noninstitutional clients, more variations will be offered. Unlike with other products that track indexes, with a TRAKR, dividend, interest and other distributions are not subtracted but remain in the index.

A TRAKR is an exchange-traded product with a duration of three to five years, and it trades on the CME Globex platform. It is nonmarginable, which means that buyers pay 100 percent of the purchase price. As a TRAKR does not make distributions during its life, the only applicable tax is the capital gains tax at the time of sale or expiration. If the product is held for more than six months, the capital gains tax rate is based on long-term holdings.

· OPTIONS ON FUTURES ·

Options on futures have the same properties as any other listed option, such as equity or index options. The difference is that exercise of an option on a future during its life will involve ownership of the future, and exercise of an option on a future at the end of the future's life will involve the product underlying the future product. To avoid redundancy and for a better understanding of the option product and how it functions, please read the options chapter of this book.

· SPAN Margin ·

Earlier in this chapter, we discussed margining of future positions. The methods used for setting standard margin and maintenance margin were discussed. The nightly mark to the market, the increasing or decreasing of variation margin, and its purpose have been explained earlier in this chapter, but future commission merchants (FCMs) and some of their institutional and other clients may have complex positions of futures and options on futures. In the case of an FCM that is carrying many strategies from several sources in one account at the clearing corporation, it would be virtually impossible to identify each and every position for margin purposes. In many cases, due to price and position changes during the day, strategies can change from moment to moment. For example, let's look at the following position (note: assumes the American form of option, which can be exercised any time during its life and that each set of option series is different):

> long 10 widget future contracts
> long 10 widget calls   short 10 widget calls
> long 10 widget puts   short 10 widget puts

The application of these positions to offset each other would depend on the trading prices of the widgets and the futures, the strike prices of the options, the delivery months of the futures, and the expiration months of the options. As the prices change, the market risks of the total position change also. For example, as the account stands now, if the short calls are out of the money and the long calls are in the money, you wouldn't apply the short call against the long future position, as that would reduce the value of the future to the strike price of the short option. (The price of the underlying product can never be higher than the strike price of a short call option position, because the strike price is the value that would be received if the call option was exercised.) If the future was selling at a price that was greater than the short call, and the long call had a higher strike price and expired on or after the short call, you would apply the long call to the short call, as that would constitute a covered position and margin would not be required. You could also apply the long call and long put as a straddle, but that might leave the short call and short put, which would require margin, and so on. As the price of the future changes, so does the relationship between it and the overlying options. One main purpose of margin in futures and options on futures is to protect the FCM from market exposure. SPAN margin does this.

SPAN margin (standardized portfolio analysis of risk) is based on software that uses algorithms to analyze complex future and option-on-futures positions to determine the minimum risk associated with that holistic position. Regardless of the strategies being employed, the software rearranges the positions to minimize overall exposure. If, due to some catastrophic event, liquidation of all positions became necessary, the result would be this dollar amount of exposure. Based on that computation, margin is charged. The FCM's own proprietary position and that of its clients are computed separately and the result settled with the respective clearing corporation each day. The FCM, in turn, uses the software in house and applies it against those clients with complex positions to determine the exposure per client. Some institutional clients run their own software to measure their exposure.

To summarize SPAN, the software ignores the intended strategies being employed. It matches or pairs the long and short positions appearing in the particular account under review so as to minimize the exposure of the overall account. When the FCM sends in its clients' positions to the clearing corporation, they appear in one account, (e.g., Stone Forrest and Rivers Clients' Account). On SFR's internal records, the "Clients' Account" is broken down on an account-by-account basis. SFR proprietary accounts are most likely also sent in as one net position (e.g., Stone Forrest and Rivers Proprietary), although depending on the type of proprietary trading SFR does, it may separate them into different accounts for control purposes (e.g., SFR Trading Account, SFR Arbitrage Account, et cetera).

· CONCLUSION ·

Futures are easily one of the most misunderstood products that we trade. The concept of setting prices far in advance of delivery and those prices being upheld mystifies many. Futures are an important product that ranges from the global perspective to the individual. That range includes our financial health, our choice of products, and our very way of life.

11

Forwards

INCLUDED IN THIS CHAPTER:

• *Introduction*
• *Forward Rate Agreements*
• *Conclusion*

· INTRODUCTION ·

The forward market is an over-the-counter market where transactions are negotiated on a contract-for-contract basis. The rate or price is set today for which a delivery will occur at a later time, usually from one to three months. As the contracts are custom made, there is very little secondary trading of the particular contract. The value of the forward market is that the quantity, quality, delivery date, delivery location, payment method, and payment location are all negotiated. For example, the quantity required for a Swiss franc future is 125,000 Swiss francs. Where could a jeweler turn if there was a need to hedge 75,000 Swiss francs that will be used three months from today as part of a payment when a shipment of watches arrives? The jeweler would enter the forward market and negotiate the terms of an agreement with a forward currency dealer. Not only would the contract be for 75,000 CHF, it would settle on the day the jeweler wanted.

Two of the primary products in this market are currency and interest rates. When comparing forward rates, the country with the lower interest rate will rise over a ninety-day period, while the country with the higher interest rate will fall. This is because if the currency of the country with the lower interest rate was invested in money market instruments of the country with the higher interest rate, after the ninety-day period had passed and the currency was repatriated, it would have gained more value than if it had remained in its domestic market. Conversely, if the higher-interest-rate country's currency was invested in the money market instruments of the lower-interest-rate country, it would have lost money by accepting the lower rate, compared with what it could have earned by remaining in the domestic market.

	Euro	British Pound Sterling	Japanese Yen	Swiss Franc
Spot	0.6268	0.5024	103.0583	1.0068
1 month	0.6292	0.5035	102.8367	1.0063
3 months	0.6292	0.5056	102.4607	1.0057
6 months	0.6321	0.5090	101.9588	1.0057
overnight LIBOR rate	3.9%	4.9%	.055%	1.95%

Note 1: The U.S. dollar overnight LIBOR rate is 2.625%.
Note 2: Those currencies with a LIBOR rate higher than that of the United States rise over time, and those with a rate lower than that of the United States fall.
Source: *Financial Times*, April 23, 2008.

The forward market for currency trading includes many more currencies than are found in the future market.

· FORWARD RATE AGREEMENTS ·

Forward rate agreements (FRAs) are over-the-counter contracts between two parties that establish an interest rate or foreign exchange rate that will be employed at a later date. For example, say Pete Cole needs to borrow euros for the next five years, starting six months from now, for use in his business. He negotiates a rate with his investment bank. At the end of the five-year period, if Pete's borrowing costs are higher that the FRA rate, the bank will pay Pete's company the difference. If Pete's borrowing costs are lower, Pete's company must pay the bank.

As another example, imagine Clydesdale Corporation is involved with floating-rate debt and wants to convert it to fixed-rate debt. It enters into an FRA with Appaloosa Bank, agreeing that Clydesdale Corporation will pay the difference between a negotiated fixed rate and a floating reference rate (such as the Federal Fund Rate or LIBOR), plus a stated number of basis points, at the end of a set period of time if the fixed rate is higher or receive payment if the fixed rate amount turns out to be lower. By entering into the FRA, Clydesdale has locked in a fixed rate as compared to the actual cost of the floating-rate debt.

· Conclusion ·

These customized products serve the needs of those who must react to specific situations. In some cases, they transfer unwanted risk; in other cases, they reduce the cost of doing business.

12

Swaps

· INTRODUCTION ·

Swaps are not a security, regulated by the Securities and Exchange Commission, nor are they a commodity, regulated by the Commodity Futures Trading Commission. They are covered by Commercial Code. As swaps are international products and generally involve the exchange of very large sums of assets, an association was formed, known as the International Swaps and Derivatives Association (ISDA), to promulgate practices that users of these products are expected to follow and adhere to. The practices are encapsulated in their master agreements, which are designed to eliminate, as much as possible, disagreements and misunderstandings as to the terms of the swap and reduce risk. The agreements are used not only in swaps, but also in many derivative products, such as collateralized debt obligations, which are discussed elsewhere in this book.

As the names implies, a swap involves an exchange of assets. This exchange generally falls into one of three categories; exchanges of currency, cash flow, or commodities. Bear in mind that you can swap anything, but generally a swap falls into these three categories.

To initiate a swap, an entity generally retains the services of a swap broker or a swap dealer. A broker acts as an intermediary between parties for a fee. A swap dealer will become an intermediary or the contra side to swap by taking down positions using other derivatives, such as forwards, futures, or options to hedge the dealer's risk.

· CURRENCY ·

Let's assume a large U.S. corporation is expanding its business and establishes an operation in the UK. At the same time a large English company has begun operations in the United States. Things are going well, and both companies want to expand their operations. They want to borrow money to be used in their new venture but want to avoid foreign-exchange risk. The U.S. company goes to a British bank and applies for an unsecured loan. The British company does the reverse. Each company wants to use its loan for operational purposes within the foreign country. They are both told that since they can close shop and return to their domestic business, they cannot take loans at the prime rate but must pay a premium.

Enter the swap broker. Each company, not knowing the other's needs, turns to the swap broker for assistance. The broker introduces the principals to each other, and after the appropriate paperwork and master agreement are completed the U.S. company goes to its U.S. bank and takes out a loan for the British company and the UK company takes out the loan from the British bank that the U.S. company needs. Then they swap the currencies.

The U.S. company, using British pounds, pays the UK company British pounds to pay off the UK loan, including the interest on the loan. Conversely, the British company pays dollars to the U.S. company, which turns around and pays off the loan at the U.S. bank.

This is a simplistic example of a currency swap. In reality, there could be a sizable difference in the amounts of the loans the two companies need, the length of time the loans are to remain open, when the interest payments are due, actions to be taken in case of default or late payment by one party, and much more. If the loans cover an extended period of time, there may be a clause that requires the parties to repay the loans to each other periodically and then renew it for the next period. Accomplishing this would give each company a comfort level that the other is solvent. All of these conditions and more are addressed in the ISDA master agreements.

The more differences that exist between the needs of the two entities, the more likely the services of a swap dealer may be called on. The dealer could position the overage between the two loans and offset it with currency futures. This would hedge the risk. If the currency rose in value, the profit the swap broker would earn on the currency would be lost in the future position. If the value of the currency fell, the money lost on the currency position would be offset by the profit on the short future position. This is an isolated example of one of many strategies afforded the swap dealer.

· CASH FLOW ·

Under the umbrella of a cash-flow swap is any swap in which, when all the terms and conditions are boiled down, what remains is the flow of cash.

EXAMPLE

Two businesses' cash flows do not match up with their needs. Marnee Travel Inc.'s busy season is around the holidays and summer. Cash flow into the company occurs in May, June, November, and December. The company's greatest need for cash is in April (for taxes) and October (for vacations and bonuses). Divad Corporation has its greatest inflow of cash in late March, early April, late September, and early October. It needs cash during the holiday season (for bonuses) and June (for vacations and to pay for acquired inventory). The problem both corporations face is the control of their internal cash flow so that cash is available when needed. They seek out a swap broker/dealer. After negotiations by all parties, the terms and amount are agreed to. Marnee agrees to loan its November/December excess cash to Divad in time for Divad's December need, and Divad agrees to loan Marnee its excess cash from its March/ April period in time for Marnee's tax needs. The same process is carried out in the other periods.

EXAMPLE

Wensat Corporation is a well-capitalized company that has borrowing needs for expansion. The company can borrow at a fixed rate of 5 percent or a floating rate of 4.5 percent. Nannyk Limited. is not as well capitalized and needs to borrow money for its operations. It can borrow at a fixed rate of 7 percent or a floating rate of 5.5 percent. Due to the nature of Nannyk's business (mortgage financing), it wants to arrange a loan for ten years at a fixed rate. This will allow it to earn the spread between the interest paid on the loan and the interest received on the fixed rate mortgages. Wensat, due to the nature of its business (funding other companies' short-term receivables) wants to borrow at a floating rate, allowing it to profit from the difference between the changing cost of interest and the changing rate being received. Wensat could simply borrow at a 4.5 percent floating rate, and Nannyk could borrow at 7 percent fixed, but as stated earlier in the book, no one likes to pay interest. Enter the swap broker.

The following arrangement is negotiated:

Wensat is to take a loan at 5 percent, and Nannyk is to take a loan at 5.5 percent floating.
Nannyk will pay Wensat its 5 percent interest cost, plus an additional 1.5 percent.
Wensat will pay Nannyk's 5.5 percent interest cost.

The net cost to Nannayk will be 5.5 percent plus 1.5 percent, or 6.5 percent fixed, as opposed to 7 percent at the bank.

The net cost to Wensat will be 5.5 percent minus 1.5 percent, or 4 percent floating, as opposed to 4.5 percent at the bank.

There are many other versions brought on by changes to situations over time. For example, in interest rates we have:

Fixed rate for fixed rate with a different payment date
Fixed for floating
Floating for floating with a different reset date
Fixed for zero
Floating for zero
In equities we have capital gains for dividend income

· COMMODITY ·

The most common commodity swap is referred to as EFP or exchange for physical. Say Pete Rolium owns oil that is on a tanker arriving in a month. As Pete has not received the actual oil, he hasn't paid for it. He finds himself in a bind, as one of his customers that was supposed to purchase oil from him has walked away from the deal; Pete has nowhere to store the oil that he is about to receive. Gus O'Line is experiencing a different problem. Due to a miscalculation, he finds his company is short on its supply of the next month's deliverable oil. His mistake was that several months ago he bought an extra oil future contract that is due for delivery in four months, when he should have bought a future that is deliverable next month. Through negotiation, Gus accepts and pays for Pete's oil in exchange for Gus's future contract.

EXAMPLE
Farmer Dell grows zaps. Miller Miler buys zaps and sells them as an ingredient to food processing companies. Zaps fluctuate around $10.00 a pound. Both parties find it too time consuming each month to record the slight differences in prices and want a flat monthly cost. Enter the swap broker. Farmer Dell is willing to use $10.00 as the monthly mark. Miller Miler is willing to use $10.02 as the monthly mark.

Month one: Farmer Dell delivers zaps to the market and receives $9.95 per pound. Miller Miler buys zaps in the market and pays $9.95 per pound. Miler pays the swap broker an additional $.07 per pound. The swap broker keeps $.02 and passes the remaining $.05 to Dell. The net cost to Miler is $1.02, and the net received by Dell is $1.00.

Month two: Farmer Dell delivers zaps to the market and receives $10.05 per pound. Miller Miler buys zaps in the market and pays $10.05 per pound. Dell pays the swap broker $.05 per pound. The swap broker keeps $.02 and passes the remaining $.03 to Miler. The net cost to Miler is $1.02, and the net received by Dell is $1.00.

The above are examples of how swaps work and why they exist. Though these examples are simplistic in their forms, swaps can be extremely complicated, with all types of caveats and entitlements. The more complex the swap, the more important it is to have the terms covered in the ISDA master agreement.

Included in the master agreement are such topics as:

1. Is the party a legal entity
2. Are they permitted to enter into this type of agreement
3. Is this agreement in conflict with any other agreement or with the charter of the company
4. Agrees that all information provided by the company is accurate
5. Deliveries will be made as stated in the confirmation
6. Payments are to be made on the due date in freely transferable funds
7. A default has not occurred and an early termination date has not been exercised
8. Deliverer's account may be changed with five days' notice
9. Netting of payments is permissible under certain conditions
10. Party will furnish all required documentation on a timely basis
11. Party will comply with all legal requirements
12. Causes of default or termination:
    Failure to pay or deliver
    Breach of contract
    Misrepresentation
13. What constitutes default
14. What happens in case of a force majeure event

And much more. As said in the opening of this chapter, the purpose of the master agreement is to clarify all terms and conditions, cover all maladies, and their remedies, and detail all penalties and restitution. It is a very thorough document.

The swap may not include all of the properties of the asset involved in the swap but only a part. Therefore, the face value of the asset may be relevant only as part of the general information. The value of the asset, which is usually referred to as its principal, is in this case referred to as *notional*. In the case where interest amounts are being swapped, the important facts of the swap have to do with the interest payments (amount, timing, payment method, et cetera), and not the "principal" of the asset. In this swap scenario, the face value or amount of value is just general information and is referred to as the asset's notional value.

The longevity of the swap may and usually does have nothing to do with the longevity of the asset. In the case of an interest-rate swap, the interest payments under the swap could cover a shorter time span than the assets paying the interest. So as not to confuse the two, the life span of the swap is referred to as its tenor.

· CURRENCY DEFAULT (CDS) ·

Currency default swaps are a different type of swap. Unlike the ones mentioned previously, where there is an exchange of some asset, such as a floating-rate income leg of a swap for a fixed-rate income leg, the CDS involves a qualified institution, which, for a fee, accepts the risk of a third party by having to pay a debt instrument's obligations should the instrument default. The CDS resembles an insurance policy more than a conventional swap. The institution accepting the fee is considered the seller of the CDS, and the one paying the fee is considered the buyer.

EXAMPLE
Loster Motor Corporation took a sizable loan from First Continental Bank several years go. The economy is currently in a downturn, and Loster Motor's market share has fallen dramatically. The bank's economists are of the opinion that the economy and Loster Motor's finances will not improve over the next three years, but First Continental is concerned about Loster Motor's ability to meet its financial commitments in the near term. It turns to Stone Forrest and

Rivers and enters into a CDS for the interest payment on the loan for the next three years. Should Loster default on the interest payments during that period, Stone Forrest and Rivers will have to pay them. For this "protection," First Continental Bank will pay Stone Forrest and Rivers a fee. Stone Forrest and Rivers's research department has been following Loster Motor's business and financials. It believes that, barring any major catastrophe, the corporation should make it through this period. Therefore, First Continental and SFR negotiate terms and enter into a three-year CDS agreement.

The use of a CDS may be a surrogate for shorting the actual loan obligation. The buyer of the CDS is anticipating a rise in the interest rate of the referenced issue. If the issuer should encounter a credit event, the spread of the CDS will widen, allowing the buyer to liquidate the position at a profit. The reverse is true if the seller of the CDS expects the spread to narrow.

The terms of the CDS are negotiated and agreed to under the International Swaps and Derivatives Association's (ISDA) master agreement, which is discussed elsewhere in the asset-backed security section of this book. The swap may cover a loan, bond, or other debt instrument. The financial entity accepting the risk ascertains the risk of the issuer of the instrument as well as the party from which they are selling the CDS. The instrument or instruments involved in the CDS are referred to as the reference issue. The CDS may cover the interest and/or principal for part of the debt life or for part of the notional value of the debt. It may cover interest payments only for a specified number of years. The CDS may only be acted upon in case of default or late payment, or whatever the parties to the agreements negotiate.

For example, loans and mortgages typically require the payment of periodic interest, and included in the payment is a gradual pay-down of the principal. A CDS may be struck for any part or all of the payments.

Bonds typically pay interest periodically and their principal at maturity. During the bond's existence, much can happen to the issuer. The bonds are exposed to internal and external maladies. Therefore, besides the payment of interest and principal, a CDS may be struck to cover certain events but not others.

Pricing of a CDS

The seller of the CDS negotiates the price based on its perception of the risk involved with the terms negotiated. The current financial crisis has caused the cost of credit default swaps to skyrocket. Even the premiums on CDSs on sovereign debt from the richest nations have increased to a historic level. The pricing of a CDS is the culmination of several factors: the base rate (usually LIBOR), the calculated risk factor, and the assumed recovery rate (what is expected to remain after failure of the referenced security).

Settlement of a CDS Contract

When booking or referring to a CDS position, the buyer of the CDS is said to be short, whereas the seller is said to be long. That is because the buyer of the CDS is deemed to have sold the referenced security. As part of the negotiation between the parties to the CDS is the method of settlement. Usually cash is the medium, but it could be a physical delivery with the referenced issue being delivered from the buyer of the CDS to the seller.

Credit Default Indexes

As with most products, there are indexes that track the credit default swap market. Among these are the CDX indexes, which cover a range of specific CDSs. The CDX.NA.IG, for example, focuses on CDSs on investment-grade issues, the CDX.NA.HY on high-yield issues. The ABX indexes follow the asset-backed market, especially the lenders who have mortgages outstanding with individuals with weak credit ratings. The indexes are administered by Markit Group Limited.

The Chicago Board of Trade trades contracts on the CDR Liquid 50 North America Investment Grade Index.

· CONCLUSION ·

The domain that can be covered by a swap contract is enormous. It is international in scope, covering any and all types of assets. What is needed is two parties, each looking for what the other party has, that are willing to swap!

13

Alternative Investments

T he term *alternative investment* is a catchall phrase for investment in any product other than stock and the usual bonds. It goes beyond the standard products that are traded. Depending on where and by whom the phrase is being used, it could include hedge funds, private equity investments, leveraged buyout instruments, arbitrage strategies, real estate, and venture capital.

· HEDGE FUNDS ·

Basically, there isn't any clear definition of a hedge fund, except that they attempt to generate profits regardless of which way the market in general is going. These are not mutual funds and are not as restricted in what they can do as other investments are. Due to their nature, investment in them is open to a select few, namely high-net-worth individuals and large institutions known as qualified institutional buyers (QIBs). The rationale behind this restriction is that this group of investors is supposed to be astute enough to avoid the pitfalls less affluent investors might fall into. Based on their wealth and assumed familiarity with investments and financial matters, it is assumed that they do not need the full disclosure of information that the general public is entitled to. To qualify, an investor must have at least $1,000,000 in liquid financial assets or an annual income of $200,000 or more in the last two years and the possibility of earning at least that in the current year. For an institution to qualify, it must manage $100,000,000 worth of securities. Included in this group are banks, employee benefit plans, insurance companies, investment companies, and any entity owned by qualified investors. To qualify, broker-dealers must own or be investing $10,000,000 on a discretionary basis in nonaffiliated securities.

The funds are private investments. The term *hedge fund* is used to cover many different unrestricted investment possibilities. Included are securities not registered with the Securities and Exchange Commission and strategies such as swaps, futures, short selling of securities, collateralized debt obligations (CDOs), and collateralized bond obligations (CBOs). As hedge funds are free to invest in riskier opportunities, their ability to use leverage is unrestricted, and with the greater use of leverage comes much greater risk.

The term *hedge fund* is misleading, as many such funds do not hedge at all. For example, many hedge funds bought shares of pooled subprime mortgages. As the possibility of default was remote, the funds did not hedge the position. As proper hedges against major defaults were not taken, when these and other mortgages defaulted, which contributed to the mortgage crisis, these funds took major losses. Hedges restrict profits or limit losses. As a matter of fact, a perfect hedge freezes the profit or losses at the time it enters into the position and remains frozen until one "leg" or both legs of the box are lifted. The reason the profit or loss remains the same is that as the underlying market changes, the profit on one side is offset by a loss on the other side. An example of a hedge would be buying a stock at $10 per share and selling the same stock short when it reached $90. This is known as short against the box. The box is that no matter which way the stock moves, an 80-point profit has been "boxed." What is made on one side is lost on the other.

Generally, hedge funds are more expensive for the investor to own than are conventional mutual fund fees as they include management and performance fees. Management fees are usually less than 5 percent of the hedge fund's net asset value. A hedge fund with $100,000,000 net asset value and charging a 3 percent management fee will collect a $3,000,000 management fee. The charging of a management fee is standard practice, and the fees are calculated annually and charged to the share owners monthly.

Performance fees are imposed by hedge funds on the shareholders also. These fees are very controversial, as they are not allowed to be exercised anywhere else in the registered security market. In addition, the fees are generally charged against realized and unrealized profits. Of obvious concern is the taking of the performance fee against unrealized profit. What if by the time the asset is disposed of, it is disposed of at a loss? The fee taken previously for the unrealized profit is not returned.

The structure of a hedge fund consists of a manager and clients (investors). The manager selects an adviser or advisers (and the adviser selects a hedge fund or hedge funds). Orders are entered through the appropriate execution routing vehicle, such as a broker-dealer. The execution vehicle used depends on the asset or strategy being employed. In a case where the hedge fund is involved with short selling, the execution vehicle will have to borrow the stock being sold short, so the hedge fund will utilize the services of a broker-dealer. In the case of buying CDOs, the services of a Structured Investment Vehicle (SIV) will probably be used.

Structure of a Hedge Fund

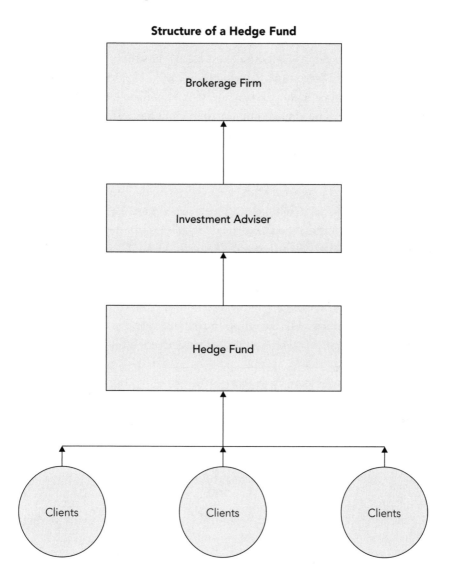

Structure of a Hedge Fund

- **Brokerage Firm**
- **Investment Adviser**
- **Hedge Fund**
- Clients · Clients · Clients

· LEVERAGED BUYOUTS (LBOs) ·

Leveraged buyout is a process by which a person or entity takes control of a company by acquiring its voting stock with borrowed funds. Other names for this practice are highly leveraged transaction and bootstrap transaction. The borrowing can be in the form of cash loans or the issuance of debt products. Due to the risks involved, the debt instruments usually pay a high rate of interest and are classified as high-yield bonds or junk bonds.

The purpose of a leveraged buyout is to permit one entity or group to acquire another company. With this vehicle, a "small fish can swallow a much bigger fish," as the majority of funding for the acquisition is borrowed funds. The ratio of debt to equity may be 30 percent equity to 70 percent debt, or higher. The assets of one or both companies are sometimes pledged against the loans. Sometimes the effect of this is to destroy the rating of the acquiring and the acquired company, as the assets of one or the other are now encumbered by the load of the debt.

To understand the genesis of a leveraged buyout, one should understand the subtle similarity between an equity (stock) owner and a debt (bond) owner. They have both made investments. The equity owner receives compensation for the investment after the bond owner has received his and after the compensation amount has been declared by the board of directors. Stockholders have some sway over the board of directors, through their individual votes and, through them, the management of the company. The larger amount the shareholder owns, the more "sway" he or she has. However, the stockholder or group of stockholders must have or control a large enough amount of votes to make a difference. A large enough block of stock aimed at one goal can force the corporation into an action it wouldn't otherwise take. The large block of stock may be keeping poor management in office, or it may be what is needed to kick bad management out of office. Either way, a small investor has little or no say in the company. Poor management has as an analogy to weak share price. Weak share price is an advertisement to attract a large block of outside investment. A successful investment by a large outside interest could cure the corporation's malady, which in turn would benefit the small investor.

The bondholder has an investment that restricts the issuer's actions through the debt's indenture (also known as the deed of trust). Those restrictions may limit the amount of additional debt the corporation can issue, the weakening of the firm's balance sheet through mergers or acquisitions, and other bond rating diluting strategies. Therefore, in comparing the two forms of investment, from this point of view there are more similarities than there are differences.

· Venture Capital (VC) ·

Among the products offered, the name *venture capital* must evoke a picture of the most exciting of investments. Just compare the words *venture capital* to *bonds* or *mortgages*. Use the term at a social function and watch the degree of interest in nearby listeners. But what is this thrill-packed product?

1. It is usually a private investment in a start-up company.
2. It is a long-term investment.
3. It is an illiquid investment.
4. It usually involves high management fees.
5. It usually takes the form of partnership.

Over time, the partnership may invest in several ventures. While it is understood that some will fail, resulting in the total loss of that particular investment, and others will just float along, generating little if any profit, if these companies ever go public, the investor has an opportunity to get at least part, if not all, of his or her investment back. Those investments in companies that are successful over time should pay off handsomely and give a much better return than conventional investments. The payoff on these will not only cover the loss and disappointment of the ones that did not work out, but also cover the initial investment many times over.

To participate in the venture-capital arena, investors MUST do their homework. They must fully understand what they are doing and what they are getting into:

1. What are the risks, and what are the rewards?
2. Can they afford to lose their entire investment?
3. Is this an emotional or a well-thought-out decision?

They must also seek out a venture capitalist firm that they are comfortable doing business with:

1. Who are the managers?
2. What is their track record?

3. How long have they been actively operating as venture-capital managers? What the individuals have done in other venues is of interest, but their experience and success in venture capital is far more important.

4. Are all the managers or principals active in the management, or are one or two listed for name recognition only?

5. What functions do the "managers" or "principals" perform? The track record of a principal who is involved solely with the operation/administration part of the business and not the investment-decision part is being compensated for the performance of those operational & administration duties and therefore would have a different history or track record than, say, those who are engaged in the investment decision process. There should be a clear delineation of duties.

6. What are the venture capitalists' fields of expertise?

7. How does this company compare to other VCs? It is also better if the investor has sufficient capital to be able to invest in several partnerships over time, so that he or she has a running inventory of these partnerships at all times. Depending on the venture-capital managers' track record, it may behoove the investor to invest with more than one venture-capital firm. An investor limiting his or her investment to one partnership is taking a huge risk, in that all the start-up companies in that partnership may fail.

Venture capital should not be confused with private equity. Venture capitalists usually invest in start-up companies. The minimum amount of investment is usually $1,000,000. The venture capitalist receives a stake in the company, usually in the form of common shares. He or she holds the stock in hopes that it will be sold into the public market through an IPO (initial public offering), at which time the venture capitalist can start to "cash out" and reap the profits. In the case of a private equity investment, the investor usually receives convertible preferred stock, which must be retained for a period of time (three–five years), after which the investor can convert the preferred stock to common stock or liquidate the position. Many times, the company needing to raise capital is attempting to raise a small amount, making a formal underwriting too expensive. The private-equity route gives the company access to needed funds without giving up a stake in the company or going through the expense of a public offering.

· SPECIAL-PURPOSE VEHICLES (SPVs) AND SPECIAL-PURPOSE ENTITIES (SPEs) ·

SPVs were formed as a way of getting loan assets off the books of banks and other financial institutions. The SPV was formed and funded as a subsidiary of the institution or as a stand-alone entity. It would buy the assets from the institution, pool the loans, securitize the pools, and sell the pool into the market as various collateralized debt obligations. (CDOs). In the CDOs were car loans, second mortgages, subprime mortgages, credit card loans, boat loans, et cetera.

The effect of the transactions was to shield the originator from default of the loan and replenish the originator's liquid assets. Many of these SPVs were established offshore as tax-exempt charitable trusts, which provided two more benefits to the originator. First, the trust being tax-exempt allowed the SPV to raise money more efficiently. And second, making the trust the sole owner of the SPV further removed the originator from the loan assets.

· STRUCTURED INVESTMENT VEHICLE (SIV) ·

Structured investment vehicles are funds that borrow money by issuing short-term securities, such as commercial paper, to acquire long-term assets. They sell shares of the fund to investors such as hedge funds. The SIV attempts to earn revenue from the interest spread between the interest paid on the short-term instruments and the higher rate earned on the longer-term assets. The SIV typically invests in asset-backed securities, which include collateralized debt obligations, credit card loans, and student loans, and mortgage-backed securities, which include fixed- and adjustable-rate mortgages and corporate bonds. As the long-term debt is financed by short-term borrowings, the management must continuously refinance the short-term borrowings. Therein lie three independent risks:

1. Short-term rates may rise to the point that they are higher than the income being received from the long-term investments.
2. The liquidity of short-term funds for this type of investment may dry up.
3. The value of the asset being sold falls, leaving the SIV with uncollaterlized loans.

The first risk, that short-term rates may increase and overtake the long-term rates being received from the assets, can happen through normal market activity. The profit margin would dry up. The manager would seek out vehicles to offset the situation. One such vehicle might be the use of credit swaps, that is, swapping out the SIV's short-term debt for long-term debt of a tenor that is perceived to satisfy the need.

The second risk is brought about either by a general shortage of short-term funds or a catastrophic event occurring within the SIV's industry that would sour the willingness of the short-term buyer to invest in these types of securities.

A third problem occurs when the value of the assets falls below the value of the long-term loan. The part of the loan that exceeds the value of the asset is unsecured and weakens the value of the SIV. This could get worse if the payer of the loan realizes that it is paying for an asset that is worth less than what is owed on it and simply walks away, leaving the SIV with an illiquid asset.

Note: Many of the products developed by the SPVs were purchased these SIVs. As the mortgage market collapsed, so did the SPVs and then the SIVs.

· CONCLUSION ·

These products were unheard of a few years ago. The information super-highway has brought them forward from obscurity. Who knows what tomorrow will bring?

14

Markets

INCLUDED IN THIS CHAPTER:

- *Introduction*
- *Order Instruction*
- *Agency vs. Principal Transactions*
- *Workings of the Market*
- *The Over-the-Counter (Principal-Type) Market*
- *Municipal Bond Market*
- *The Third Market*
- *The Fourth Market*
- *ECNs and Alternative Trading Systems (ATS)*
- *Dark Pools*
- *Conclusion*

· INTRODUCTION ·

The markets are not a mystery. The more liquidity there is in a market, the more realistic and reliable the prices are. As the liquidity diminishes, the prices become more uncertain. The security market is the same as any other auction market. The prices are set by supply and demand. The buyers want to pay as little as possible. The sellers want to receive as much as possible. When the two sides agree, there is a trade. The markets aren't stagnant. They are dynamic and ever changing.

The basic frame and simplest form of the "current" market is the quote and size. The quote in any auction market is composed of a bid and an offer.

The bid is the highest price anyone at that moment wants to pay, and the offer is the lowest price anyone will accept. These have been "announced." Other interested parties may have not committed their bid or offer, as they want to wait and see the market activity or their pricing is away from the current market. In an active market there will be bids below the current bids and offers above the current offer. But the current market is composed of only the highest bid and the lowest offer.

The other part is known as size. It represents the number of trading lots available at that price. The quote is always displayed first, then the size. For common stock, a quote of "26.30–.50" translates to the bid being $26.30 per share per trading (round) lot of 100 shares, and shares being offered at $26.50 per share per trading lot. A size of "50 × 80" would translate into 5,000 shares (50 times the trading lot of 100 shares) composing the bid and 8,000 shares (80 times the trading lot of 100 shares) composing the offer. The display would look like this:

Bid	Offer
26.30 −	.50
50	× 80

In the United States, the standard trading lot for common stock is 100 shares. This is known as a round lot. In the UK, the trading lot is 1,000 shares. However, the United States trades in dollars, and the UK trades in pence ($1 = 100 cents; £1 = 100 pence), and of course, other countries have their own standards. As the trading lot is 100 shares in the United States, the last two zeros are dropped from the stated size. Therefore, a size of "50 × 80" in common stock really stands for 5,000 shares composing the bid and 8,000 shares composing the offer.

· ORDER INSTRUCTION ·

Time Limits

Orders can be entered as:

Day Orders
These expire at the end of the day of entry if not executed.

Good Till Canceled (GTC) Orders

Also known as (open orders), they remain in force in the marketplace and maintain their standing in the order of entry until they are executed in the market or canceled by the originator.

Good Thru (time period)

These orders remain in force for a stipulated period of time if not executed (good thru month, good thru week, et cetera) At the end of the time period, the order is automatically canceled.

It should be noted that many broker-dealers report pending orders on their clients' monthly statements as a reminder of their existence. A pending order, regardless of the terms and conditions, is a live liability to the order's originator.

Types of Orders

Markets and Market

What is the current market? For a buyer, the current market is the offer of $26.50. That is the lowest price that we know of at which anyone will sell that stock at this moment. For someone wanting to sell shares, the market is the bid of $26.30. That's the highest price others want to buy at. You cannot buy from buyers; you must buy from sellers. Likewise, you cannot sell to a seller; you must sell to a buyer. Again, for a seller the current market is $26.30 per share. That is the highest price anyone wants to buy the stock for. You cannot sell the stock at $26.50, as that is where other sellers are. A customer entering a "market" order is saying that he or she is willing to accept the "current" market. Buy market orders accept the current offer; sell market orders accept the current bid.

As the bid represents the highest price at which anyone has announced a willingness to purchase the stock at, once the supply (size) composing the bid is used up, the next-lower bid will take precedence. The same is true of the offers. Once the supply composing the offer is taken, the next-higher offer takes precedence.

In the above example, had someone bought the stock at the offer price of $26.50 and turned around immediately and sold it, the person would have a trading loss of 20 cents per share. The difference between the bid and the offer is known as the spread. For the person to be even, tradingwise, the quote would have to increase until the new bid equaled the $26.50 currently being offered. This excludes fees and other charges associated with the transaction. As the bid moved up from $26.30 to $26.50, the offer would have moved up also.

The more active a market is, the tighter (smaller) the spread of the quote should be. The less active, the wider the quote is. With many interests trying to buy and sell the stock, their competitiveness will keep the spread of the quote close.

Limit

With quote $26.30–$26.50, Ed Ukate wants to buy shares of the Loster Corporation, but he is not willing to pay $26.50. Ed enters a buy order with a higher price than the current bid of $26.30, let's say $26.40 for 3,000 shares. Ed now has the highest bid, so the quote would change to $26.40–26.50, the bid side of the size would change to 30, and the price and size of the offer would remain the same. If someone is willing to sell at $26.40, a trade will occur. If someone else sees that bid and wants to pay more, that person could buy the stock at $26.50 or enter a buy order with a limit price higher than $26.40 and lower than $26.50. (Note: Stocks in the United States can trade at $.01 intervals.) Say the order is entered halfway between $26.40 and $26.50. The quote would now be 26.45–26.50, and the size would represent the orders behind the quote.

If Ed thinks the current bid was too high, he can enter a buy limit order with a lower price than the current bid, in hopes that the price of the stock will fall in value. If his assumption is wrong, and the market price doesn't fall in value until it's reached his bid (the price on his limit order), his order will never be "exposed" to the marketplace and never be executed.

The opposite is true for a sell. Say Rose Thorns wants to sell her stock. She sees the quote of $26.40–.50 and thinks she can get a better price than $26.40 but realizes that offers of $26.50 have already been made. She enters an offer at $26.45 for her 10,000 shares of stock. The quote changes to $26.40–.45, and it is her offer. The offer side of the size changes to 100 (10,000 shares).

However, if Rose thought the price, in general, was too low, she could enter a limit order above $26.50 and hope for the price to rise so that her limit price could be exposed to the market.

Therefore, a buy limit order sets the maximum to be paid per share, whereas a sell limit order sets the minimum to be received. Use of limit orders requires a special need, such as protection during a very fast-moving and volatile market in that security, a strategy involving other products, or a very thinly traded marketplace where the spread between the bid and offer is unusually wide and/or the quote is not firm. But under normal market conditions, the use of a limit order is questionable.

Let's run through this again.

Ed

Order Entered	Quote	Size
	26.30–.50	50 × 80
buy 3,000 @ 26.40		
	26.40–50	30 × 80

Rose

Order Entered	Quote	Size
	26.40–.50	30 × 80
sell 10,000 @ 26.45		
	26.40–45	30 × 100

At this point, let's assume Randi Miles enters an order to sell 1,000 shares at the market when the market is 26.40–.45, 30 × 100.

Order Entered	Quote	Size	Execution
	26.40–.45	30 × 100	
sell 1,000 @ mkt			sold 1,000 @ 26.40
	26.40–.45	20 × 100	

After that execution, let's assume Don Kei enters a buy order for 1,000 shares at the market.

Order Entered	Quote	Size	Execution
	26.40–.45	20 × 100	
buy 1,000 @ mkt			bought 1,000 @ 26.45
	26.40–.45	20 × 90	

Stop

Stop orders, also known as stop-loss orders, are memorandum orders. The term *memorandum order* means that the order does not have any standing in the marketplace until its price is elected by another.

For example, say Don Kei, the above-mentioned client who bought 1,000 shares of stock at $26.45 per share, has concerns that the price of the stock may fall. Due to the nature of his work, he doesn't have access to timely pricing information. Don decides that he wants to get out of the position if the price drops 3 points to $23.45. If he enters an order to sell the stock at the $23.45 limit when the quote is 26.40–.45, the order will be executed at the $26.40 price on a 23.45 limit because the current market price satisfies the terms of Don's order. That is not what Don intended to do, but that is what the order's instruction was. Don meant to enter an order that said, "Do nothing until the price of the stock falls to 23.45 or below; then sell my stock." He should have entered a "stop order," because that is the instruction conveyed by that type of order. The order would read, "Sell 500 shares at 23.45 Stop." The first time the stock traded at $23.45 or below, the order would change from a sell stop order to a sell market order and would be executed against the then-current bid.

There is a negative side to stop orders. The stop price is a "trigger" price that must be reached or passed before the order is activated. The stock has to trade at a triggering price just one time to activate the market order. Two negative results are as follows.

William Fold is watching the price movement of Invicter Products. Bill owns the stock at $25 a share. It is now trading at $30 per share, and he wants to protect his profit. He enters a sell stop order at $29. Over the next couple of days, the market in general is weak and the stock's price slips down to $29 per share and then turns upward. The fact that it traded one time at $29 triggers Bill's sell order as a live market order, and it gets executed. As Bill watches, the price of Invicter common stock rises as the market in general rises. The temporary negative impact on Invicter's price had nothing to do with the company but had to do with market sentiment.

Terry Kloth owns shares of Dynamo. He purchased them at $23, and Dynamo is now trading at $39, down from a high of $45. He is debating whether he should close out the position and take the profit or see if the stock comes back. He decides to place a sell stop order and uses an arbitrary price of $38 as the stop price. The stock lingers around $39 per share for a few more days and then opens one morning at down 50 percent on some horrific news. His stop order gets executed at around $19 per share.

Stop Limit

Stop limit orders are stop orders that become limit orders when their price is reached or passed. They are best used by professional traders. Guy Zendolls is a technical analyst who has been tracking Whipper Corporation common stock. The stock has had an interesting trading pattern. The stock has been having trouble breaking through the $51 price. It keeps approaching it and then loses some value, only to rise again to approximately $51 and then fall again. Guy believes that if it breaks through the $51 "barrier," it could reach $55 or higher. However, Guy is also concerned that it could close today at $50 per share and then some unexpected good news overnight could cause the stock to open for trading tomorrow close to $55 or higher. Therefore, a regular stop order would not be beneficial, as he would be buying the stock at the price he is looking to sell it at, or worse. Guy enters the following order: "Buy 10,000 shares of Whipper at $51.10 Stop, 51.50 limit." This gives Guy the benefit of a stop order, in that it can be entered above the current market as a memorandum order, as well as the protection of a limit order in case the stock runs up suddenly. If it breaks through the $51 barrier to $51.10 the most he will pay is $51.50. If it does close today at $50 per share and opens tomorrow above $51.50, Guy will not receive an execution.

Short Sale

A short sale is one in which a sale is made using borrowed stock with the expectation of buying it back at a lower price at a later date. Ellie Phant has been following Rigg-a-Mortiss Corporation and thinks the stock will fall 20 percent in value. With Rigg-a-Mortiss trading at $80 per share, Ellie arranges through her broker-dealer to sell the stock short.

When Elllie contacts the broker-dealer, it arranges to borrow the stock on her behalf. It can borrow the stock from another financial institution or its own proprietary positions or from a client who has signed the proper legal documents and whose account currently permits the borrow.

If Ellie's judgment is correct, and the stock falls in value, Ellie will buy the stock in the open market and close out the short sale. Ellie's broker-dealer will take the stock that Ellie purchased and return it to the source it was borrowed from.

But what can go wrong with Ellie's short sale? First, the price may rise instead of fall. As it rises, Ellie will face a bigger and bigger loss. If it rises high enough, the broker-dealer will issue a margin call for Ellie to deposit more collateral (money or other securities) in her account. This cycle could continue until Ellie can no longer take any more of a loss, goes into the market to buy the stock, and closes out the short sale. At this time, her "paper loss" becomes a real one.

Another thing that can go wrong is that Rigg-a-Mortiss Corporation becomes involved in some corporate action such as a merger, acquisition, or tender offer and the supply of loanable stock dries up. Ellie may be forced to close out the short position, as the stock she has borrowed is being called in by its owner and the broker-dealer cannot borrow it anywhere else.

A final factor is caused by a recent federal rule known as SHO. Occasionally, a broker-dealer cannot deliver stock against a sale. Under SHO, should a broker-dealer's fail to deliver remain open (undelivered) for thirteen consecutive business days, the broker-dealer must close out the position by buying in the affected position.

Naked short selling, or uncovered short selling, is a practice that has regulators concerned. It is done either by deliberately selling stock short without a solid source for delivery or by accidentally having located borrowable stock that becomes unavailable when needed. The former is a violation of federal rules; the latter is a usual business practice.

Because there is a three-day cycle between the day the trade occurs and when the stock is needed for delivery, it is possible that stock that was available for loan on the trade date may not still be available on the settlement date. For example, broker-dealer Giant Reckor and Crane calls broker dealer Stone Forrest and Rivers to see if it can borrow stock. At that moment of the day, one of SFR's trading accounts owns the stock, and it agrees to make the loan. Later the same day, a trader sells the stock as part of a normal trading activity. Giant Reckor and Crane has sold the stock short when it was told Stone Forrest and Rivers would lend it. On the settlement date, Stone Forrest and Rivers needs the stock to settle its trader's sale, and therefore it is not available to Giant Reckor and Crane, which must now borrow the stock elsewhere. If GRC is unable to borrow the stock, it inadvertently has a naked short. Recently, the SEC has proposed rules that would tighten the "borrow" even further by making the short seller be sure of the borrowed stock's availability on the settlement date. Under rule SHO of the Securities and Exchange Act of 1934, securities cannot be sold short if they appear on the "threshold" list. Threshold securities are equity securities that have an aggregate fail-to-deliver position for five consecutive settlement days at a registered clearing agency (e.g., National Securities Clearing Corporation) totaling 10,000 shares or more and equal to at least 0.5 percent of the issuer's total shares outstanding. The list can be found at www.nasdaq.com.

Short Against the Box

Let's assume client Pete Cole bought 10,000 shares of Whinn Whon Limited at $10 per share in January. The stock is trading at $90 per share in September. Pete doesn't want to sell the stock because he wants to postpone the taxable event until the following year. Pete sets up a short sale for 10,000 shares of Whinn Whon. His account is now is long (owns) 10,000 shares and short (owes) 10,000 shares. Whichever way the price of the stock moves, Pete will profit on one side and lose on the other the same amount. The position is "boxed." If the stock rises in value, the long side is better off and the short side loses; if the stock falls in value, the short side profits but the long side loses. Whatever his profit or loss is (in this case a profit of 80 points) will remain until one or both of the "legs" of the box are taken off at a later time. Pete can close out the position and retain his 80-point profit, or, if he likes the way the stock is moving, he can buy in the short sale and continue earning money on the rising price on the long position. Or if the stock is losing value, he can sell out the long stock and make additional profit on the short sale.

Say the acquisition was at $10 and the short sale at $90, for a net $80 profit. The stock rises to $100 when Pete decides to close out the short sale.

Buy side		Sell side	
current stock value	$100	cost of stock buyback	$100
cost of purchase	− 10	short sale price	− 90
profit	$90	loss	$10
net profit	$80		

Pete sells the long stock at $50.

Buy side		Sell side	
proceeds of sale	$50	short sale price	$90
cost of purchase	− 10	current value	− 50
profit	$40	profit	$40
net profit	$80		

The company goes bankrupt, making the stock worthless.

Buy side		Sell side	
value of stock	$ 0	short sale price	$90
cost of purchase	− 10	current value	− 0
loss	$10	profit	$90
net profit	$80		

No matter what the stock is trading at, an 80-point profit is locked in, or boxed!

Fill-or-Kill (FOK)

Institutions, arbitrageurs, trading firms, and others sometimes employ strategies that require simultaneous and/or instantaneous execution. They must use orders that clearly specify their intentions. One of these special orders is known as a fill-or-kill order. This order must be filled immediately in its entirety or it is to be canceled. Note: Some markets no longer accept this type of order.

Immediate or Cancel (IOC)

Like the fill-or-kill order, this order must be acted on immediately. The difference is that this order will accept execution on any part of the order's quantity, and that portion not executable immediately will be canceled.

All or None (AON)

This is another variation of the fill-or-kill order. Like the fill-or-kill, this order must be filled in its entirety, but instead of having to be filled immediately, it must be filled over a stipulated period of time, such as a day. The broker or trader that accepts this order has agreed to fill it. If he or she is unable to, he or she owns the acquired shares, not the originator of the order. In the case of a sell AON order, the broker or trader owns the unsold shares. Note: Some markets do not allow this type of order.

Not Held (NH)

Each marketplace has its own set of rules and regulations. They govern the handling of orders, such as a buy market order, which must be filled against the current offer, or a sell market order, which must be filled against the current bid. But let's say the quote and size are 35.30–35.50, 100 × 100 and client Sal Amanda enters the market wanting to buy 50,000 shares "at the market." Ten thousand shares will be immediately executed at 35.50. Then the remainder will be executed against the next-higher offers until the order is filled. After the completion of the order, the market price of the shares will return to true current value. To avoid overpaying for large buy orders or receiving less than true market value for sell orders, Sal should enter a "not held" order, which relieves the broker or trader from the execution rules. The order will be executed using the best judgment of the broker or trader, in piecemeal over time, assuring Sal a fair price.

In addition, had Sal thrown the 50,000 share order on the market, either as a market order or, if Sal wanted to try the limit order route, as a limit order, any good seller of size would have backed away from the market to see how badly Sal wanted the stock. The higher the price Sal was willing to pay, the more money the seller would receive. Therefore, as the large order sellers pulled away, Sal would have been left trading with a lot of small executions. By entering the NH order, Sal's representative disguises the size of the order and has the time to "work it off" by entering and leaving the market with parts of the order.

Step
Step orders are a series of limit orders entered at ever-increasing (buy order) or decreasing (sell order) prices.

Spread
Spread orders are most common in trading exchange-listed options and futures. The strategy is explained in more detail in the chapters on particular products. But for here and now, an option spread order is equal numbers of long and short put or call positions on the same underlying product but with different contract terms. For example:

> Long 5 calls on Invicter Corp. expiring in April with a strike price of 50
> Short 5 calls on Invicter Corp. expiring in April with a strike price of 60

Usually, the less expensive option is being used to reduce cost if it is the short option or reduce risk if it is the long option

In futures, a spread order is long one future contract month and short a different future contract month on the same product or long a future contract month and short a related future contract month (such as soybeans and soybean oil). Depending on the setup of the position, the owner expects the difference between the two to widen or narrow so that when the position is closed out, a profit will exist.

Straddle
Straddle orders are used in listed options. A straddle order means long or short equal numbers of puts and calls on the same underlying product with the same (straddle) or different (combination) contract terms. For example:

Long 10 calls on Zappa Corp. expiring in May with a strike price
of 35

Long 10 puts on Zappa Corp. expiring in May with a strike price
of 35

The call and put are bought if the straddle is a long position. If both the put
and the call are sold, it is a short position.

· AGENCY VS. PRINCIPAL TRANSACTIONS ·

Trades are executed on an "agency" or "principal" basis. Those two words in
the financial industry have the same meaning as they do in other industries. For example, a real estate agent or an insurance agent does not own
the product he or she is offering and receives a commission for his or her
services. In the case of a real estate agent, the commission is subtracted
from the proceeds received from the sale of the property. An insurance
agent's compensation is subtracted from the premiums paid by the policy-
holder. Automobile dealers and appliance dealers operate on a principal
basis. They own the inventory they are selling and therefore have a financial interest in the product. Their compensation is based on the markup
added to the wholesale price of the item being sold. The same is true in the
financial industry.

When clients buy or sell securities on an "agency" basis, the broker-
dealers or financial intermediaries charge a commission. They are operating as brokers, or as conduits between buyer and seller. As such, they do
not have any financial interest in the transaction. When they are operating
on a principal basis, the price of the transaction includes a markup for buy
trades or a markdown for sell trades. As principals, they do have a financial
interest in the product, as they are selling it from their inventory or buying
it for their inventory accounts.

Common stocks that trade on a stock exchange are traded on an agency
basis, with very few exceptions. The quotes that are reflected are the prices
at which trades can occur. For example, say the quote on Zipper common
stock is 35.50–35.70. A buy market order for 100 shares would be filled and
reported at a price of 35.70. The client's trade confirmation would read as
follows:

Bought 100 shares of Zipper Corp. of America at 35.70

First money $3,570.00 [100 shares × 35.70]
Commission   70.00 [assuming a 2 percent commission charge]
Fee   10.00 [most firms charge processing fee]

Net money $3,650.00

If the over-the-counter quote for Downe Detubes Corporation common stock was 27.50–27.75, a broker-dealer acting as principal on a sell trade would include the markdown of $70 as part of first money, with a note on the client's confirmation stating that there was a charge of $70. The client's trade confirmation would look like this:

Sold 100 shares of Downe De Tubes Corp. at $26.80.

First money $2,680.00
Fee   10.00

Net money $2,670.00

We acted as principal on this trade and charged a fee of $70.

Or the markdown would appear on the confirmation as a charge in the same way that the commission on an agency trade is reflected:

First money $2,680.00
Charge   70.00
Fee   10.00

Net money $2,670.00

We acted as principal on this trade, and the charge is part of first money.

A big difference between agency and principal trades to the customer arises in the case of limit orders. The quote reflected in many principal-type markets is a "wholesale" quote, to which the markup or markdown must be applied to get the "retail" price. In the above example, had a customer entered a limit order to buy at $27.75 or sell at $27.50, the order would not have been executed because those prices didn't include the markup/markdown. In an agency transaction, commission is added to or subtracted from the execution price, not embedded in the price as it is in a principal transaction, so an agency trade would have been executed, whereas a principal trade would not have been. Therefore, individuals who place orders at the same or nearly the same price as a bid or offer should be cognizant of whether it is going to be a principal or agency transaction.

· WORKINGS OF THE MARKET ·

Now that we have covered some of the types of orders, let's put them to work and see how the market works. We will use an agency-type market where the highest announced bid and lowest announced offer are the current quote and the number of shares of common stock composing the quote is the size. (Note: As we trade in 100-share lots, the last two zeros are dropped.)

Step No.	Action	Results	Price	Bid	Offer	Bid Size	Offer Size
1	Buy and sell orders are paired off to establish opening quote and size. Those pending orders that do pair off are executed, leaving opening bid offer and size.	Opening quote and size		23.25	23.55	80	100

(continued)

Step No.	Action	Results	Price	Bid	Offer	Bid Size	Offer Size
2	Order entered to buy 1,000 shares at 23.30	Not executable. Order's price higher than current bid, so it becomes the new bid and size.		23.30	23.55	10	100
3	Order entered to buy 1,000 shares at market	Order executed against offer at 23.55. Size changes.	23.55	23.30	23.55	10	90
4	Order entered to sell 2,000 shares at 23.60	Nothing changes, as order has higher offer price than current market. Order is noted.		23.30	23.55	10	90
5	Order entered to sell 5,000 shares at 23.45	Order not executed but causes offer and size to change, as offer price is lower than current offer.		23.30	23.45	10	50
6	Order entered to buy 25,000 shares at 23.20	Nothing changes, as price of order is below current bid. Order is noted.		23.30	23.45	10	50

(continued)

Step No.	Action	Results	Price	Bid	Offer	Bid Size	Offer Size
7	Order entered to buy 5,000 shares at 23.45	Order executed at offer price. As it consumes all shares offered at that price, next-lowest-priced order(s) becomes new offer.	23.45	23.30	23.55	10	90
8	Order received to buy 20,000 shares at 23.40	No execution. Order replaces current bid, as its limit price is higher.		23.40	23.55	200	90
9	Order received to sell 10,000 shares at 23.70	Nothing changes, as order's limit is higher than current offer. Order is noted.		23.40	23.55	200	90
10	Order received to buy 10,000 shares at 23.55	9,000 of 10,000 shares executed against current offer. Remaining 1,000 shares become new bid. Offer becomes next lower-price offer. Order was entered in step 4.	23.55	23.55	23.60	10	20

(continued)

Step No.	Action	Results	Price	Bid	Offer	Bid Size	Offer Size
11	Order received to buy 25,000 shares at 23.60 FOK	Order canceled, as it calls for immediate execution of 25,000 shares and there are only 2,000 offered.		23.55	23.60	10	20
12	Order is received to buy 20,000 at 23.65	2,000 shares bought at 23.60 (offer). Remaining 18,000 become new bid, and order received in step 9 becomes the new offer.	23.60	23.65	23.70	180	100
13	Order received to sell 50,000 shares at 23.65 IOC	18,000 of the 50,000 shares sold at 23.65. Remaining 32,000 shares canceled. Next highest bid becomes new bid.	23.65	23.55	23.70	10	100
14	Order received to buy 3,000 shares at 23.60	Nothing executed. Quote and size change.		23.60	23.70	30	100
15	Market closes	Volume 35,000 shares Range: High 23.65 Low 23.45	Last sale 23.65	23.60	23.70	30	100

This is a static presentation of a trading day. The interaction between participants, the inter- and intramarket communications, and many other facets of a real market have been removed. There is also the assumption that previously entered orders are still active and have not been canceled. However, even in this basic form, the steps presented are correct.

An interesting facet of human behavior is how investors perceive their execution in relation to the stock's "last sale." Let's look at two investors. One bought the stock "above the last sale" and is annoyed because he feels that he was taken. The other bought the stock "below the last sale" and is happy because he received a "better price." Why did the one who is annoyed buy the stock in the first place? The stock was acquired on the expectation that it would rise in value. If it is bought at a price higher than the last sale, which way is it going, up or down? Why is the investor annoyed? The investor should be happy. And as to the one who is happy that the stock was bought below the last sale, which way is that stock going? That investor should be annoyed because the stock is moving downward.

The market that we have looked at is a hypothetical exchange market. These markets are considered to be of the agency type, where the members operate as brokers, executing orders for their clients. Therefore, the bids and offers are projected to be those of orders from those wanting to buy or sell securities and not from dealers who are acting as market makers and making two-sided markets (bid and offer). In an agency-type market (also known as an auction market), the highest bid and the lowest offer have priority over any lesser bid or higher offer. The highest bid and lowest offer compose the quote and must be addressed before any other bid or offer in that marketplace can be traded against. For example, say the quote is 34.20–34.50, there are 5,000 shares behind the bid, and there are 20,000 shares behind the offer. The next-lower bid is 34.15, and there are 10,000 shares behind that bid. A sell order for 10,000 shares is entered "at the market." The bid at 34.15 can fill the order, whereas the bid at $34.20 cannot. The highest bid is $34.20 for 5,000 shares and is the dominant bid. The next bid is $35.15 for 10,000 shares. The seller can execute the order one of two ways. One, the seller can sell 5,000 shares to the bid at $34.20 and 5,000 shares to the bid at $35.15, giving the seller two execution prices or include the $34.20 bidder in a sale of 10,000 shares at $34.15, getting one price for the lot and saving the bidder the cost of $.05 per share on the purchase of their 5,000 shares; a savings of $250 (5,000 × $.05 = $250).

While the seller lost the opportunity to earn the $250, the seller has in return one execution price, one trade to record, to reconcile, to figure tax consequences on, et cetera.

Over the years, the character of the markets have changed. What was once a retail-type market, with customers buying shares of stock in hundred-share lots, grew into an institutional-type market, where blocks of tens of thousands of shares of stock could be contained in one order. The volume of trading on regional exchanges also grew, making it difficult to assure the clients of broker-dealers that they were receiving the best prices. Arbitrageurs regularly took advantage of the idiosyncrasies between markets and took profit from $\frac{1}{8}$ to $\frac{1}{4}$ point on the price differences between the market prices at each marketplace.

Intermarket Trading System

To ensure that clients received the best price possible, the equity markets installed the Intermarket Trading System (ITS). Under this system, all the exchanges had to post the best bid and offer and their sizes through one central facility. The ITS system would post the best bid and best offer from among all the exchanges. Therefore, the bid and its size could be from the New York Stock Exchange (NYSE) and the offer and its size could be from the Chicago Stock Exchange (CHX). Orders routed to any of the marketplaces would respond to the best market price, regardless of the origin of the order. Marketplaces participating in the program were the American Stock Exchange, the Chicago Stock Exchange (then known as the Midwest Stock Exchange), the Cincinnati Stock Exchange, the New York Stock Exchange, the Pacific Coast Stock Exchange, and the Philadelphia Stock Exchange.

· THE OVER-THE-COUNTER (PRINCIPAL-TYPE) MARKET ·

More securities trade in the over-the-counter market than on listed exchanges. In addition, due to advancements in technology, many exchanges have moved away from the trading floor concept and offer electronic order routing, execution, and reporting systems, so it is hard to distinguish the over-the-counter from the electronic one. The basic difference is that the exchanges offer a broker market, whereas the over-the-counter market offers a dealer market. Simply put, in an exchange market, the highest bid and lowest offer "has the floor" and must be satisfied before trades can take place below the then-current bid or above the then-current offer. In the over-the-counter market, as the quote is primarily made up by dealers (market makers), the size of the order plays an important role in the execution. Let's look at Zapp common stock that trades in the over-the-counter environment.

ZAPP

	Bid	Offer	Size
Dealer A	45.20	45.60	50 × 50
Dealer B	45.30	45.70	100 × 100
Dealer C	45.40	45.80	80 × 80

The quote and size for the stock would appear as "45.40–.60, 80 × 50."

As these are negotiated markets, a broker-dealer with 1,000 shares to buy would go to Dealer A first, as Dealer A has the lowest offer price that can fill the order. A broker-dealer with 10,000 shares to buy would go to Dealer B first, as Dealer B has the best price for the size order the broker-dealer wants to trade. A broker-dealer with more than 10,000 shares to buy would call all three dealers to see which one would give the best price for the entire lot. It might be Dealer A, who, though not interested in the stock for his or her own trading inventory, knows of a party who might be interested in selling a lot of that size given an attractive price.

Therefore, unlike in the exchange markets, where the best bid or offer must be satisfied before you can trade around it, in the over-the-counter market, the best price that satisfies the terms of the order will prevail.

Many of the securities that trade in the over-the-counter market do not have enough depth of issue to support ongoing trading. Therefore, market makers (dealers and traders) will take down inventory and trade the instruments against their own customers and against other broker-dealers that are trading the instruments for themselves or on behalf of their own clients.

Market makers try to earn revenue on the "turnaround," which is the spread between their bid and their offer. A market maker's stock quote of 34.50–34.60 will gross the trader $10.00 per 100 shares bought and sold or sold and bought. Market makers will maintain a position in a security depending on their opinion of the issue. If they think the price of the issue will rise, they will maintain a "long" (ownership) position. If they think the value of the product will fall, they may maintain a short position. The goal is to complete the turnaround before the prices change.

Market makers earn a profit when they are right in their judgment and incur a loss when they are wrong. Market making is analogous to any other business. Market makers need inventory that people are interested in and want to trade. They must also be competitive pricewise. Traders are specialists in their product. A corporate bond trader cannot sit down and begin to trade options, nor can an option trader sit down and trade municipal bonds, and so on. To be successful, traders must understand their products, the markets in which they trade, and their public (whom they are trading for or against). It is the details therein that lead to success or failure.

Corporate bonds and U.S. Treasury bonds are issued in bullet form. This means that an entire issue is offered under one heading, e.g., "$10,000,000 ACHO 5% FA 20XX." In the industry we identify securities through the use of numbers. Our domestic numbering system is called CUSIP (Committee on Uniform Security Identification Procedure), and the international numbering system is called ISIN (International Security Identification Numbers). Domestically, every dollar of principal in this bond is the same as every other dollar of principal in the same bond. The classical municipal bond is issued in serial form. Take, for example, a bond called "$500,000,000 Centertown NL Waterworks." It might include several issues:

Amount	Coupon	Pay Dates	Maturity Date	Yield to Maturity
$10,000,000	5%	JJ	20XA (5-Year)	5.20%
$10,000,000	5%	JJ	20XB (6-year)	5.00%
$10,000,000	5.10%	JJ	20XC (7-year)	5.00%
$25,000,000	6.00%	JJ	20XO (20-year)	6.00%

Each issue is a stand-alone issue with its own identification numbers. As each issue is small in size, the demographics of a "muni" offering are that it is sold and over time pieces come back to the market.

· MUNICIPAL BOND MARKET ·

Due to the unique characteristics of municipal bonds, namely, individual issues of relatively small size, a particular issue cannot sustain trading. Investors are looking for certain characteristics in a muni that will satisfy their needs. First, the interest payments must not be taxed by the federal, state, or local governments. That limits what state of issuance an investor will consider. Second, the investor will consider the duration of the bond. Third, the investor will consider the bond's rating. And so on. The more criteria the investor puts forward, the fewer the choices of bonds will be. When the broker or other client representative reads the list of available muni bonds that satisfy the investor's needs, he or she omits the price and gives instead the yield to maturity. The investor is assumed to understand the relationship between the yield to maturity and the debt's coupon rate. The closer the basis price is to the coupon rate, the closer the instrument is to trading at par. If the basis price is higher than the bond's coupon rate, the bond is selling at a discount to par. If the basis price is below the coupon rate, the bond is selling above par. If they are the same, the bond is trading at par. *Par* is synonymous with the face amount. A $1,000-face-amount bond selling at par is at $1,000. U.S. Treasury bills are also quoted on a yield-to-maturity basis. The concept of basis pricing is covered in more detail in the municipal bond section of the debt chapter.

· THE THIRD MARKET ·

As the participation of institutions (mutual funds, pension funds, trust accounts, hedge funds) grew, the traditional exchange markets could not absorb the size of these transactions, so trading of securities listed on the exchanges moved away from the exchanges and into the over-the-counter environment forming the "third market." Broker-dealers that were exchange members, those that were nonmembers, and other institutions would trade exchange-listed securities in an over-the-counter environment. The only caveat was that exchange members had to "clean" off exchange specialists' books pending orders that could be executed at that time. As the market grew, nonmember firms began to "take down" blocks of stock from other firms and institutions and, using their contacts, complete the trades. Many times they would guarantee a price for the block and proceed to work against the guarantee. If the transaction was completed at a better average price than the guarantee, the intermediary firm profited; if it misjudged and the average price was worse than the guarantee, it incurred the loss.

· THE FOURTH MARKET ·

The fourth market is a spin on the third-market concept. In this market, institutions trade with institutions, without the facilitation of a broker. Market makers can deal directly with institutions, and vice versa. Communications between parties were carried on by an electronic communication network (ECN) such as SelectNet, Instinet (acquired by NASDAQ), and ArcaEx (acquired by the NYSE).(Note: ArcaEx is an exchange registered with the Securities and Exchange Commission and provides for the trading of over-the-counter stocks and options.)

· ECNs AND ALTERNATIVE TRADING SYSTEMS (ATS) ·

The term *fourth market* has been replaced by *ECNs* or *ATS*. ECN stands for electronic communication network. ATS stands for alternative trading system. The two go hand in hand. ATS are electronic trading platforms. Besides the ones mentioned above, there are BATS, Turquoise, Direct Edge ECN, Bloomberg's Tradebook, and others. These trading platforms can provide access to liquidity pools globally. They are trade-matching facilities, and their execution capability, liquidity, speed, and cost are paramount to their survival. Trades executed through these systems are done away from exchanges and do not get involved with the exchange's systems, prices, or order routing and execution facilities.

ECNs in the equity segment of the market must be registered with the Securities and Exchange Commission as alternative trading systems. Participants include banks, institutions, broker-dealers, and market makers. There are trading platforms for equities, currencies, and different types of debt instruments. The participants place orders into the system. These orders are usually limit orders. The orders are exposed to other participants. If an order is accepted, a trade occurs. Some trading systems permit price and/or quantity negotiations. The benefits that these systems offer are cost, anonymity, and speed of execution.

ECNs have a fee schedule that is lower than that found in the conventional marketplace. Some even pay a rebate for order flow and/or liquidity. The originator of the order is unknown to the perspective contra party. The reverse is true also. No one knows who wants to buy or sell at a particular moment. After a trade has occurred, the ECN sets itself up as the contra party. Even at that point, the true buyer doesn't know the true seller. The trades are reported to the respective clearing facilities for ultimate settlement. If a trade cannot be consummated at one ECN, it may be sent electronically to another. Again the originator will remain anonymous. In the search for liquidity, broker-dealers have begun to aggregate sources for supply. This has given way to the concept discussed in the next section.

· Dark Pools ·

A fairly new concept is "deep pools" of liquidity. Financial institutions and block-trading firms access each other's networks to locate pools of securities to be traded. These transactions are occurring away from the marketplace. They permit the parties to the trade to negotiate a price that will move the block, without concern for other orders. These trades are usually consummated at one price, making them less expensive to process, clear, and settle. There are crossing networks that permit participants to pass through to other dark pools, which adds even more liquidity.

The liquidity pools can be independent, broker-dealer–owned, or owned by a consortium.

· CONCLUSION ·

An ever-changing and dynamic part of the financial world, the markets have gone from a central meeting place in which to establish a fair price to a computer-driven executing platform that can receive an order, locate the other side, and execute it in a fraction of a second.

15

Equity Margin

· INTRODUCTION ·

The term *margin* takes on different meanings from product to product. In equities and corporate, municipal, and government debt it is ownership margin. In options, it takes the form of protection margin. In futures, margin is nothing more than a good-faith deposit, and so on. The intricacies of margin go much deeper than the space of this discussion permits. But the following should serve to clear up some of the mystery that surrounds the topic.

First of all, margin passes through three levels of regulations before it is applied to a client. At the federal level there is the Federal Reserve Board (FRB), the Securities and Exchange Commission (SEC), and the Commodity Futures Trading Commission (CFTC). The next level is the industry's self-regulatory organizations (SROs), led by the Financial Industry Regulatory Authority (FINRA), and the last level is the financial institution's own "house" rules. The rules at each level may be as stringent as or more stringent than those at the previous level, but never less stringent.

A client may have a "cash account" or a "cash and margin account." The type of account a client has depends on the purpose of the account. Some types of accounts, such as custodian accounts, are not permitted to be margin accounts. Within the cash and/or margin account, the client may be permitted to do other forms of trading. The type of trading permissible is controlled by regulation, what levels of trading the broker-dealer will permit, and the broker-dealers forms the client has completed. In addition to regulation and required forms, the client must satisfy the financial institution's own rules and requirements.

A customer choosing to purchase stock in a cash account is supposed to pay for it by the third business day and no later than the fifth business day after the trade date. Purchases in a margin account must be paid for by the third business day after the trade date.

The purpose of margin is twofold. One is to give the client leverage. With the margin requirement for equities at 50 percent, a client with a fixed sum of money to invest can acquire twice as much stock using margin, by borrowing the other half, as he or she could by paying for the securities in full. The other purpose is to permit the client to enter certain types of trading, such as short selling.

EXAMPLE

Client has $6,000 to invest.

Trade in a cash account	*Trade in a margin account*
100 shares of PUP @ $60	200 shares of PUP @ $60
$6,000 Current market value	$12,000 Current market value
−6,000 Equity	−6,000 Equity
$0 Money line	$6,000 Money line (loan)

While the client can earn two times as much with the margin purchase, the client can also lose twice as much. Even though he or she only paid for half of the purchase, the client owns all of the securities. On the amount borrowed, the client will pay interest via his or her account being charged at the end of the month.

The margin requirement for each type of security is different. This book will use equity securities to explain the mechanics of margin.

· Minimum Equity Requirement ·

According to the FINRA rules, before a firm can lend money to a client, the client must satisfy a $2,000 minimum equity requirement. That means that a client whose first purchase in a new margin account is for $1,500 worth of securities must pay for them in full. If that first purchase was for $2,100, the client would have to deposit $2,000 and the firm would lend the remaining $100. As the margin rate for common stock is 50 percent, the rate would kick in when the client purchased $4,000 worth of stock or more. It is important to note that many firms will not allow a client to open a margin account until the client can satisfy a much higher threshold. This higher threshold is necessary in today's market to protect the client and the firm alike from the account going into default.

Regulation T, or Reg. T, is the Federal Reserve's regulation covering the lending of money by broker-dealers to customers. It contains other requirement as well. The Reg. T margin requirement for common stock is 50 percent. Each class of security is assigned its own margin rate, depending on liquidity and volatility. Nonmarginable stock is said to have a margin requirement of 100 percent, which means the buyer must deposit the entire amount of the purchase price. Broker-dealers and banks have the right to set higher rates on an account-by-account basis if they perceive that the account's portfolio represents a higher-than-normal risk.

Whatever the margin rate for a type of security is, the loan value is its complement. If a client must deposit 50 percent (the margin rate), the firm can arrange to lend the other 50 percent (loan value). If the margin rate was 25 percent, as it is on investment-grade corporate bonds, the loan value would be 75 percent. The two together must always equal 100 percent. Broker-dealers have the right to charge a higher margin rate if they are of the opinion that the security position poses a greater-than-normal risk, but they may never charge a lower margin rate than required by the rules.

· PURCHASE OF A STOCK IN A
MARGIN ACCOUNT ·

Reg. T Excess and Buying Power

Let's assume a client, Amy Strate, purchases 1,000 shares of PUP stock at $30 per share. Amy deposits the minimum of 50 percent, or $15,000. Amy's account appears as follows:

Long 1,000 PUP @ $30 per share

Current market value (CMV)	$30,000
Equity (EQ)	−15,000
Debit balance (loan)	$15,000

Equity, in this case, is defined as what the client would receive if all security positions were converted and added to cash.

Pup increases to $40 per share. Now Amy's account looks like this:

Long 1,000 PUP @ $40 per share

Current market value (CMV)	$40,000
Equity (EQ)	−25,000
Debit balance (loan)	$15,000

At $40 dollars per share, Amy's equity rises to $25,000. For the equity in Amy's account to be at margin (50 percent) it would have to be $20,000. Therefore, her account has an excess equity of $5,000 or, using the loan side of the account, Amy can borrow up to $20,000 (50 percent of $40,000) but has only borrowed $15,000. Amy can borrow the remaining $5,000 as cash or use it to acquire more securities or do nothing. If she borrows the $5,000, the equity in her account will decrease to $20,000 and the debit balance will increase to $20,000, leaving her account as follows:

Long 1,000 PUP @ $40 per share

Current market value (CMV)	$40,000		= $40,000
Equity (EQ)	−25,000	− $5,000	= −20,000
Debit balance (loan)	$15,000	+ $5,000	= $20,000

What if Amy borrowed the excess $5,000, brought it to another broker-dealer, and deposited the money in her account there? What is the maximum dollar amount of stock that Amy could acquire with that money? The answer is $10,000. The margin conversion of excess is called buying power. As the margin rate is 50 percent, the converted excess to buying power is 2X excess. Say Amy purchases 100 shares of ZIP at $100 per share. Her account at the other broker will look as follows:

Long 100 ZIP @ $100 per share

Current market value (CMV)	$10,000
Equity (EQ)	−5,000
Debit balance (loan)	$ 5,000

If Amy can acquire the ZIP stock at a different broker-dealer using money that was borrowed from her account at the initial broker-dealer, she should be able to do the same transaction with the initial broker-dealer:

Long	1,000 PUP @ $40 per share		100 ZIP @ $100 per share	
Current market value (CMV)	$40,000		$10,000	= $50,000
Equity (EQ)	−25,000	− $5,000	+5,000	= 25,000
Debit balance (loan)	$15,000	+ $5,000	+$ 5,000	= $25,000

Amy bought the $10,000 worth of ZIP by borrowing $5,000 against the value of PUP and $5,000 against the value of the new ZIP shares. Her account is back in perfect margin.

Long 1,000 shares PUP @ $40 = $40,000
Long 100 shares ZIP @ 100   =   10,000

CMV = $50,000
− EQ =   25,000

Debit balance = $25,000

The equity and the debit balance are both at 50 percent. The margin conversion of excess is called *buying power*. In this case, the $5,000 excess allowed the purchase of $10,000 worth of securities without the client having to deposit any additional funds.

As the market value of the stock continues to climb, more excess is created, which in turn can be used as buying power, borrowed as cash, or left alone. Each time the excess is used, however, the debit balance (loan) increases. The client is paying interest on the debit balance, as the client would on any loan. The interest is charged on a monthly basis.

Maintenance

Let's assume the value of the securities in Amy's account began to decrease in value. FINRA rules say the equity in the account cannot be less than 25 percent of the market value; conversely, the debit balance cannot be more than 75 percent of the market value. With the account as it now stands, to what level can the market value fall before the firm will have to call the client for more collateral (cash and/or fully paid-for margin securities)? As the market value decreases, so does the client's equity. The debit balance remains untouched by changes in the market value. Therefore, focusing in on the debit balance of $25,000, since it cannot be more than 75 percent of the market value, the equity cannot be less than 25 percent, which is $8,333.33 (25 percent is $\frac{1}{3}$ of 75 percent, and $\frac{1}{3}$ of $25,000 is $8,333). If the debit balance is $25,000 (75 percent) and the equity is $8,333.33 (25 percent), then market value cannot be less than $33,333.33 (100 percent).

Market value	$33,333.33 (100%)
Less equity	8,333.33 (25%)
Debit balance	$25,000.00 (75%)

The previous computation is based on FINRA requirements. Broker-dealers use a maintenance rate that is higher. Theirs is known as a "house requirement." The house rate may be 30 percent or 35 percent. The higher rate is used for several reasons, including the fact that if a client's account falls below "house," the firm is not in immediate violation of regulatory requirements. For a financial institution using 30 percent as the point to call for additional collateral, the account's figures would be:

Market value	$35,714.29 (100%)
Less equity	10,714.29 (30%)
Debit balance	$25,000 (70%)

Call for Collateral

Using regulatory requirements (equity at a minimum of 25 percent), let's suppose the market value in the above account fell below the $33,333.33 to $30,000. The account would be "on call for more collateral." The account would now stand as follows:

Market value	$30,000 (100%)
Less equity	5,000 (16.67%)
Debit balance	$25,000 (83.33%)

A market value of $30,000 requires equity of $7,500 (25 percent). As the equity is currently $5,000, the client will receive a call for $2,500. When the money is received, the account will look as follows.

Market value	$30,000 (100%)	$30,000 (100%)
Less equity	5,000 (16.67%) + 2,500 =	7,500 (25%)
Debit balance	$25,000 (83.33%) − 2,500 =	$22,500 (75%)

What if the client deposited securities instead of cash? The client would have to deposit enough fully paid-for marginable securities so that the loan value (50 percent) on those securities would satisfy the call. A call of $2,500 would require a deposit of $5,000 worth of stock, because the maximum loan value on the stock is only 75 percent. The stock being deposited would be applied 100 percent to the market value and the equity. As the account is on call, the stock being received has a "release" of 75 percent. Therefore, $5,000 will release $3,750 (75 percent).

When the stock is added to the account:

Market value	$30,000 (100%)	+ $5,000 =	$35,000 (100%)
Less equity	5,000 (16.67%)	+ $5,000 =	10,000 (28.6%)
Debit balance	$25,000	0	$25,000 (71.4%)

However, the 75 percent release from the $5,000 is $3,750. When added to the $5,000 equity it is $8,750, which satisfies the 25 percent of market value maintenance requirement ($35,000 × .25 = $8,750).

After the stock deposit, the balance in the account meets or exceeds the minimum requirement.

What if the client liquidated securities to meet the call? As only 25 percent of the stock's value can be attributed to equity, the client would have to liquidate four times the amount of the call, or $10,000 ($2,500 × 4). The account would look like this:

Market value	$30,000 (100%) − $10,000	=	$20,000 (100%)
Less equity	5,000 (16.67%)	=	5,000 (25%)
Debit balance	$25,000 (83.33%) −$10,000	=	$15,000 (75%)

The resulting account balances exceed the maintenance requirements, but the $2,500 call has been satisfied by the loan value of the newly deposited marginable stock.

· SHORT SALE OF STOCK ·

A short sale of stock is the opposite of a long purchase. Besides the fact that a buyer of stock wants the price to increase, whereas the short seller wants it to decrease, the buyer of stock on margin is borrowing money to acquire the stock and therefore has a debit balance in his or her account. The short seller is borrowing stock and therefore has a credit balance. A debit balance in the customer's account signifies an asset to the firm, as the client owes the firm the debit amount. A credit balance in the customer's account signifies a liability, as the firm owes the client money. In addition, the client's equity in a long margin account is a result of the interaction between the market value of the securities and the money line (debit/credit balance). The equity in a short margin account is the money line residing in the margin account.

In the case of a sale of securities, the buyer doesn't care if the seller is delivering stock that he or she owns (long sale) or borrowing the stock to make delivery (short sale). In either case, the buyer wants the stock. Selling stock short might be done for two reasons. Both require the borrowing of stock to make the delivery. In the first instance, the seller is selling stock that he or she does not currently own in the expectation of buying it back at a later date at a lower price. In the second case, the seller is implementing some tax strategy, arbitrage, or hedge.

Say Mark Tyme has been watching the Rapid Internet Module (RAM) Company and the movement of its stock, which is currently trading between $58–$60 a share. Based on Mark's research, he believes that the company will not do too well over the next few years and thinks the stock could fall to the mid-$40s. Mark, who doesn't own the stock, wants to sell 1,000 shares short and contacts his broker, who, through the firm's operations area, arranges to borrow the required stock. The 1,000 shares are sold at $59 per share, and the borrowed stock is delivered to the buyer.

Mark must deposit Reg. T margin of 50 percent into his margin account, with the short sale residing in Mark's short-type account. Mark's account looks like this:

Margin Account	Short Account
$29,500 credit (50%)	SS 1,000 RAM @ 59 = $59,000
	$59,000 credit

Note: The $59,000 in the short account does not belong to the client. It is "booked" there as collateral against the stock that was borrowed on behalf of the client. The monetary value in the short account must represent the current market value of the stock at all times, as it is what will be used to "cover" (buy in) the short sale when it is closed out.

Let's assume the stock falls in value to $49 per share. All that is required in the short account to secure the borrowed stock is $49,000. The $49,000 is subtracted from the $59,000, and the $10,000 difference is moved over to Mark's margin account:

Margin Account   *Short Account*
$39,500 credit   SS 1,000 RAM @ 49 = $49,000
                          $49,000 credit

The margin required for a short sale of 1,000 shares of stock at $49 is $24,500 (50 percent of $49,000). Mark's margin account has a credit balance of $39,500. As only $24,500 is required for margin, Mark's account has Reg. T excess of $15,000 ($39,500 − $24,500 = $15,000). Mark may withdraw this money; unlike a long purchase, this is not a loan but Mark's money (credit balance). Or Mark may use the excess in the same way he would if the excess was created in a long account.

The best outcome for Mark's investment would be if RAM became worthless. Then all of the money that is locked in Mark's short account would move over to Mark's margin account. Mark would then close out the short position by purchasing the worthless stock and closing out the position or waiting for the stock to be written off by the firm.

But what if the stock rose in value? Money would be taken from Mark's equity in his margin account and moved into his short account to keep the borrowed security secured. At some point, Mark would run out of money in his margin account. The rules do not let the situation deteriorate that far. The rules state that the equity in a margin account cannot be below 30 percent of the market value. Short sales of stock below $10 per share cannot be below 30 percent of the market value or $2.50, whichever is higher.

With the account as it stood at the time the short sale was made, Mark's equity was $29,500. The maintenance requirement was $17,700 (30 percent of the market value), giving Mark a cushion of $11,800 ($29,500 − $17,700 = $11,800).

Margin Account   *Short Account*
$29,500 credit (50%)   SS 1,000 RAM @ 59 = $59,000
                          $59,000 credit
Maintenance $17,700

Suppose the stock rose one point to $60 per share.

$1,000 would be transferred from the margin account to the short account to keep the borrowed security secure. At the same time, the maintenance requirement crawled by $300 (or $.30 per share). Mark's cushion is now $10,500 ($60,000 × .30 = $18,000 and $28,500 − $18,000 = $10,500), a reduction of $1,300 (or $1.30 per share). This would repeat for each point the stock moved against Mark until the equity in the account and the maintenance requirement crossed.

If the stock rose from $59 to $60, the account would look like this:

Margin Account	Short Account
$28,500 credit	SS 1,000 RAM @ 60 = $60,000
	$60,000 credit
Maintenance $18,000	

To discover that crossover point, we will take the "cushion" and divide it by $1.30 per share, or in this case, since there are 1,000 shares, $1,300. Because $10,500 divided by $1,300 is 8.077, if the stock rose 8.077 points, the account would be on call. After moving $8,077 from Mark's equity position in his margin account to his short account, we have the following balances:

Margin Account	Short Account
$20,423 credit	SS 1,000 RAM @ 68.077
	$68,077 credit
Maintenance $20,423	

Caution: **When you purchase stock on margin, the most likely circumstance in which you will have to close out the position is if the stock's price decreases and you no longer want to support the increasing maintenance requirement. When you sell short, a similar situation could arise; the stock price might continue to rise and you might no longer want to satisfy the increasing maintenance requirement. Short sales carry another risk; the supply of loanable stock could dry up, forcing the short seller to buy the stock back in and return it to the lending party. The short seller has no control over this, and it is part of the risk assumed by selling short.**

While a short sale is in place, the short seller must keep the security lender whole. If the company pays a dividend, it will pay it to only one owner, and the buyer of the short-sold stock is that owner, because he or she owns the stock. The stock lender must look to the short seller for remuneration. Therefore, the short seller has an out-of-pocket expense, as he or she must pay the stock lender the dividend it is entitled to. The same is true with any other corporate distribution. If there is a rights offering, the short seller must go into the market and buy and deliver the required number of rights due the stock lender, and so on. The only corporate action the short seller cannot act on is the right to vote. The voting privilege has passed from the lending owner of the stock to the new buyer. There isn't any way for the short seller to make the lender whole. The new owner has that right, whereas the security lender has forfeited that privilege.

· SPECIAL MEMORANDUM ACCOUNT (SMA) ·

A special memorandum account (SMA) is not special, nor is it an account. Other than that, it is properly named. It is a memo field that records events that were not used at the time they occurred but could (under certain circumstances) be used at a later date.

For example, say Amy Strate bought 1,000 shares of PUP at $30. The stock rose to $40, giving Amy $5,000 excess. Amy could have used the excess to acquire $10,000 worth of ZIP, but what if she didn't? The $5,000 would be stored in the SMA. The $5,000 would remain in Amy's SMA until she used it. The account's condition at any given time would be the determining factor. As Amy used the SMA, the debit balance in her account would increase. Therefore, if her SMA grew to a huge balance, or if the market value fell, she could only use that portion of the SMA that would not trigger a margin call for more collateral.

Let's add another two clients, Randi Miles and Craig Zemann. Both purchased 1,000 shares of Wow at $40 per share in their margin accounts and met the Reg. T (50 percent) requirement.

Randi Miles Account - SMA		Craig Zeeman Account - SMA	
CMV	$40,000	CMV	$40,000
Equity	−20,000	Equity	−20,000
Debit	$20,000	Debit	$20,000

(continued)

Randi Miles Account - SMA			Craig Zeeman Account - SMA		
The stock rises to $50.					
CMV	$50,000		CMV	$50,000	
Equity	−30,000		Equity	−30,000	
Debit	$20,000		Debit	$20,000	
Loan value	$25,000		Loan value	$25,000	
Debit	−20,000 Reg. T		Debit	−20,000 Reg. T	
Reg. T Excess	$5,000		Reg. T excess	$5,000	

Craig withdraws the excess, and Randi does not.

CMV	$50,000	$5,000	CMV	$50,000	$0
Equity	−30,000		Equity	−25,000	
Debit	$20,000		Debit	$25,000	

The stock rises to $60.

CMV	$60,000	$5,000	CMV	$60,000	$0
Equity	−40,000		Equity	−35,000	
Debit	$20,000		Debit	$25,000	
Loan value	$30,000		Loan value	$30,000	
Debit	−20,000		Debit	−25,000	
Reg. T excess	$10,000		Reg. T excess	$5,000	

Craig withdraws the excess, and Randi does not.

CMV	$60,000	$10,000	CMV	$60,000	$0
Equity	−40,000		Equity	−30,000	
Debit	$20,000		Debit	$30,000	

Note: As $5,000 was already captured in Randi's SMA when the stock rose to $50 per share only the excess generated when the stock moved from $50 to $ 60 per share ($5,000) is added to Randi's SMA.

The stock falls in price to $50 per share.

The loan value at $50 per share is $25,000. Randi's account has a debit balance of $20,000 and therefore has a Reg. T excess of $5,000. However, Craig has borrowed $10,000 during this period and is not being called for money. So why can't Randi? She doesn't. The stock falls in price to $40 per share.

Maintenance requirement on Craig's account

CMV	$40,000 (100%)
Equity	−10,000 (25%)
Debit	$30,000 (75%)

If Randi had borrowed the $10,000 that is in the SMA, her account would be the same as Craig's is now. Therefore, since Craig was allowed to borrow $10,000, there isn't any reason why Randi shouldn't be allowed to do the same.

Focusing on Craig's account, if the market value in his account fell to $38,000, Craig's account would be on call:

1) Current market value = $38,000
   Equity   = −8,000 (21%)
   Debit   = $30,000 (79%)

2) Equity must be equal to or greater than 25 percent of the market value.
   25% of $38,000 = $9,500
   Current equity is = $8,000
   Deficit   = $1,500

A maintenance call goes to Craig's for $1,500 and Craig satisfies it.

3) Current market value = $38,000 (100%)
   Adjusted equity   = −9,500 (25%)
   Adjusted debit   = $28,500 (75%)

Let's focus on Randi's account. If the market value fell to $38,000, Randi's account would not be on call:

1) Current market value = $38,000 (100%)

   Equity   = −18,000 (47%)

   Debit   = $20,000 (53%)

2) Equity must be equal to or greater than 25 percent of the market value.

25% of $38,000	= $9,500
Equity in account	= $18,000
Excess over minimum ($18,000 − $9,500)	= $8,500

3) If Randi withdrew the excess, the account would have the same balance as Craig's account did after he satisfied the maintenance call.

CMV	$38,000
Equity	$9,500
Debit	$28,500

While Randi's account does not have any Reg. T excess, it does have an SMA of $10,000. If Randi used the entire SMA balance, her account would have the same balances Craig's account had when it went on call for additional collateral. Randi can use the part of the SMA that will not cause a call. The sum that can be used is the amount of equity ($8,500) that is above what is required to support the market value (25 percent of $38,000 = $9,500).

Randi's account before the use of the SMA:

Debit	= $20,000
Loan value	= $19,000 (50% of the market value)
Reg. T excess =	$0

Randi's account after withdrawing $8,500 from the SMA:

SMA	= $10,000	CMV	$38,000
Withdrawal	= −$8,500	Equity	−$9,500
SMA Balance =	$1,500	Debit	$28,500

This is an example of "house excess," or the amount the account's equity exceeds the house requirement.

The SMA plays an important role in the operation of a margin account. In addition to being adjusted for Reg. T excess increases, it is also adjusted for sales in a client's accounts, for dividends and interest payments, and more. For example, when a stock purchase is made in a margin account, the 50 percent requirement must be satisfied. When that stock is sold, 50 percent of the proceeds of the sale may be removed or released to SMA. The only time the SMA is reduced is when the account's principal uses it.

· Portfolio Margin ·

The Securities and Exchange Commission has recently granted owners of accounts with large positions a new way to calculate their margin requirements. This is currently a pilot program that is based on computer program risk models. The account's positions are looked at holistically rather than on a position-by-position basis, and an assessment of possible risk is made. Based on that assessment, margin is charged. The computer model that is used must be approved by a self-regulatory organization (SRO) such as FINRA.

16

Option Margin

INCLUDED IN THIS CHAPTER:

- *Introduction*
- *Uncovered Option Position*
- *Spreads*
- *Straddle (Combination)*

· INTRODUCTION ·

The purpose of this section is to give the reader a basis for comparing equity margin (ownership margin) to option margin (protection margin). If there isn't any risk to the firm, either at present or during the life of the option position, margin is not required. If an option is bought that has less than nine months of life, the purchase must be paid for in full. An option issued for longer than nine months (known as a long-term equity anticipation security, or LEAPS) may be purchased on margin. The margin requirement is 75 percent. A writer (seller) of a covered option, one that is backed by the security or a long (owned) option with more value and equal or longer time remaining, is called a covered option. Margin is not required for the short option.

The formula for the margin requirement on an uncovered written equity call option is 20 percent of the underlying market value, plus the premium, less the out-of-the-money sum or 10 percent of the underlying market value plus the premium (whichever is greater), with a minimum of

$250 per option contract. The formula for the margin requirement on an uncovered put is the same, except it is 10 percent applied to the option exercise price instead of the market price in the second uncovered option computation.

· UNCOVERED OPTION POSITION ·

EXAMPLE

Sonny Raye sells 1 call PUP Apr 50 @ 2. PUP is now trading at $47 per share. Nobody would call in 100 shares of PUP and pay $50 per share (the exercise price of the option) when PUP is trading at $47. Therefore, PUP is "out of the money" by 3 points. The margin calculation for this uncovered call is:

20% of the underlying value ($4,700)	$ 940.00
plus the premium	200.00
	$1,140.00
less the out-of-the-money sum	−300.00
	$ 840.00

OR

10% of the underlying value ($4,700)	$470.00
plus the premium	200.00
	$670.00

with a minimum of $250 per contract

Using whichever is greater, the margin requirement is $840.00.

EXAMPLE

Peg Bord sells 1 put BOW Jul 60 @ 1, with BOW trading at $62 per share. Nobody would buy BOW common stock at $62 per share and "put it out" at $60 per share, so the option is out of the money by 2 points. The margin calculation for this uncovered put is:

20% of the underlying value ($6,200)	$1,240.00
plus the premium	100.00
	$1,340.00
less the out-of-the-money sum	−200.00
	$1,140.00

OR

10% of the exercise price ($6,000)	$600.00
plus the premium	100.00
	$700.00

with a minimum of $250 per contract

Using whichever is greater, the margin requirement is $1,140.

· SPREADS ·

Option spreads are more intricate. A spread is defined as having equal numbers of long and short options of the same type (put or call) but different series. If the long option expires on or after the short option and is the more valuable one, no margin is required; the account's principal pays the required difference.

EXAMPLE
Patty Kaick buys 1 call ZOW Nov 30 @ 6 and sells 1 call ZOW Nov 35 @ 2. Patty pays the difference of 4 points. The 30-strike-price call is the more valuable one (the lower-strike-price call with the same amount of time remaining always has the greater value), and they both expire the same month. There isn't any exposure to the firm, so margin is not required.

EXAMPLE
Lauren Auder buys 1 put RAM Jul 30 @ 4 and sells 1 put RAM Nov 25 @ 3. Even though the 30-strike-price put has more value, the put that was sold expires after the long put, opening the firm to risk for the period after the long put expires. Lauren pays the difference of 1 point and must post margin on the short (sold)

option as if the sold option were an uncovered position. RAM is trading at 27. The margin calculation is:

20% of the underlying value ($2,700)	$ 540.00
plus the premium	300.00
	$ 840.00
less the out-of-the-money sum	−200.00
	$ 640.00

OR

10% of the exrcise price ($2,500)	$250.00
plus the premium	300.00
	$550.00

with a minimum of $250 per contract

Using whichever is greater, the margin required is $ 640.

EXAMPLE

Rob Abank buys 1 put DOG Nov 50 @ 2 and sells 1 put DOG Nov 55 @ 4. DOG is trading at 53. The short (sold) option position has more value, but as the long (bought) options expire with or after the short option, spread margin is applied.

Spread margin is the difference between the strike prices of the two positions or the margin required on the short option if it was an uncovered position, whichever is less.

The difference between the strike prices of 55 and 50 is 5, or a total of $500 for 100 shares.

The margin calculation for an uncovered option is as follows:

20% of the underlying value ($5,300)	$1,060,00
plus the premium	400.00
	$1,460.00
less the out-of-the-money sum	0
	$1,460.00

Note: The option with the strike price of 55 is in the money, as the stock can be acquired at $53 per share and "put out" at $55 per share.

OR

10% of the exercise price ($5,500)	$550.00
plus the premium	400.00
	$950.00

Use whichever is greater (with a minimum of $250 per contract), in this case $1,460.

In spread margin, the lower of the difference between strike prices (here, $500) or the calculation for an uncovered margin (here, $1,460) is used, as it represents the minimum necessary to cover the risk to the firm. Therefore, the margin required for this position is $500 because that represents the maximum the firm and customer have at risk.

Assuming the stock is trading at $47, and someone exercises the put against the client's short (sold) 55-strike-price position. The client must take in the stock, which is only worth $4,700, and pay $5,500. The client turns around and exercises the 50-strike-price option that he owns, delivers out of the stock that he paid $5,500 for, and receives $5,000 against the delivery of the exercise, for a loss of $500, which is what the margin requirement is.

· STRADDLE (COMBINATION) ·

A straddle is the buying or selling or positioning of equal numbers of puts or calls. If both positions have the same series description, it is a "straddle." If they are different, it is referred to as a combination.

EXAMPLE
Allie Wei buys 1 Call ZIP Aug 50 @ 5 and buys 1 Put ZIP Aug 45 @ 2, for a total cost of 7 points. As this combination contains a long position call and a long position put, Allie pays for both options in full, and margin is not required as there isn't any risk to the broker-dealer.

Carol Leiner sells one call WIP Mar 60 @ 3 and sells 1 put WIP Mar 60 @ 2. WIP common stock is trading at 62. As this straddle contains a short put and a short call, the margin requirement is the uncovered margin from the greater side, plus the premium from the other side.

	Call	Put
20% of underlying value	$1,240	$1,240
plus the premium	300	200
	$1,540	$1,440
less the out-of-the-money sum	0	−200
	$1,540	$1,240

OR

	Call	Put
10% of underlying value	$ 620	exercise price = $ 600
plus the premium	300	200
	$ 920	$ 820

with a $250-per-option minimum

Take the requirement from the greater side ($1,540) plus the premium from the other side ($200) to arrive at the requirement ($1,740).

As there are many possible combinations that include the use of options entirely or partially, margin is always calculated to the minimum risk.

For example, if the position is long 100 shares of stock and short 2 calls, one call is covered and you would compute margin on the other call as an uncovered option.

If the customer is long stock long and short equal numbers of puts and calls, rearrange the position so the account is boiled down to the lowest possible risk. This may be accomplished by pairing the calls or puts off as spreads, pairing the puts and calls off as straddles, et cetera.

There are other applications for margin, as there are other products that have options traded on them.

17

Future Margin

· INTRODUCTION ·

A future margin is a good-faith deposit.

The third type of margin is more of a good-faith deposit than any of the above. It has its roots (no pun intended) in the agricultural industry, when farmers would sell their crops before they were grown so that they could lock in the revenue they would receive at delivery time months later. On the other side was the product user, who was trying to cap the cost of the commodity and not be suddenly surprised by a spike in prices or other risks.

· FUTURE MARGIN ·

The exchange on which the product trades sets the margin. It is based on a concept known as value at risk. By tracking a product, the frequency of sudden, severe price changes can be monitored and the product's price range determined. The range is then applied to the margin formula.

For this example, the product used will be a fictional one called widgets. The six-month widget is trading at $1 per widget. The exchange has set the contract size at 100,000 widgets. Standard margin is set at $5,000 per contract, and maintenance margin is set $2,000 per contract.

Day 1:

Bill Zender	Bea Quick
buys 1 widget 6-mo.	sells 1 widget 6-mo.
contract @ $1	contract @ $1

At the present time there are four interests involved: (1) Bill Zender, (2) the firm representing Bill Zender, (3) Bea Quick, and (4) the firm representing Bea Quick. Bill's contract states that Bill will not pay more than $100,000 for the widgets, and Bea's contract states that she will receive $100,000 and her money back when she delivers the widgets

Bill and Bea both post the standard margin of $5,000.

Bill Zender		Bea Quick	
long 1 widget 6-mo. contract @$1		short 1 widget 6-mo. contract @ $1	
standard margin	$5,000 credit	standard margin	$5,000 credit
Account Balance	$5,000 credit	Account Balance	$5,000 credit

Day 2: Widgets close at $1.01. Bill has a paper profit of $1,000. Bea has a loss of the same amount. To allow both firms to honor their clients' contracts, Bea's account is charged $1,000 and Bill's account is credited the amount. This process is known as variation margin.

Bill Zender		Bea Quick	
Price at $1.01		Price at $1.01	
long 1 widget 6-mo. contract @ $1		short 1 widget 6-mo. contract @ $1	
standard margin	$5,000 credit	standard margin	$5,000 credit
variation margin	+1,000	variation margin	−1,000
Account Balance	$6,000 credit	Account Balance	$4,000 credit

The daily adjustment, known sometimes as P&S-ing, is performed so that the firms can honor the contract. Suppose delivery is to occur at $1.01. Bea is supposed to receive $100,000 for the widgets and her $5,000 margin deposit back. The delivery is made at $1.01 for $101,000 plus the funds that are in her account ($4,000) for a total of $105,000. Bill's contract states that he will pay $100,000 for the widgets. Bill has already deposited $5,000 for standard margin, so he deposits $95,000 more to fulfill his commitment. The firm takes the $100,000 plus the $1,000 variation margin and acquires the widgets at $1.01 per widget. What happened to Bea's loss of $1,000? Bea could have received $101,000 had she not had the contracts and sold them at delivery time. Bill's profit is buried in the fact that he paid $100,000 for $101,000 worth of widgets.

Day 3: Widgets close at $0.99. Bill's and Bea's accounts must be adjusted for the 2-point drop in price from the previous day to enable their firms to honor their contracts.

Bill Zender	*Bea Quick*
Price at $.99	Price at $.99
long 1 widget 6-mo.	short 1 widget 6-mo.
contract @ $1.00	contract @ $1.00
standard margin $6,000 credit	standard margin $4,000 credit
variation margin −2,000	variation margin +2,000
Account Balance $4,000 credit	Account Balance $6,000 credit

If delivery was to occur at $.99, the firm representing Bea would deliver the widgets and receive $99,000. The firm would add to the $99,000 the $6,000 balance in Bea's account, for a total of $105,000, exactly what Bea is owed. In effect, Bea would have been paid $100,000 for $99,000 worth of widgets. Bill would still owe $95,000 to fulfill the terms of his contract. The firm would take Bill's $95,000 and the $4,000 balance from Bill's account and acquire the widgets for $99,000. Bill would have paid $100,000 ($5,000 initially, then $95,000 later, for a total of $100,000) for $99,000 worth of widgets.

Day 4: Widgets continue to lose value and close at $.96 per widget. When the accounts are adjusted to reflect the latest price, Bill's account balance will be below $2,000, which is the maintenance level, and will trigger a call.

Bill Zender	*Bea Quick*
Price at $.96	Price at $.96
long 1 widget 6-mo.	short 1 widget 6-mo.
contract @ $1	contract @ $1.00
standard margin $5,000 credit	standard margin $5,000 credit
variation margin −4,000	variation margin +4,000
Account Balance $1,000 credit	Account Balance $9,000 credit

Unlike equity and option margins, where a maintenance call is issued to bring the account back to the minimum level, in futures the maintenance call is used to bring the account back to standard margin. Therefore, Bill will get a call for $4,000. When it is received in his account, the account will have these balances:

Bill Zender
long 1 widget 6-mo. contract @ $1.00
standard margin $9,000 credit
variation margin   −4,000
_____

Account Balance $5,000 credit
_____

Day 5: Widgets fall to $.95, and the accounts are adjusted:

Bill Zender	Bea Quick
Price at $.95	Price at $.95
long 1 widget 6-mo. contract @ $1	short 1 widget 6-mo. contract @ $1
standard margin $9,000 credit	standard margin $5,000 credit
variation margin −5,000	variation margin +5,000
_____	_____
Account Balance $4,000 credit	Account Balance $10,000 credit

If delivery occurred at $.95, Bea's widgets would be delivered through the firm representing her contract, and she would get paid $95,000. The firm would take that money, add to it the $10,000 balance remaining in Bea's account, and pay her $105,000. In effect, Bea has received $100,000 for the widgets, as the contract calls for, and her $5,000 back. As Bill has now paid $9,000, he owes $91,000 more. He pays the $91,000 to the firm representing his contract, which in turn takes the $91,000 and the balance in his account of $4,000 and buys the widgets for $95,000. In effect, Bill has paid $100,000 for the widgets.

A word of caution: In the previous examples, we compared a buyer and a seller. We will now compare a buyer and a greedy buyer to point out a serious pitfall.

Bill Zender
long 1 widget 6-mo.
 contract @ $1.00
standard margin $5,000 credit
  —————
Account Balance $5,000 credit
  —————

Tom Aytto
long 1 widget 6-mo.
 contract @ $1.00
standard margin $5,000 credit
  —————
Account Balance $5,000 credit
  —————

Widgets increase in price to $1.05.

Bill Zender
Price at $1.05
long 1 widget 6-mo.
 contract @ $1.00
standard margin $5,000 credit
variation margin   +5,000
  —————
Account Balance $10,000 credit
  —————

Tom Aytto
Price at $1.05
long 1 widget 6-mo.
 contract @ $1.00
standard margin $5,000 credit
variation margin   +5,000
  —————
Account Balance $10,000 credit
  —————

Tom realizes that if he used the variation margin he could buy a second contract, as standard margin is $5,000 per contract. However, by doing so, he would negate his $1.00-per-widget contract, as he has removed the firm's ability to honor that price. He would have two contracts at $1.05 and be making $2,000 per point instead of $1,000.

Bill Zender
Price at $1.05
long 1 widget 6-mo.
 contract @ $1.00
standard margin $5,000 credit
variation margin   +5,000
  —————
Account Balance $10,000 credit
  —————

Tom Aytto
Price at $1.05
long 2 widget 6-mo.
 contract @ $1.05
standard margin $10,000 credit
variation margin   0
  —————
Account Balance $10,000 credit
  —————

The widgets continue to gain value. At $1.10, the two accounts have these balances:

Bill Zender	*Tom Aytto*
Price at $1.05	Price at $1.05
long 1 widget 6-mo.	long 2 widget 6-mo.
contract @ $1.00	contract @ $1.05
standard margin $5,000 credit	standard margin $10,000 credit
variation margin +10,000	variation margin +10,000
Account Balance $15,000 credit	Account Balance $20,000 credit

Tom takes his variation margin and buys two more contracts, so that he now has 4 contracts at $1.10 and is making $4,000 a point.

Bill Zender	*Tom Aytto*
Price at $1.10	Price at $1.10
long 1 widget 6-mo.	long 4 widget 6-mo.
contract @ $1.00	contract @ $1.10
standard margin $5,000 credit	standard margin $20,000 credit
variation margin +10,000	variation margin 0
Account Balance $15,000 credit	Account Balance $20,000 credit

The market for widgets falls to $1.06. Now the accounts' balances are:

Bill Zender	*Tom Aytto*
Price at $1.06	Price at $1.06
long 1 widget 6-mo.	long 4 widget 6-mo.
contract @ $1.00	contract @ $1.10
standard margin $5,000 credit	standard margin $20,000 credit
variation margin +6,000	variation margin −16,000
Account Balance $11,000 credit	Account Balance $4,000 credit

As maintenance is $2,000 per contract, Tom's account needs a minimum balance of $8,000 ($2,000 × 4 contracts = $8,000). Tom receives a call to bring the account back to standard margin ($5,000 per contract × 4 contracts = $20,000 − the balance of $4,000 that is in the account = $16,000). His $5,000 investment is now costing Tom $16,000. Even if Tom liquidated the position, he would still owe $16,000, having owned 4 contracts at $1.10 and sold them out at $1.06. Bill, on the other hand, liquidates the one contract at $1.06 and walks away with a $6,000 profit on a $5,000 investment.

· SPAN Margin (Standardized Portfolio Analysis of Risk) ·

Future traders use options on futures to augment their positions. Those who trade against the public respond to public orders and limit their risk by offsetting these transactions with future options and the different future months that are trading. In addition, some strategists may be "running" three or more strategies at one time. Of concern to the firm is what risks or exposures are inherent in the multitude of positions. SPAN margin looks at the account as a unit, not as positions. The future exchanges use SPAN margin to assess their members, the margin requirements for their net customer positions, and the members' own positions being carried by the exchanges' clearing corporation. The member firms, in turn, run the same SPAN program or a more stringent version of it against their larger-positioned clients to determine their individual requirements. SPAN basically rearranges the positions in an account so as to minimize the exposure.

· Conclusion ·

This section has presented the three major forms of margin: ownership margin, as used in stocks and bonds, protection margin, as used in products such as options, and good-faith deposits, as used in futures. The theory behind these forms of margin is applicable to the vast majority of products that we trade. However, regardless of what the "rules" say, a broker-dealer or other financial institution has the right to be more stringent with its requirements, even to the point of demanding full payment.

Summary

T his book has taken you through a wide range of products; it should have provided you with a foundation that permits you to comprehend conversations with those more product savvy. We've covered the issuance, nuances, and characteristics of the various products. From this base you can expand your knowledge in the areas needed, rather than flounder and waste time searching for what you want.

In the equity portion of the book, common and preferred stocks were addressed, as were rights, warrants, ADRs, and GDRs. The book then focused on the debt market. Product similarities and differences that exist among the issues were explained, as was the interest-sensitive market as a whole. The characteristics and qualities of mortgage-backed and asset-backed securities were delved into, and mutual funds and exchange-traded funds were delineated. Derivatives were delved into, including their usage and evolution. All major products were covered.

It is apparent that some of the products offered by the industry have been abused. They were sound in thought but abused in practice, when their structure and purpose was applied to unsound foundations and practices. We are paying for that now. Let's make sure mistakes like that do not repeat themselves.

Glossary

ABC fund: Mutual fund that offers investors different methods to acquire their shares.

ABCP: See *asset-backed commercial paper.*

acquisition: When one company buys another company, and the acquiring company remains. It maintains the continuity of its books and records.

adjustable rate: The interest or dividend rates are reset periodically based on the current rates at that time.

adjustable-rate preferred stock: A preferred stock in which the rate of dividend is changed periodically so as to keep the interest-sensitive preferred stock in line with the current interest rates.

adjustable-rate mortgage: A mortgage in which the rate of interest is changed over the life of the mortgage based on the current rates.

ADR: See *American depositary receipt.*

ADS: See *American depositary receipt.*

ad valorem: A fee or tax based on an asset's value.

agency: A transaction where a broker assists in the execution of an order without taking financial responsibility or having market exposure.

alternate trading systems: Sometimes referred to as ECN, this is an electronic trading system for large blocks of securities to be traded away from traditional marketplaces.

American depositary receipts (shares): A receipt, issued in the form of shares, issued by a U.S. bank, that represents the ordinary shares of a foreign company that the bank is holding against the receipts.

American form of option: An option that can be exercised any time during its life. Compare with *European form of option.*

arbitrageurs: Professional traders who take advantage of a temporary anomaly in the marketplace.

ARM: See *adjustable-rate mortgage.*

ARPS: See *adjustable-rate preferred stock.*

ARS: See *auction rate securities.*

asset: That which is owned by or owed to the entity.

asset-backed commercial paper: Commercial paper backed by business receivables, usually outstanding from ninety to one hundred eighty days.

ATS: See *alternate trading system.*

auction rate securities: Longer-term municipal debt, corporate debt, or perpetual preferred stock whose payment rate (interest or dividend) is set through periodic auctions. The auctions are of the Dutch format.

avoirdupois ounce: 28.349523 grams. Industrial weight measure. Compare with *troy ounce.*

back-end load: A sales charge imposed by certain mutual funds when the mutual fund share owners sell shares of that fund.

balloon maturity: The part of a serial bond offering where a large percentage of the debt matures at the end of the series.

BAN: See *bond anticipation note.*

banker's acceptances: A money-market instrument used in international trade. It is created when the importer's bank accepts responsibility for payment of goods when received.

basis points: The term used to express interest rates and changes in interest rates (e.g., 100 basis points = 1 percent, 25 basis points = ¼ of a percent, etc).

basis price: The pricing convention used in some debt instruments, which is presented on the basis of its yield to maturity.

beneficial owner: The actual owner of a security.

bid: The part of a quote representing the highest price anyone will pay.

binary option: An option that is usually traded in the over-the-counter market that sets an event or monetary amount as the strike price. If the strike price is reached and the option is exercised, the option will pay a predetermined amount.

block order: An order to buy or sell 10,000 shares or more.

block-trading firm: A broker-dealer that makes markets to service large transactions for financial institutions and other holders of large positions.

bond: A long-term debt instrument issued by governments and corporations with a maturity date of ten to thirty years from the date of issuance.

bond anticipation note: A short-term instrument, issued by a state or municipality as interim funding prior to a bond offering.

break-point sales: A point at which the sales charge in a mutual fund investment decreases to a lower level.

broker: An agent that acts on behalf of its clients, buying or selling issues in the marketplace.

broker-dealer: A license obtained from the Security and Exchange Commission that establishes the type of security business the broker-dealer will conduct with the public.

buying power: The margin conversion of excess. The amount a client can buy on margin without having to deposit additional funds.

callable: See *call feature.*

callable bond: See *call feature.*

callable preferred: See *call feature.*

call feature: A feature that can be found in some corporate preferred stocks and bonds and municipal bonds that permits the issuer to retire the bond before the maturity date.

call option: An option that grants its owner the privilege to buy the underlying issue at a price and time or time period determined by the contract.

cap option: An option that offers limited exposure to the writer. The cap is entered above the strike price on a call or below the strike price of a put. If the underlying closes at or higher (call) than the cap price, at or lower (put) than the cap price, the option is automatically exercised.

cash account: An account of a client in which all purchases must be paid for in full and all securities had to be owned prior to sale.

cash dividend: A periodic taxable distribution of currency by a corporation to shareholders.

cashing out: The selling of one's stock, received as compensation, to derive the cash benefit.

cash management bills: Bills issued by the U.S. Treasury, usually with a duration measured in days or weeks.

CBO: See *collateralized bond obligation*.

CDO: See *collateralized debt obligation*.

CDS: See *credit default swaps*.

certificates of deposit: Unsecured short-term debt issued by commercial banks and other financial institutions. The larger-denominated ones, known as jumbo CDs, are tradable.

chartered market technician exam: A qualification examination required to be passed before the industry will recognize an individual as a technical analyst.

clearing corporation: An industry utility whose purpose is to expedite settlement of transactions.

closed-end mutual fund: A mutual fund that issues its shares to the public until a specific investment level is reached. It then closes and trades like common stock, with the share price determined by supply and demand.

CMO: See *collateralized mortgage obligation*.

collateralized bond obligation: A pool of bonds that are securitized by a special-purpose vehicle (SPV); because of the diversification of risk, the pool becomes investment grade.

collateralized debt obligation: A pool of debt, namely bonds, notes, loans, and other assets. Due to the possible mixture of debt that can be in a CDO, each one has to be evaluated on its own.

collateralized mortgage obligation: A pool of mortgages set up in tranche format. Each tranche has its own time span and interest rate. These securitized products are issued by government-sponsored enterprises (GSEs) and nongovernment entities.

collateral trust bond: A corporate bond backed by assets other those of the issuer.

commercial paper: Unsecured short-term debt of a corporation, usually issued for one year or less.

Committee for Uniform Security Identification Procedures (CUSIP) number: A nine-digit security identification code. The first six digits identify the issuer, the next two identify the issue, and the last is a check digit.

common stock: The voting stock of a corporation, evidencing ownership.

competitive underwriting: A process used in municipal bond offerings where underwriters bid (compete) for the "deal."

conduit: A vehicle that passes financial material from point A to point B.

convertible bond: A debt instrument that can be exchanged (converted into) a different security, usually common stock.

convertible preferred stock: A feature of some preferred stocks that allows the share owner to covert the preferred shares into another security of the issuer.

corporate bond: Long-term debt of a corporation issued for between ten and thirty years.

corporate note: Intermediate-term debt of a corporation, issued for between one and ten years.

coupon rate: The interest rate a debt instrument carries in its description and at which it will pay interest to its owner based on the face amount of the debt.

covered bonds: Bank-issued corporate-type bonds backed by a dedicated group of loans.

credit balance: 1. The amount of money in a client's account that is owed to the client according to the books and records of the issuing entity. 2. In accounting, the logical balance position for liabilities and revenue accounts.

credit default swaps: One qualified institution for a fee accepts the risk of paying interest and/or principal due on a debt instrument should the instrument go into default.

credit risk: The ability of the issuer to meet or not meet its debt obligations.

cum rights: The condition of common stock shares involved in a rights offering prior to the rights officially being issued. The common stock is said to be trading with rights (cum rights).

cumulative preferred stock: Preferred stock whose unpaid dividends accumulate and must be paid before the common stock can receive a dividend.

cumulative voting: A practice that permits a shareholder to aggregate votes and apply them to a specific situation. For example, a shareholder of 500 shares of stock who is asked to select three of six board of director candidates can vote 1,500 votes (3 × 500) for one candidate.

currency options: Put and call options that have foreign currency as the underlying product.

current yield: Interest rate divided by current dollar price.

CUSIP: See *Committee for Uniform Security Identification Procedures.*

dark pools: Electronic communication networks that seek out inventory for large transactions are assembled and traded away from any exchange.

dated date: The day that interest on a newly issued debt instrument begins to accrue.

day order: An order that, if not executed during the day entered, it will be canceled at the end of that trading day.

dealer: A market maker (trader) who commits and risks capital in trading issues against its own clients and other broker-dealers.

debenture bond: A corporate bond that is supported by nothing but the good name of the issuer.

debit balance: 1. The amount of money in a client's security account that is owed by the client to the firm, according to the books and records of the firm. 2. In accounting, the logical balance for asset and expense accounts.

deed of trust: A document stating the terms and features of a debt issue.

default risk: Market risk plus credit risk, which are the two exposures to loss that the debt owner faces. See also *market risk* and *credit risk*.

dollar price: The price of a debt instrument, presented as 10 percent of actual value.

due bills: An IOU used in financial transactions involving stock splits where the additional shares have not yet been issued.

Dutch auction: A type of auction in which bids and offers are totaled, both price and quantity, and at the point that the bids and offers are equal, trading occurs with all those eligible (bids that were at that price or higher and offers that were at that price or lower).

ECN: See *electronic communication network*.

electronic communication network: A communication network between participants aimed at facilitating trades by doing away with the middle person, which in most cases is a broker.

equipment trust: A corporate bond backed by a corporation's equipment, such as airplanes, train cars, and computer hardware.

equity: 1. That portion of a client's account that the client would receive if all securities were converted and added to cash.

2. Ownership in a corporation or other business.

3. Amount of value an owner would receive after all debts, liens, and other claims have been satisfied.

ETF: See *exchange-traded funds*.

European form of option: An option that can only be exercised at the end of its life. See also *American form of option.*

excess: See *margin excess.*

exchange-traded fund: A fund based on an index. The fund acquires the shares included in the index and sells the index shares to the public, which trades the fund shares like stock, on exchanges in a real-time, real-price environment.

ex-distribution date: The first day of trading on which the owner of a security has received a distribution. The distribution is usually in the form of securities.

ex-dividend date: The first day of trading on which a buyer of a stock is not entitled to receive the dividend.

ex-rights: The period during a rights offering after the rights have been issued. The stock is said to be trading "ex-rights."

expense: That which is used up in an attempt to generate revenue.

factor tables: A listing of outstanding pools of debt that contains a percentage figure used to determine the present outstanding principal of each pool.

Fannie Mae: See *Federal National Mortgage Association.*

Federal Home Loan Mortgage Company: A government-sponsored entity whose function is to buy mortgages in the secondary market and keep them in its portfolio or pool them and sell them as mortgage-backed securities.

Federal National Mortgage Association: A publicly traded government-sponsored entity that acquires mortgages in the secondary market, most of which are insured by the Federal Housing Administration, and resells them to the public.

fill-or-kill order: An order that instructs the trader or broker to execute the entire order immediately or, if the market cannot absorb it at that moment, to cancel the order.

Financial Industry Regulatory Authority: Primary self-regulatory organization (SRO) financial institutions such as broker-dealers. Created out of a merger of NYSE and NASD regulatory arms.

FINRA: See *Financial Industry Regulatory Authority.*

floating-rate instruments: The instruments interest or dividend rate is reset periodically to reflect current market conditions.

FOK: See *fill-or-kill order.*

foreign exchange: The conversion of one currency into another.

forward: A short-term over-the-counter instrument that locks in a price or rate applicable at a later time.

forward rate: A rate set today at which a currency exchange will occur at a later date.

fourth market: An electronic marketplace where institutions and other financial entities trade with one another without the need of a third-party intermediary. Trades are routed over an electronic communications network (ECN).

Freddie Mac: See *Federal Home Loan Mortgage Company.*

front-end load: A sales charge imposed by some mutual funds on the buyers of their shares.

fundamental research: Information that focuses on the company, its management, its industry, and economic conditions. Uses a company's financial reports to extract key ratios and percentages from which to make recommendations.

funds: Another name for currency or cash. Also used to refer to mutual funds and exchange-traded funds.

futures: A product traded on exchanges that sets the price today at which a delivery will be made at a later date.

gasoline blendstock: A mixture of gasoline and 10 percent ethanol.

GDR: See *global depositary receipts.*

general obligation bonds: Municipal bonds backed by the full taxing power of the issuer.

global depositary receipts: Receipts issued by international banks into one country's financial market for foreign securities that are traded in their domestic market. Similar to ADRs.

Government National Mortgage Association: A division of Housing and Urban Development that issues pooled government-guaranteed mortgage-backed securities.

hedge: Offsetting positions taken on to minimize risk at the cost of maximizing profit.

hedge fund: Basically, an unregulated pooling of money or other assets that is able to pursue investment opportunities not available to the regulated investment manager.

hedger: General term for a participant who reduces the risk of loss by offsetting a position with a contra position, which is usually a derivative product. Often used in futures when the participants offset the risk of adverse pricing when a product is delivered by using a future contract to lock in a delivery price.

holder: Another name for the owner of an option contract.

house excess: The dollar amount of an SMA that is in excess of the minimum "house" equity requirement. Used in margin accounts.

immediate-or-cancel order: An order that instructs the trader or broker to execute the amount available at that moment and cancel the rest of the order.

indenture: A document stating the terms and features of a debt issue.

indication of interest: The term used to express a client's interest in acquiring a new issue before it is actually trading.

initial public offering: The first time a class of securities is brought to the public market. This is usually accomplished through a formal process known as underwriting.

interest: Cash flow stemming from a debt instrument.

International Security Identification Number: A twelve-digit identification code that is used internationally to identify the issuer, issue, and country of origin of a security.

Investment Company Act of 1940: Set rules and regulations for investment companies.

IOC order: See *immediate-or-cancel order.*

IPO: See *initial public offering.*

iShares: The name given to a group of ETFs created by Barclays Global Investors.

ISIN: See *International Security Identification Number.*

joint venture: The pooling of assets to accomplish a specific goal. Generally the venture is short term and focused on a one-time event.

lead underwriter: The underwriting manager who is responsible for overseeing the distribution of a new issue.

letter of credit: A payment guarantee issued for a client and backed by the bank's creditworthiness. The client pays a fee for the letter whether it is used or not. When used and a loan exists the client pays interest on the amount owed. Used to satisfy daily loan needs with a counter party.

letter of intent: A service offered by some mutual funds that sets the sale charge to the amount of investment stated in the letter of intent.

liability: That which is owed by the entity.

LIBOR: See *London Interbank Offer Rate.*

limit order: An order that sets the maximum price to be paid or the minimum price to be received on an order.

liquidating a position: The closing out of an established position. More commonly used in the options and futures markets, where participants can enter into long or short positions with equal ease.

loan value: The maximum the broker-dealer can lend on a transaction.

London Interbank Offer Rate: An international interest rate used as a standard to set interest rates on loans, short-term instruments, and other financing, both in the international market and within a country's domestic market.

long position: A position that is owned.

maintenance margin: The minimum amount to which the security in a margin account can fall before additional collateral is called for.

managing underwriter: Either the lead manager responsible for overseeing the entire distribution of a new issue or one of the managers working on the distribution.

margin: The margin requirements differ from one type of security to another and represent the minimum amount of equity a client must have in his or her account at all times.

margin account: An account that permits its principal(s) to leverage transactions through borrowings.

margin call: A call for additional collateral needed in a margin account when the equity in the account falls below allowable limits.

margin excess: The amount by which the equity in a margin account exceeds the margin requirement or the amount by which the debit balance (amount loaned) is below the loan value (amount that could be loaned).

margin rate: The minimum a client must have available against a transaction.

market order: An order that accepts the current offer of the quote, if it is a buy order, or accepts the current bid, if it is a sell order.

market risk: The effect that changes in current interest rates have on the market price of a debt instrument or the exposure to price changes.

market technician association: An association of technical analysts that promulgates good market practices and administers qualification examinations for technical analysts.

mark to the market: A process by which the value of a position is updated to its current price.

MBS: See *mortgage-backed security*.

merger: When two or more companies merge to form a new company. The new company may use the name of one of the former companies, but it is still a new company. A new set of books and records are developed.

money market securities: Securities issued for a period of one year or less.

mortgage-backed security: Government-insured or guaranteed mortgages (GNMA) or those issued by government-sponsored entities (GSEs) (such as FHLMC and FNMA) that are combined into a pool and sold to the public.

mortgage bond: A corporate bond backed by long-term fixed assets of the issuer, such as real estate.

MTA: See *market technician association*.

municipal debt: Short-term debt (two years or less) is referred to as notes; bonds are two years or more, issued by state and local governments. Debt issued by municipalities.

mutual fund: The pooling of capital in an attempt to achieve specific goals. The fund may take several forms. The most common is the open-end mutual fund.

NASD: See *National Association of Security Dealers*.

National Association of Security Dealers: An industry regulator promulgating rules and regulations, auditing broker dealers, and leveling disciplinary actions against members. It is part of the Financial Industry Regulatory Authority (FINRA).

negotiated underwritings: The formal underwriting process for new corporate issues. The terms of the underwriting are negotiated between corporate management, the underwriters, and other key interests.

net worth: The accounting value of an entity.

New York Stock Exchange: See *NYSE Euronext*.

NH order: See *not held order*.

no-load funds: Mutual funds that sell their shares directly to the public without imposing a sales charge.

nominee name: A security registered to the name of an industry-recognized entity operating on behalf of the beneficial owner.

noncumulative preferred stock: Dividends that are not paid by the issuer are lost, without any obligation of the issuer to pay them to the shareholders at a later date.

note: Intermediate term debt instrument issued by corporations and governments with a life expectancy from one to ten years. Municipality issues start at a shorter term.

not held order: An order that releases the trader or broker from the marketplace's execution rules and allows for the use of one's own judgment.

NYSE: See *NYSE Euronext.*

NYSE Euronext: Is a result of the combination of the New York Stock Exchange and Euronext N.V. It combines six cash equities exchanges in five countries and six derivatives exchanges. The marketplace offers trading in cash equities, equity and interest rate derivatives, bonds as well as distributing of market information.

offer: The part of a quote representing the lowest price a seller is willing to accept.

offering circular: A document explaining the terms and conditions of a new security offering, as in a Reg. A distribution.

open-end mutual fund: A mutual fund that makes a continuous offering of its shares to the public and stands ready to buy its shares back on demand. Its share price is determined by the net asset value of its portfolio.

open interest: The total number of derivative contracts (e.g., options, futures) that are in the positions of that product's participants' accounts at a given moment. This world exists in a balanced environment. Buyers' positions must equal sellers' positions.

option: A product that gives its owner the privilege to do something if he or she want to.

Option Clearing Corporation: The clearing corporation for exchange-traded options in the United States.

OTC: See *over-the-counter.*

over-the-counter: A dealer-type market where terms of the contract are negotiated between parties. Generally one party is a client, the other is a dealer in that product.

over-the-counter option: A put or call whose contracted terms are negotiated between two parties and not regimented or preset by the Options Clearing Corporation.

par: When a debt instrument is trading at its face value, it is said to be trading at par.

parity: When the price of one instrument is equal to its conversion value of another instrument.

participating preferred: Preferred stock on which the dividends paid will increase when certain preestablished conditions exist.

payable date: The date set by an issuer on which a distribution will be made.

PERC: See *preferred equity redemption stock*.

PN: See *project note*.

preference shares: See *preferred stock*.

preferred equity redemption stock: A type of preferred stock that will convert to either cash or the underlying stock at the end of its life.

preferred stock: Equity ownership of a company, like common stock, that pays a stipulated rate of dividend and therefore trades like a bond.

preliminary prospectus (aka red herring): A document used to solicit underwriters and others into a new security offering.

principal: 1. An owner. 2. The face amount of a debt instrument. 3. A trade executed against a broker-dealer.

prior preferred stock: A preferred stock that has prior claim to dividends and assets over other preferred stock and common stock.

program trading: A basket of securities replicating an index is bought/ sold against future contracts that are sold/bought attempting to profit from the future's price discount/premium against the cost of carry.

project note: A short-term instrument issued for interim funding by municipalities for projects such as hospitals and schools.

prospectus: A document required to accompany most corporate new issues.

proxy: A substitute voting form used by common stockholders who cannot attend the annual meeting.

put option: An option that grants its owner the privilege of selling the underlying item at a price and at a time or during a time period set by the contract.

quote: The highest bid and lowest offer of an issue in that marketplace.

RAN: See *revenue anticipation note*.

RBOB: See *reformulated blendstock for oxygen blending*.

real estate mortgage investment conduit: A pool of qualified residential and commercial mortgages that are securitized and sold CMO style. Unlike other such instruments, a REMIC is exempt from federal income tax. Investors are not.

record date: The date on which one must be legal owner of an issue to be eligible for distribution or other action.

recovery rate: The amount that is expected to be available after failure of a debt instrument.

redemption: Retiring debt using cash.

red herring: See *preliminary prospectus.*

reference debt or security: The debt instrument(s) that behind a credit default swap.

reformulated blendstock for oxygen blending: Gasoline that is awaiting the addition of ethanol.

refunding: Retiring one debt using the proceeds of a new debt.

Reg. A: See *Regulation A.*

Reg. T: See *Regulation T.*

Reg. T excess: The amount by which the equity in a margin account exceeds the margin required percentage or the amount by which the loan value of the securities in a margin account exceeds the debit balance (loan).

Regulation A: The regulation governing a new issue of no more than $5,000,000, of which no more than $1,500,000 worth of stock can be sold to insiders.

Regulation T: Federal Reserve Board regulation setting the amount a broker-dealer can lend on a security transaction, as well as the segregation requirements of securities.

REMIC: See *real estate mortgage investment conduit.*

repo: See *repurchase agreement.*

repurchase agreement: A financing tool involving the pledging (selling) of high-quality debt instruments vs. payment. It usually involves a broker-dealer or other financial institution pledging securities with a nonfinancial institution, with the understanding that they will be "repurchased" at predetermined fixed terms.

resistance level: A term used in technical analysis denoting a price point a stock has had and would have difficulty rising above.

retail price: The price at which the public can transact business.

return on investment (ROI): Usually expressed as a percentage of the profit or earnings made on an investment.

revenue: Income received from the main activities of an entity.

revenue anticipation notes: Notes issued by states and municipalities as interim funding while awaiting the collection of revenue from fees and tolls.

revenue bonds: Municipal bonds whose scheduled payment of interest and return of principal at the end of their lives are derived from a revenue source such as a toll road.

reverse repo: The opposite side of a repurchase agreement. The temporary acquisition of high-quality securities vs. payment, with the understanding that they will be "resold" at predetermined fixed terms.

reverse split: When a corporation consolidates its outstanding shares, thereby causing the market price of the stock to rise. For example, the owner of 1,000 shares of a $0.10 stock in a 100-for-1 reverse split would own 10 shares of a $10 stock. While the total value doesn't change, the $10 stock has greater public appeal.

rights: Issued to existing shareholders, permitting them to subscribe to new shares of the same issue. Rights are short term and can be traded.

rights of accumulation: A service offered by some mutual funds by which the sales charge is reduced as the accumulated investment passes predetermined levels.

ROI: See *return on investment.*

Rule 144A: Rule permitting the issuance of securities to qualified institutional buyers and select high-net-worth individuals through a scaled-down offering procedure.

sales charge: A term usually applied to mutual funds that carry a sales charge or "load."

separate trading of registered interest and principals of securities: The splitting of a Treasury bond into two instruments, one a zero-coupon bond based on the principal and the other an income instrument paying interest periodically.

serial bond: A bond composed of several component bonds maturing sequentially.

short against the box: Selling short a security and not delivering the same security owned, setting up a perfect boxed situation that will be acted on at a later time.

short position: A position that is owed.

short sale: Selling stock not owned and that must be borrowed, with the anticipation of reacquiring it at a lower price at a later date.

sinker: See *sinking fund.*

sinking fund: A feature found with some debt instruments in which the issuer will buy its debt instruments in the open market and retire them. The issuer uses net earnings to pay for these purchases.

SIV: See *special investment vehicle.*

size: The quantity of the current bid or offer of a quote.

SMA: See *special memorandum account.*

SPAN margin: See *standarized portfolio analysis of risk.*

SPDRS: Standard & Poor's depositary receipts, a series of ETFs managed by State Street Global Advisors.

SPE (Special-purpose entity): See *special-purpose vehicle.*

special dividend: A corporate payout to stockholders, declared by corporate management, that is over and above the normal payout schedule.

special memorandum account: The part of a margin account that stores or tracks monetary events that were not acted upon at the time of occurrence.

special purpose vehicle/special purpose entity: An entity established by an underwriter of derivative products that has the purpose of packaging the component parts of the derivative product into a security and issuing securitized product.

spin-off: When a company divests itself of subsidiaries or parts of the overall company and the parts become stand-alone companies.

spot market: Dealing in actual physicals today requiring delivery of the commodity at the end of the product's settlement cycle (e.g. currency trades settle two business days after trade.)

spot rate: The current conversion rate of one currency into another.

spread: The difference between the bid and the offer of a quote, an option strategy consisting of a long and short put or call on the same underlying product, a future strategy consisting of two different delivery months on the same or related products.

SPV: See *special-purpose vehicle.*

standard margin: The per-contract amount required to establish a margin position. A term used in customer accounts that are involved with futures.

standard portfolio analysis of risk (SPAN): A holistic method of assessing risk in future accounts with large positions and offsetting strategies. Used in future product positions.

standard voting: Policy allowing the owner of common stock to vote on a per-share basis for each event. (See also *cumulative voting.*)

stand-by underwriting: A process used between a broker-dealer or other financial institution and an issuer whereby underwriters agree to take in any portion of the issue not absorbed through normal channels.

stock dividend: A nontaxable distribution of company shares that increase the number of shares outstanding but lowers their price. Corporate capitalization remains the same.

stock split: When a corporation splits its stock because the price has gotten to be too high for the general public to afford and/or the corporation wants to increase the float of the outstanding shares. In a 3–1 split, 100 shares trading at $90 per share will become 300 shares trading at $30 per share.

stop order: A memorandum order with a limit price that becomes a market order when its stop price is reached or passed.

straddle: Long or short positions in calls or puts having the same underlying product and the same series. In options, a long straddle expects the movement of the underlying to outperform the cost of the position. A short straddle expects the underlying to underperform the proceeds received.

STRIPS: See *separate trading of registered interest and principals of securities.*

structured investment vehicle: An ongoing, open-ended, fixed-income fund that invests in asset-backed securities. As old assets mature, the fund uses the proceeds to acquire new assets.

support level: A term used in technical research to denote a price point below which a stock's price has not fallen since the previous support level was reached.

TAN: See *tax anticipation note.*

tax anticipation note: Short-term issue of a state or municipality used in the anticipation of collecting taxes from individuals and corporations.

TBA: See *to be announced.*

technical research: Research that focuses on the behavior of a company's stock over time in relation to the market or to other securities in the same industry and other relevant or related activity from which the analyst can render a recommendation.

tender offer: When a person or entity makes a bid that is above the current market price for a substantial number of shares of a company. The size of the offer can be stated as a percentage of the outstanding stock.

tenor: The assumed longevity of a debt instrument as it differs from its actual maturity (e.g., the assumed pay-down of a mortgage vs. its actual final payment date) or the period of a debt instrument's payments quartered by another party.

third market: When institutions, exchange members, and non–exchange members trade large blocks of exchange-listed stocks among one another.

to be announced: A term applied to the period of time between when a pool of mortgages are approved and when they are actually in force. At that time, the pool number is assigned by GNMA or other entity and the pool can be delivered into the market.

total return asset contract: A future contract that tracks an index composed of stocks, bonds, currencies, and other financial products. It is a total return product: Dividends and other distributions are calculated into the price.

TRAKR: See *total return asset contract.*

tranche: One section of an offering, such as a CMO, that has defined parameters that separate it from other tranches of the same issue.

transfer agent: The keeper of the registration of securities. The registration can be in the actual owner's name (beneficial owner) or in the name of an entity acting on behalf of the owner (nominee).

triple tax free: Income that is not taxed by the federal, state, or local governments. The interest paid on some municipal bonds is triple tax free.

troy ounce: 31.1034768 grams. A measure used in precious metals. See also *avoirdupois ounce.*

12b-1 fee: A fee that originally permitted mutual funds that didn't charge a sale fee (no-load fund) to use part of their assets for marketing. It's now used by all types of mutual funds for a multitude of marketing and operational purposes.

uncovered writer: In the case of a call option, a writer that does not own the underlying security the call option is written on. In the case of a put option, a writer that is not short the underlying security the put option is written on.

underwriter: One who buys a new issue from the issuer for the sole purpose of selling it. An underwriter's ownership of the issue does not constitute primary ownership. The party the underwriter sells it to is the primary owner.

United States Treasury bills: Short-term debt of the federal government, with the longest instrument maturing one year from issuance. They are discounted instruments and trade at a yield-to-maturity basis.

United States Treasury bond: Long-term debt of the federal government, with maturities from ten to thirty years. These instruments pay interest every six months and trade at dollar prices.

United States Treasury note: Intermediate-term debt of the federal government issued with between two and ten years until maturity. These are interest-bearing instruments, with interest paid every six months, and trade at dollar prices.

unit investment trust: A specific type of product that is acquired under a trust, then pooled and broken into units that are sold to the public.

value date: The day on which foreign exchange transactions are due to settle and currency changes hands.

variation margin: A mark-to-the-market process used in future accounts that permits the honoring of the contract terms.

voting trust certificate: When there is a need to control the votes of common stockholders, a trust is set up offering voting trust certificates in exchange for stockholders voting shares. The common stockholder loses nothing but the right to vote.

VTC: See *voting trust certificate.*

WAC: See *weighted average coupon.*

WALA: See *weighted average loan age.*

WAM: See *weighted average maturity.*

warrant: A long-term instrument, initially offered temporarily with another product, forming a unit, that permits its owner to buy an issue of the issuer at a predetermined price.

weighted average coupon: A term used for GNMA IIs and other multi–interest rate pooled debt to express the total interest payment that will be received, divided by the size of the pool. The debt that composes the larger part of the portfolio will have the greatest effect on the total payment.

weighted average loan age: In some mortgage-backed securities, the constituent loans have differing maturities. This calculation is used to compute the average life of these mortgages. The term is also used to refer to the average life remaining in an existing pool of mortgages.

weighted average maturity: A term used in pooled mortgages where the anticipated depletion of the mortgages is less than the original depletion date of the actual mortgage.

when issued: A temporary state in the offering of some securities when the security is traded in the market even though it has not been issued.

whole loan: A term that refers to the acquisition or sale of a loan in its entirety, such as the purchase of a particular outstanding mortgage.

wholesale price: An inter–broker-dealer price at which certain broker-dealers can trade among themselves. To this price a markup or commission must be applied to obtain the retail price.

writer: The seller or granter of an option contract.

yield: The amount returned on an investment (e.g., the amount of interest paid on an investment in debt or the amount of crops a field can produce).

yield to call: The return on the investment if a debt instrument was called in by the issuer ahead of the maturity date.

yield curve: The tracking of debt yields over time.

yield to maturity: The return on investment that can be expected if a debt instrument is held until it matures.

zero-coupon bond: A deeply discounted debt instrument whose interest is not paid out until maturity.

Index